C0-BYV-632

IMPERIAL DIPLOMACY
IN THE ERA
OF DECOLONIZATION

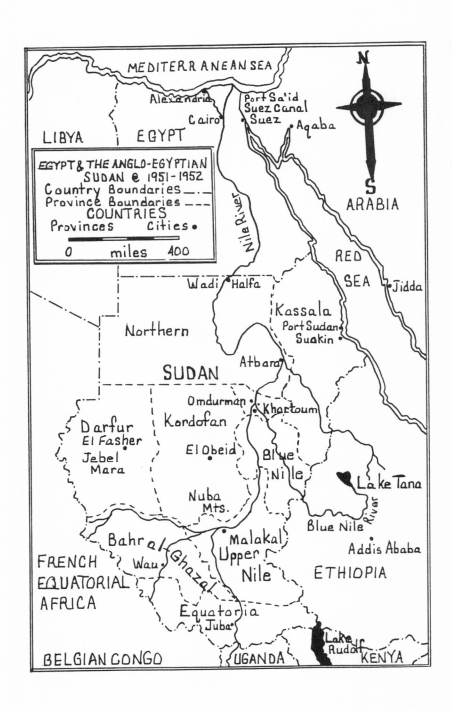

IMPERIAL DIPLOMACY IN THE ERA OF DECOLONIZATION

The Sudan and Anglo-Egyptian Relations, 1945–1956

W. TRAVIS HANES III

WITHDRAWN
FAIRFIELD UNIVERSITY
LIBRARY

Contributions in Comparative Colonial Studies,
Number 30

FAIRFIELD UNIV LIBRARY

JAN 2 4 1997

Greenwood Press
Westport, Connecticut • London

Library of Congress Cataloging-in-Publication Data

Hanes, William Travis.
    Imperial diplomacy in the era of decolonization : the Sudan and
Anglo-Egyptian relations, 1945–1956 / W. Travis Hanes III.
       p.   cm.—(Contributions in comparative colonial studies,
ISSN 0163–3813 ; no. 30)
    Includes bibliographical references (p.   ) and index.
    ISBN 0–313–29341–4 (alk. paper)
    1. Egypt—Foreign Relations—Great Britain. 2. Great Britain—
Foreign relations—Egypt. 3. Sudan—Foreign relations—Great
Britain. 4. Great Britain—Foreign relations—Sudan. 5. Egypt—
Foreign relations—Sudan. 6. Sudan—Foreign relations—Egypt.
I. Title. II. Series.
DT82.5.G7H36 1995
327.62041—dc20   94–7421

British Library Cataloguing in Publication Data is available.

Copyright © 1995 by W. Travis Hanes III

All rights reserved. No portion of this book may be
reproduced, by any process or technique, without the
express written consent of the publisher.

Library of Congress Catalog Card Number: 94–7421
ISBN: 0–313–29341–4
ISSN: 0163–3813

First published in 1995

Greenwood Press, 88 Post Road West, Westport, CT 06881
An imprint of Greenwood Publishing Group, Inc.

Printed in the United States of America

The paper used in this book complies with the
Permanent Paper Standard issued by the National
Information Standards Organization (Z39.48–1984).

10 9 8 7 6 5 4 3 2 1

To the Memory of

BEN MURRAY
and to
JOHN J. CONNOLLY

this book is dedicated with respect,
admiration, and gratitude

Contents

Preface

This project could not have been completed without the help of many people. First and foremost, I must thank Professor William Roger Louis at the University of Texas, whose wisdom, patience and scholarship has inspired me during the last fifteen years. His seminars have been a model of the Socratic method. In addition, I must thank the members of his senior graduate seminar in British Imperial History for their willingness to put up with draft chapters and revisions. I am particularly indebted to Col. Robert B. Osborn, Dr. David P. Billington, Claire Anderson, Dr. George Kelling, Dr. Bill Brands, and Dr. Pierre Cagniart. I have also benefitted greatly over the past decade in Austin from the friendship aand support of Professor Gail Minault, Professor Brian Levack, and Dean William Livingston. Thanks of a special sort must go to Professor Hafez Farmayan, a friend as well as mentor whose urbanity, grace and gentility are matched only by his devotion to his students. Not least, I wish to express my gratitude to Professor Ronald Robinson for his friendship, his camaraderie and encouragement, his vast knowledge, and the keenness of his intellect and insight.

Others who have helped me along the way include Dr. Peter Woodward, the late Mr. Albert Hourani, Mr. Norman Daniel, Professor Robert O. Collins, Professor John Lamphear, Professor Robert Fernea, and Dr. Bushra Hamad. I am especially grateful to Professor Martin Daly, perhaps the most knowledgeable scholar of the condominium period, who read the original draft and provided extremely helpful detailed commentary. The staffs of the Public Record Office in London, the Sudan Archive at Durham University, and Rhodes House Library in Oxford made the research for this study much less painful and considerably more pleasurable than might have been the case. I am also greatly indebted to Sir Gawain Bell for his willingness to answer a multitude of questions about the Sudan Service and Sir James Robertson. It is with some sadness that I express my appreciation to the late K.D.D. Henderson, who departed this life in the midst of our correspondence. I regret that I experienced his vitality and wit only at second hand through his letters. It should be recorded that even after more than thirty years away from the Sudan, the Sudanese remained in his thoughts to the end: most prominent in his funeral service were the prayers written by Sir Douglas Newbold for the peoples of the Sudan.

In London I am indebted for the loving friendship and care of the family Calvert—Maria, Colin, Olivia and Amy—without whom, quite frankly, I would have been lost. In London too I wish to thank Professor and Mrs. J. B. Kelly, and especially Saul, for their hospitality and friendship, as also the Aziz family, "Bunny" and Elizabeth, who reminded me that there is life beyond the Public Record Office. In Durham, I owe many thanks to the Fellows and staff of St. Aidan's College. As ever, I continue to benefit from the lessons learned in the classroom and at home from Herb and Taffy Bodman of Chapel Hill, North Carolina. I am also especially grateful to Mr. David H. Fado, M. Phil., who indexed and edited the entire manuscript. Needless to say, any errors are entirely my responsibility.

Last but certainly not least, I wish to record my gratitude and love for my wife, Sally, and my son, Kyle, who never quite gave up on what turned out to be a marathon rather than a sprint. This book owes much to their spirit of endurance and support, and willingness to forego the pleasures of a "normal" family life. I hope its completion may repay some of their investment.

Austin, Texas
March, 1995

IMPERIAL DIPLOMACY
IN THE ERA
OF DECOLONIZATION

Introduction: The Problem

In December 1945, the Royal Egyptian Government formally requested a revision of the 1936 Anglo-Egyptian Treaty that had officially regulated Anglo-Egyptian relations for the previous ten years. It was the opening gambit in a game that would result eight years later in a new Anglo-Egyptian Agreement on the Sudan, followed shortly by the final evacuation of the Nile Valley by Britain. The game itself finally ended three years after that in the Suez crisis of 1956, an event that nearly destroyed the Conservative Party, that did destroy the career of Anthony Eden, that divided British families almost as bitterly as the Civil War had divided American families a century earlier, and that is viewed by many as the watershed in Britain's decline from global power to second-rate status.

The name Suez, of course, conjures up images of the great canal which was Britain's lifeline to her eastern empire, even after Indian independence removed the premier jewel from the imperial diadem. For thousands of First and Second World War veterans from nearly all the allied countries, Suez also brings to mind that vast military zone covering hundreds of square miles, with its air bases, army bases, munitions dumps, repair facilities, cinemas, and barracks, which was the heart of the British and Allied presence in the Middle East and North Africa. For Egyptians, Suez carries the bitter national memory of the seventy-year British occupation of their country, and the moment of triumph when the greatest of modern Arab leaders, President Gamal Abdel Nasser, claimed the Suez Canal for Egypt, putting an end once and for all (or so he hoped) to foreign domination of his country.

Given the centrality of the Canal Zone and its strategic importance in all Anglo-Egyptian relations, not to mention postwar Egyptian relations with the Western powers in general, it is little wonder that military and strategic considerations have overshadowed almost all discussions and interpretations of Anglo-Egyptian relations between the end of the Second World War and the 1956 crisis. The irony is that while Anglo-Egyptian relations during this period did

indeed break down, it was not primarily over the Suez question. Indeed, the
military issue was actually resolved, at least tentatively, several times, the first
as early as the summer of 1946. In fact, despite considerable efforts on the part
of the British Government, especially Labour Foreign Secretary Ernest Bevin, to
accommodate Egyptian nationalist demands for a new, equal treaty relationship
between Britain and Egypt, all efforts to renegotiate the 1936 treaty foundered on
a very different issue—the status of the Sudan.

Between 1945 and 1953, all Anglo-Egyptian treaty negotiations broke down
over three related questions: who had sovereignty over the Sudan? who should
administer the Sudan? and should the Sudanese themselves be guaranteed the
right to full self-determination? Not until after the 1952 Egyptian Revolution
had swept away the old regime in Cairo, along with its adamant claim to sole
sovereignty over the Sudan, were these problems finally resolved and an
acceptable Anglo-Egyptian Agreement reached concerning the condominium.
Resolution of the Sudan problem in turn paved the way for final Anglo-Egyptian
agreement and the complete British evacuation of the Nile Valley. This
prolonged failure to reach agreement over the Sudan, however, was not the fault
of either Britain or Egypt so much as of the condominium government in
Khartoum itself. This study, therefore, is about the remarkable intervention by a
supposedly subordinate colonial administration in the foreign relations of the
two governments legally responsible for its existence.

The argument of this monograph is, quite frankly, revisionist. Over the past
decade several major studies involving the British Labour Government of 1945–
51 and its policies toward Egypt and the Middle East have attempted to resurrect
the reputation and personality of Labour Foreign Secretary Ernest Bevin. Bevin
has been portrayed, not without reason, as a hardheaded negotiator who yet held
to certain fundamental principles. He has been credited, for example, with
pursuing a noninterventionist policy in the Middle East, especially in Egypt,
which, because of the Suez Canal and the great military base in the Canal Zone,
was the key to Britain's position in the entire region. In the Sudan, too, Bevin
has been credited with maintaining a proper moral position despite tremendous
pressures, because he could not bring himself to agree to Egyptian claims in the
condominium that would have precluded Sudanese self-determination and
ultimate independence. While such an interpretation may seem correct in its
broad outlines, a closer examination of Bevin's treatment of the Sudan issue, the
"brick-wall" to use his own phrase, in his efforts to renegotiate the Anglo-
Egyptian Treaty of 1936, does much to refute the image so carefully and
sympathetically built up.[1]

One of the main themes that will emerge in the following pages is the
argument that, despite all his public rhetoric to the contrary, Bevin was in fact

---

1. For sympathetic views of Bevin see especially Wm. Roger Louis, *The British
Empire in the Middle East, 1945-51: Arab Nationalism, the United States, and Postwar Imperialism* (Oxford, 1984); and Lord Bullock, *Ernest Bevin: Foreign Secretary,
1945-1951* (New York and London, 1983).

fully prepared to buy his Egyptian treaty at the expense of the Sudan, so long as he did not appear to be doing so publicly: what prevented him was the obstinate opposition of the Sudan Government, an essentially "colonial" regime of British administrators. It may be that the case of the Sudan was a unique one, an aberration in an otherwise stainless career of trying to translate the Labour Party ideals into practical foreign policy. Or it may be that too much has been made of Bevin's idealism, and that he was first and last simply a hard-working Foreign Secretary, doing his best to maintain British imperial interests in a world in which British weakness inescapably limited the ability to achieve those interests. Such ultimate conclusions, however, are beyond the scope of this present study: this is not a book about Ernest Bevin, but about his policies toward Egypt and the Sudan and the men who defied those policies, thereby destroying Britain's chances for a new relationship with Egypt.

What is attempted here is a reconstruction of the means by which Bevin's policy toward the Sudan, and hence toward Anglo-Egyptian treaty revision, was actually forced not by the foreign secretary himself, but by the expatriate British administrators of the Sudan condominium government.

The dominant theme of this book concerns the unique role played in postwar Anglo-Egyptian relations by the Sudan Political Service, the elite British administrators who formed the backbone of the Sudan Government. As will be seen, the independent Sudan owes its very existence to these expatriate "colonial" officials who were in many ways more vehement proponents of Sudanese "nationalism" than the Sudanese themselves. Having developed over the years their own unique version of the history of both Egyptian-Sudanese relations and Anglo-Egyptian relations, they refused to allow Sudanese interests (as the Political Service conceived them) to be subordinated to those of either co-dominus. That a colonial administration could actually affect relations between two such "independent" powers was due primarily to the unique nature of the Anglo-Egyptian relationship, and the peculiar condominium status of the Sudan, which in turn was responsible for giving the Sudan Government an independence of action virtually unknown in any other colonial territory.[2]

---

2. On the role of the Sudan in Anglo-Egyptian relations, see especially L.A. Fabunmi, *The Sudan in Anglo-Egyptian Relations 1800-1956* (London, 1960) (Fabunmi's Nigerian perspective is particularly interesting). Other volumes that are indispensable for the themes in this study are M. W. Daly's masterful *Imperial Sudan: The Anglo-Egyptian Condominium, 1934-56* (Cambridge, Eng., 1991); R. O. Collins, *Shadows in the Grass: Britain in the Southern Sudan, 1918-1956*, (New Haven and London, 1983); Peter Woodward, *Condominium and Sudanese Nationalism* (New York, 1979); Muddathir Abdel Rahim, *Imperialism and Nationalism in the Sudan: A Study in Constitutional and Political Development, 1899-1956* (Oxford, 1969); Mohammed Omer Beshir, *Revolution and Nationalism in the Sudan* (London, 1974); and Gabriel Warburg, *Islam, Nationalism, and Communism in a Transitional Society* (London, 1978). In a different class are accounts of former Sudan administrators themselves, both British and Sudanese, especially Sir Harold MacMichael, *The Sudan* (London, 1954); J.S.R. Duncan, *The Sudan's Path to*

ORIGINS AND NATURE OF THE "CONDOMINIUM"

Designed solely as a means of cloaking British control over the strategically important headwaters of the Nile, the 1899 Anglo-Egyptian Agreement on the Sudan provided the basis for Britain to administer the territory it had just reconquered from the Mahdist state that had itself overthrown the previous Egyptian regime in 1885. The agreement placed all power, civil and military, in the hands of a governor-general nominated by the British Foreign Office and appointed by the khedive (later the king) of Egypt. Ostensibly, the agreement acknowledged both Egyptian and British rights in the Sudan on an equal basis. In fact, Egyptian money had paid for most of the reconquest, the Egyptian army had supplied the bulk of the troops, and after the reconquest Egypt continued to subsidize the administration of the territory until after the First World War—but Egyptians were frustrated in all efforts to participate equally in its administration.[3]

Despite their obviously dominant position in both Egypt, which they had occupied militarily in 1882, and the Sudan, British statesmen insisted on describing the government of the Sudan as a "condominium" between two supposedly equal powers, primarily as a means of "obfuscating," as Lord Salisbury once put it, the international status of the territory, in an effort to defuse both European and Egyptian criticism of British "expansionism." The facade of condominium status was particularly significant because it meant that the Sudan could not legitimately be placed under the aegis of the British Colonial Office. Both the reconquest and the subsequent establishment of the condominium regime were handled by the British Agency and Consulate in Cairo, a Foreign Office responsibility. Yet, the condominium was always something of a stepchild as far as Whitehall was concerned, considerably less important than the true imperial interest, Egypt. Moreover, neither the Foreign Office nor the Consulate was organized to supervise the kind of administration needed to rule such a vast territory. Consequently, the Sudan Government soon became a virtually autonomous entity, hiring its own staff and ruling the Sudan under an increasingly nominal control by the co-domini. Such independence in

---

Independence (London, 1957); Mekki Abbas, *The Sudan Question: The Dispute over the Anglo-Egyptian Condominium, 1884-1951* (London and New York, 1952); Sir James Robertson, *Transition in Africa* (London, 1974); Sir Gawain Bell, *Shadows on the Sand* (London and New York, 1983); and Glen Balfour-Paul, *The End of Empire in the Middle East* (Cambridge, Eng., 1991).

3. For British motives see especially G. R. Sanderson, *England, Europe, and the Upper Nile, 1882-1899* (Edinburgh, 1965). The best scholarly accounts of the foundations of the condominium and its early years are Gabriel Warburg, *The Sudan under Wingate* (London, 1971), and especially M. W. Daly's comprehensive *Empire on the Nile: The Anglo-Egyptian Sudan 1898-1934* (London, 1986).

Khartoum, however, proved to be a major obstacle to stability in Anglo-Egyptian relations.[4]

The first governor-general, Lord Kitchener, established a colonial government drawn essentially from the Egyptian army, of which he was also the Sirdar (commander-in-chief). Military administration, however, was soon deemed unsatisfactory by Lord Cromer, the British consul general in Cairo and, under the occupation, the virtual ruler of Egypt. Not only was military rule expensive, but a mutiny in Omdurman in 1900 demonstrated the vulnerability of a regime dependent on European officers who had little or no understanding of their own "native" (primarily Egyptian) troops, much less the local Sudanese population. Consequently, in 1901 the first civilian administrators began to be recruited from British universities. Unlike the military administrators, Cromer expected that these scions of the British ruling class would learn the local languages and customs of the Sudan and thereby establish a more efficient government, as well as one with greater "legitimacy" in the eyes of the Sudanese. Not least, Arabic-speaking Englishmen would obviate the need for the condominium administration to rely too heavily on Egyptians. As the military administrators retired, died, or were transferred, particularly during the First World War, the Sudan Government fell further and further into the hands of this civilian Sudan Political Service.[5]

The difference between military and civilian rule in the Sudan was significant. Where military officers served on secondment, and fully expected to return eventually to their regiments, members of the Political Service committed themselves to lifetime careers in the Sudan. Consequently, even more than the British Colonial Service, the Sudan Political Service became extremely parochial and paternalistic. Political officers usually spent their entire careers in one of the two major regions, the Arabized and Muslim North or the African and "pagan" South. As a result, they developed an attachment to the land and a knowledge of the peoples of the Sudan to an extent virtually unknown in the other territories of the Empire, with the possible exception of India. This attachment, combined with the relative autonomy of the Political Service, resulted in a unique sense of independence and "mission" for the Sudan Government, which the Political Service eventually came to dominate.[6]

---

4. Ibid.

5. For Cromer's views on civilian administration, see also Cromer to Salisbury, 8 June 1900, FO 633/6, PRO, as well as Cromer's introduction to S. Low's *Egypt in Transition* (London, 1913). For an account of the Omdurman mutiny see especially M.W. Daly, "The Egyptian Army Mutiny at Omdurman, January- February 1900," *Bulletin of the British Society for Middle Eastern Studies* 8, no. 1 (1981): 3-12.

6. There is some disagreement among scholars over the exact nature and attitude of the Sudan Political Service. R. O. Collins, in "The Sudan Political Service, a Portrait of the Imperialists," *African Affairs* 71 (1972), argues that the Political Service was composed of men "born and reared in the atmosphere of the country gentry," in effect a modern "squirearchy" transplanted to the Sudan. In "The Education of an Elite Imperial Administration: The Sudan Political Service and the British Public School

As for the Egyptian co-dominus, under the British governors-general and the influence of the Sudan Political Service, Egyptians were always relegated to the lowest posts of the administrative and technical services and were deliberately excluded from the ranks of the Political Service itself. Such blatant discrimination, combined with the growing independence of the Political Service and the Sudan Government, seemed to many Egyptians proof that Britain's real policy was to detach the Sudan from Egypt altogether and to turn it into a British colony. Such a possibility worried even "moderate" Egyptians, since the Sudan controlled the lifeblood of Egypt, the waters of the Nile. Equally important, however, was the general Egyptian perception that the Sudan historically belonged to Egypt and that the British, whatever their own reasons, had only helped to restore Egyptian sovereignty over a wayward and rebellious province. As Egyptian nationalism became more acute in the years following the First World War, so too did Egyptian demands for the "Unity of the Nile Valley" become more strident.[7]

Perhaps the single most important dispute between the co-domini was the question of sovereignty over the Sudan. Egypt insisted that the condominium agreement had provided for administration only of the Sudan and that sovereignty had always resided solely in the Egyptian Crown. Britain and the Sudan Government, on the other hand, maintained that the reconquest had given Britain an equal claim with Egypt to sovereignty, as Lords Cromer and Salisbury had put it "by right of conquest." Among Egyptian nationalists, feelings ran high on this issue. In 1910, Butros Ghali, the Egyptian foreign minister who had signed

---

System," *International Journal of African Historical Studies* 15, no. 4 (1982), on the other hand, J. A. Mangan argues that Collins makes too much of the "country gentry" origins of the Political Service: Mangan instead locates their devotion to ideals of service in their public school and Oxbridge backgrounds. The two interpretations need not be mutually exclusive: the most important point that emerges from both is the innate "countrified" paternalism of the Political Service. The British administrators accepted as axiomatic that the Sudan would always be primarily an agrarian and pastoral country; whether their own origins were middle-class or country gentry, in the Sudan they functioned as an elite aristocracy in an essentially rural setting. In the process of defining their purpose and establishing their methods for ruling a "country" people like the Sudanese, they drew on two principal sources: their idealized (indeed mythologized) conception of the British landed aristocracy; and their education in the classics. Blending the two traditions, they came to see themselves as a combination of philosopher-kings, guardians, and benign feudal barons or clan chiefs—in short, objective and disinterested "Fathers of the people." Above all, they increasingly justified themselves by developing a theory of "trusteeship" as the basis for their rule over the Sudanese. For a valuable sociological discussion of the Political Service see also A.H.M. Kirk-Greene, "The Sudan Political Service: A Profile in the Sociology of Imperialism," *International Journal of African Historical Studies* 15 no. 1 (1982).

7. See especially Fabunmi, *The Sudan.*

the 1899 agreement, was assassinated by Egyptian nationalists, at least partly for having "given away" the Sudan. In 1919, although not perhaps the primary cause of the Egyptian revolution, "Unity of the Nile Valley" certainly became one of the main inspirational slogans of the nationalist revolt. In 1922, when an exasperated Britain unilaterally terminated the protectorate it had established over Egypt during the First World War and declared Egyptian independence, the Sudan was one of four areas "reserved" for the discretion of His Majesty's Government. Partly in consequence, in 1924 Sir Lee Stack, the governor-general of the Sudan and a leading proponent of its separation from Egypt, was himself gunned down in the streets of Cairo by extreme Egyptian nationalists. In the aftermath of the assassination, in Khartoum a revolt of the XIth Sudanese battalion of the Egyptian army had to be bloodily suppressed.[8]

Stack's assassination, and its aftermath in Khartoum, were a watershed in the history of both the Sudan and the Anglo-Egyptian relations. They not only precipitated the complete eviction of the Egyptians from the condominium (not to mention creating a new martyr for the Political Service) but also led to persistent efforts by Khartoum to torpedo any Anglo-Egyptian rapprochement that included changes in the condominium. For the next twelve years both the legacy of the murder and the sovereignty question bedeviled Anglo-Egyptian relations, preventing all efforts to negotiate a treaty acceptable to both sides. The most that could be achieved, primarily because the question of sovereignty was simply ignored, was an agreement concerning the use of Nile waters, an agreement that balanced the needs of both Egypt and the Sudan. The fundamental issues in Anglo-Egyptian relations, however, remained unresolved. Not until 1936, on the brink of a European war and after the Italian invasion of Ethiopia the previous year had alarmed not only Britain and Egypt but also the Sudan Government, were the co-domini able to "normalize" their relations in a new Anglo-Egyptian treaty of military alliance.[9]

Like Stack's assassination, the Anglo-Egyptian Treaty of 1936 was a watershed both in Anglo-Egyptian relations and in the history of the Sudan. Anxious for the military alliance, Britain agreed to restore the *status quo ante* Stack's assassination in the Sudan. Worried by the Italian conquest of Ethiopia, most in the Sudan Political Service understood the importance of an Anglo-Egyptian alliance, but they also feared that London would "sacrifice" the Sudan to achieve it. Partly to allay such concerns, at the instigation of the governor-general, Sir Stewart Symes, the new treaty officially proclaimed, for the first time, that the purpose of the condominium was to provide for the "welfare" of the Sudanese. Moreover, on Symes's recommendation, the agreement also specified that Egyptians, British, and other "foreigners" would be appointed to only those posts in the Sudan for which there were no qualified Sudanese available. In short, Khartoum managed to forestall Egyptian claims for greater administrative participation in the condominium by advancing those of the

---

8. Ibid.
9. Ibid.

Sudanese themselves. Even so, agreement was reached only by avoiding the problem of sovereignty over the Sudan altogether. "Nothing in this article," declared the Sudan clause of the treaty, "should prejudice the question of ultimate sovereignty in the Sudan." Despite the disclaimer, many Egyptians remained convinced that the British intended eventually to separate Egypt and the Sudan completely.[10]

Egyptian fears concerning the Sudan were not without foundation, but the threat came less from the British Government than from the Sudan Administration, which emerged during the interwar period as a major force in Anglo-Egyptian relations in its own right. Although the Egyptians did not credit it, the growing independence of the Sudan Political Service was a two-edged blade. Theoretically, the Sudan administrators were recruited under the auspices of the British Foreign Office and controlled by the foreign secretary; in fact, imbued with their own mythology and inspired by their own martyrs, like Gordon and Stack, they became virtually a self-perpetuating elite giving their allegiance solely to the governor-general, the Sudan Administration, and their own conception of the best interests of the Sudanese. In short, Political Service priorities were utterly different from those of the British Government and soon came to focus on the development of a separate national identity in the Sudan, completely independent from that of Egypt.

From the perspective of the Foreign Office, on the other hand, the Sudan was never an end in itself but was always an adjunct to the larger Egyptian question. Egypt controlled the Suez Canal, Britain's imperial lifeline to the Indian and Asian possessions. Moreover, Cairo gradually became the linchpin of all British plans for defending and controlling the entire Middle East. Not least, British predominance in Egypt was to many one of the most potent symbols of Britain's status as a global imperial power. The veranda of Shepherd's Hotel in Cairo was as necessary to the imperial self-image as any Indian durbar honoring the king-emperor. To most in the Foreign Office the form of Britain's presence in the Sudan was considerably less important than the substance of British influence in Egypt. From this perspective, the condominium made a useful bargaining chip in the high-stakes game of Anglo-Egyptian relations. Fully aware of their different viewpoints, the Political Service remained worried about infiltration of the condominium by the "slippery Gyppos," despite treaty provisions advancing the rights of the Sudanese.

The course of the Second World War, and particularly the attitude of Egyptian leaders, including King Farouk, did little to calm the fears of the Sudan Government. Although during the early years of the war, officials in the Sudan were preoccupied with defense matters and the invasion of Kassala province from Italian Ethiopia, by 1943 Ethiopia had been captured, Erwin Rommel had been

---

10. See especially Fabunmi, *The Sudan*, chapters 4 and 5. The quotation is from the treaty itself in Cmd. 5360 (1937). For a general discussion of the 1936 treaty, see also H. A. Ibrahim, "The Sudan in the 1936 Anglo-Egyptian Treaty," *Sudan Notes and Records* 54 (1973).

driven back from Egypt, and as far as the Sudan was concerned, the war had generally receded. As victory approached, there was a general expectation in Khartoum that Egypt would soon demand an early renegotiation of the 1936 treaty, including the clauses dealing with the status of the Sudan. Egypt's tardy declaration of war on the Axis powers was viewed contemptuously by the Political Service as a purely cynical move to ensure a seat in the new United Nations organization. The British elections of 1945, and the installation of a Labour Government in London, also increased the anxiety of the predominantly Conservative British administrators of the Sudan Government. Many feared that the new cabinet under Clement Attlee, especially the Foreign Office under Ernest Bevin, in its avowed aim to "equalize" Anglo-Egyptian relations and to pursue a policy of "partnership" in the Middle East, might give in to Egyptian demands for the "Unity of the Nile Valley." As will be seen, such fears were not groundless.[11]

THE NATURE OF THE POSTWAR PROBLEM

As far as the Sudan was concerned, Anglo-Egyptian negotiations after the Second World War fell roughly into four periods: the first began in December 1945 with Egypt's demand for renegotiation of the 1936 treaty and ended with the final Egyptian rejection of Britain's position on the Sudan in March 1947. The second phase began with Egypt's appeal to the United Nations in the summer of 1947 and ended the following year with Britain's unilateral approval of a new Sudanese Legislative Assembly, as part of the Political Service effort to establish the Sudanese irrevocably on a path of independence from Egypt. After abortive attempts to restart negotiations in 1949, the third phase occurred between 1950 and the Egyptian revolution of 1952, largely as a result of American pressure on Britain and Egypt to resolve their differences in the face of cold war strategic exigencies. Finally, the fourth phase began against the background of the Egyptian Revolution and the fall of the Egyptian monarchy and ended with the signing of a new Anglo-Egyptian Agreement on the Sudan early in 1953. Even that was not the end of the story, however, for over the next three years Britain and Egypt jockeyed for position in the self-governing Sudanese state as each attempted to influence the direction the Sudanese would take after complete independence. The final outcome became clear only on 1 January, 1956, when the Sudanese Government unilaterally declared its independence from both co-domini.

The fundamental channels along which Anglo-Egyptian relations would flow were essentially set in stone during the first phase. Between 1945 and 1947, the Sudan Government in Khartoum was able to force both Britain and Egypt to

---

11. Robertson, *Transition,* chapter 6. The best accounts of Bevin's policy and the ethos of the Labour Government are Louis, *The British Empire,* and Lord Bullock, *Ernest Bevin.*

commit themselves either for or against the principles of Sudanese self-government and self-determination. Consequently, the emphasis in the following analysis will fall most heavily on the role of the Sudan Government during this first period of Anglo-Egyptian negotiations. During the next two phases, appeal to the United Nations and the negotiations of the early 1950s, the Political Service pursued a policy of internal Sudanese constitutional development designed primarily to establish an insurmountable bulwark against Egyptian claims to the Sudan. At the same time, it had to maintain a constant vigil against all efforts of the British Embassy in Cairo and the Foreign Office in London to water down the "pledges" guaranteeing ultimate self-determination for the Sudanese. During the third phase, Khartoum's obstinacy made any chance for concessions over the Sudan virtually impossible, and Anglo-Egyptian relations went into a kind of stasis, as Bevin, on the verge of death, finally retired, and the Labour Government itself began to wind down.

The advent of the Conservative Government, with Anthony Eden as Foreign Secretary, in October 1951 did little to change the situation. If anything, it reinforced the position of the Sudan Government, since the Conservatives had made a point of supporting Sudanese self-determination during their election campaign. Even so, Eden too did his best to "negotiate" some settlement of the Sudan problem only to experience the same frustration with Khartoum as his Labour predecessors. Not until the revolutionary regime of General Muhammad Neguib repudiated the old claim of Egyptian sovereignty over the Sudan, during the fourth and final phase, was Anglo-Egyptian agreement at last made possible on terms that even the Political Service could not effectively resist. As will be seen, for the Political Service it was to be a Pyrrhic victory.

THE POLITICAL SERVICE AND THE ROLE OF SUDANESE NATIONALISM

In its opposition to any Anglo-Egyptian agreement that might compromise its own plans for the future of the Sudan, the most potent weapon in the Sudan Government's arsenal was the magic wand called Sudanese "nationalism." It is important, therefore, to make a disclaimer in this introduction about the treatment of Sudanese nationalists in the following pages. Although fascinating as a story in its own right, the history of Sudanese nationalist development is beyond the bounds of this study. In fact, the real content of Sudanese nationalism was less important to the course of Anglo-Egyptian relations after the war than was the "spin" the Sudan Political Service could put on it for the benefit of the co-domini. Indeed, although this is not the place for it, it might well be argued (polemically no doubt) that Sudanese nationalism itself was largely a creation of the Political Service as a part of its struggle against any Anglo-Egyptian agreement that would jeopardize its agenda in the Sudan. Yet while the development of Sudanese nationalism will be dealt with here only as it impinges on the main story of the Sudan Government's ongoing "poker game" with Egypt and Great Britain, it is essential to bear in mind in the following pages the main cleavages along which Sudanese nationalism divided in the postwar period.[12]

The development of a modern nationalist movement in the Sudan during the condominium period was complicated by several internal factors. In many ways, the rise of Mahdism during the latter part of the nineteenth century, which culminated in the fall of Khartoum and the conquest of the Sudan from its Egyptian masters, displayed Sudanese "nationalist" overtones in the face of Turco-Egyptian "imperialism." During the first twenty years of the condominium, one of the greatest fears of the Sudan Administration was a recrudescence of Mahdism. Mahdism, however, for all its emphasis on what appeared to the British to be a very worldly political activity, was also primarily a religious movement. While the British tried to deal with it as they would with any political phenomenon that challenged the foundation of their rule, Sudanese opposition to Mahdism had profoundly religious overtones. In particular, those tariqas (religious brotherhoods) already established in the Sudan at the time of the initial Mahdist rising in the 1880s, and threatened by its religious tenets, opposed all efforts to reestablish Mahdist influence in the Sudan. The most prominent of these brotherhoods was the Khatmiyya, under the leadership of Sayyid 'Ali al-Mirghani, whose family had been forced to flee to Egypt during the Mahdiyya. Consequently, Sudanese nationalism after the First World War became entangled in the sectarian rivalry between the Khatmiyya under al-Mirghani and "neo-Mahdism" under Sayyid 'Abd al-Rahman al-Mahdi, a posthumous son of Muhammad Ahmad al-Mahdi.[13]

From the beginning, sectarian differences provided the backdrop of Sudanese political development, but it was the British Administration of the Sudan itself that fostered the emergence of a modern nationalist movement. Although the Mahdists conquered the Sudan and drew the numerous tribes of the north into the Mahdist state, they never completely stamped out opposition to their rule. Nor did all Muslims in the Sudan convert to the Mahdist creed. Neo-Mahdism, under 'Abd al-Rahman, also remained a largely sectarian movement. A modern nationalist movement, on the other hand, came from those Sudanese trained and educated in the western tradition by the government itself, which initially hoped

---

12. See, for example, Abdel Rahim, *Imperialism and Nationalism*; Beshir, *Revolution and Nationalism*; and Warburg, *Islam, Nationalism, and Communism*. More recent accounts have begun to question the central role of indigenous Sudanese nationalism in decolonization, though still not sufficiently for the present author. See especially Woodward, *Condominium*; and Daly, *Empire on the Nile and Imperial Sudan*.

13. For Mahdism and the most important "orthodox" Islamic sects in the Sudan see J. S. Trimingham, *Islam in the Sudan* (London, 1949). British fears of a Mahdist revival and the armed risings that fueled them are dealt with extensively in Daly, *Empire on the Nile*, chapters 3 and 7. See also H. A. Ibrahim, "The Mahdist Risings against the Condominium Government, 1900-1927," *International Journal of African Historical Studies* 12 no. 3 (1979).

to use them to replace Egyptians in the lower echelons of the administration. It was from these "effendis," as the British called them, that modern Sudanese nationalism appeared on the stage of Sudan politics.[14]

The first stirrings of this modern nationalism were felt in the years immediately following the First World War. A Sudanese officer of Dinka origins in the Egyptian army, 'Ali 'Abd al-Latif, began a campaign with the slogan "Sudan for the Sudanese." He was promptly put in jail. The movement did not end there, however. In 1924, as Anglo-Egyptian tensions were reaching a crisis, 'Abd al-Latif, who had been released, now reappeared, this time advocating an alliance with Egypt as the best means of obtaining independence from the British Administration of the Sudan. After numerous protests, including a strike by the cadets of the military academy in Khartoum, the whole movement culminated at the time of Stack's assassination in Egypt with the revolt of the XIth Sudanese in Khartoum. The revolt provided the Sudan Administration with all the proof it needed that the effendia could not be trusted and that the future of British rule in the Sudan must depend on the "traditional" and "tribal" leaders of the Sudanese. In the aftermath of the 1924 rising, indirect rule through traditional Sudanese leaders, the "tribal" *shaykhs* and "chiefs," became the sole basis of administrative policy in the Sudan.[15]

From the suppression of Sudanese nationalism in 1924, and the government's shift away from dealing with the western-educated Sudanese elite, until the Anglo-Egyptian Treaty twelve years later, Sudanese nationalism remained largely quiescent. There were no significant challenges to government authority based on any nationalist principles or slogans. The effendia were largely ignored by the administration and were considered useful only as potential adjuncts to the increasing number of native administrations being formed under "traditional" Sudanese leaders. Not until the appointment of Sir Stewart Symes to replace Sir John Maffey as governor-general in 1934 did the position of the effendia or the development of Sudanese nationalism receive any stimulus.

Symes determined to reverse the trend of indirect rule and native administration in the Sudan and to pursue instead a policy of reform and increased material prosperity for the Sudanese through economic development and modernization. Working against the tide of opinion in the Sudan Political Service, the new governor-general revived educational programs for the Sudanese and proclaimed his intention to bring trained Sudanese into the highest echelons of the administration. "Devolution," the slogan of indirect rule, meaning devolution of authority to the "traditional" Sudanese leaders, was transformed into "dilution,"

---

14. See M. W. Daly, *British Administration and the Northern Sudan, 1917-1924: The Governor-Generalship of Sir Lee Stack in the Sudan* (Leiden, 1980), chapter 2, part 2.

15. Ibid. For a discussion of the institution of indirect rule and subsequent reforms, see especially Gaafar Bakheit, *British Administration and Sudanese Nationalism, 1919-1939* (Cambridge, 1965). For the same themes in the Southern Sudan, see also Collins, *Shadows*.

by which Symes meant replacement of non-Sudanese with trained Sudanese members of the intelligentsia and a corresponding democratization of the autocratic native administrations. Nevertheless, progress was slow as the Political Service generally dragged its feet.[16]

The signing of the 1936 treaty marked a turning point, both in the development of Sudanese nationalist sentiments and in the attitude of the Sudan Political Service toward dilution and Symes's modernizing policies. With the possibility of a renewed Egyptian participation in the administration, most in the Political Service, and especially in the central secretariats in Khartoum, preferred the promotion of Sudanese. At the same time, educated Sudanese themselves felt slighted at having been ignored during the Anglo-Egyptian negotiations for the treaty. The Sudan clause declaring that the purpose of the condominium was the "welfare of the Sudanese" seemed to most of them to imply that they were incapable of taking care of themselves or participating in their own government. Determined that such a snub should not happen again, and with the full blessing and cooperation of the administration, which now saw Sudanese nationalism as a counterweight to Egyptian claims, in 1938 the educated Sudanese formed the Graduates' General Congress to represent "enlightened" Sudanese opinion to the government and the co-domini.[17]

To the dismay of the Sudan Administration, the Graduates' Congress soon became embroiled in the sectarian rivalry between Sayyid 'Abd al-Rahman and Sayyid 'Ali al-Mirghani. As the two sayyids each sought to influence the new body, a third element emerged in the Congress, devoted to neither of the sects but rather to a secular nationalism. Its leader was Isma'il al-Azhari, the future prime minister of the Sudan. Yet despite al-Azhari's commitment to a non-sectarian nationalism, he and his followers, the Ashiqqa Party, found it practically impossible to remain outside the Mahdist/Mirghanist struggle.

The main issues of Sudanese politics after the Second World War revolved around two questions: the best means of getting rid of the condominium regime; and opposition to or support of Sayyid 'Abd al-Rahman. So long as the two points remained connected, nonsectarianism had little chance of success. From the Sudanese perspective there were three possibilities: collaborate with the Sudan Government; woo Egyptian support; or reject both Egypt and the British and remain in a political wilderness. None of the major nationalist groups believed that they could effectively oppose both co-domini at the same time. All three major groups, the Mahdists, Mirghanists, and Ashiqqa, sought to play the co-domini against each other. At the same time, however, the question of looking to Egypt for support against the Sudan Government raised the further question of the Sudan's relationship with Cairo: was the Sudan, as Egyptians insisted, an integral part of the northern kingdom, or was it a separate entity? Many among the Ashiqqa believed that the Sudan and Egypt must be bound

---

16. Ibid.

17. For the 1936 treaty, see Ibrahim, "The Sudan in the 1936 Anglo-Egyptian Treaty," and H. A. Ibrahim, *The 1936 Anglo-Egyptian Treaty* (Khartoum, 1976).

together in at least some form, reflecting their ties of kinship, culture, and historical experience. The adamant refusal of the Mahdists to recognize any form of Egyptian sovereignty or dominance in the Sudan, however, effectively drew the battle lines.

It became progressively clear that Sayyid 'Abd al-Rahman had thrown in his lot with the Sudan Government. The Khatmiyya, opposing the Mahdists, joined the Ashiqqa, for sectarian and tactical reasons, in looking to Egypt as an ally. Given this fairly rigid political structure, the Sudan Government maneuvered as best it could, using political, economic, and administrative initiatives to achieve the goals of the Political Service and to salvage something of their influence in the future of the Sudan.

From the perspective of the Sudan Political Service, the Mirghanist/Mahdist split was both useful and dangerous. It was useful because it permitted the government to argue that no single group within the Sudanese nationalist movement could speak for the entire country; therefore the government must decide for itself what the best interests of the Sudanese might be. At the same time, the sectarian split forced the administration to compete with the Egyptians for the support of the two groups. While the Mahdists were unlikely ever to come to terms with any admission of Egyptian ascendancy in the Sudan (for obvious historical reasons), this was certainly a potential danger where the Khatmiyya was concerned. If the Sudan Government too openly supported the Mahdists, their natural anti-Egyptian allies, they would drive Sayyid 'Ali al-Mirghani and his followers into the arms of Egypt. Sectarianism therefore limited the extent to which the Sudan Government could raise the flag of Sudanese nationalism as a counter to Egyptian claims in the condominium, even as it gave them a weapon with which to prevent any wholesale British sellout to Egypt in exchange for an acceptable military alliance with Cairo. It was a weapon that members of the Political Service used as best they could—until it turned in their hands without warning, cutting the legs from under them and destroying all their plans for the future of the Sudan.

THE IMPORTANCE OF PERSONALITY

Finally, to understand the role played by the Sudan in Anglo-Egyptian relations after the Second World War, it is essential to bear in mind the structure and personalities of the Sudan Government. The 1899 Anglo-Egyptian Agreement concerning the Sudan had placed all power, civil and military, in the hands of the governor-general. As the military regime gave way to the civilian Sudan Political Service after the First World War, however, the governors-general themselves gradually retreated from involvement in the day-to-day affairs of government, instead leaving the details of administration in the hands of the so-called Three Secretaries—heads of the Financial Secretariat, the Legal Secretariat, and the Civil Secretariat. The civil secretary in particular, from being the least important of the Three Secretaries, emerged after 1924 as the leading administrator in the condominium. Consolidation of power in the hands of the civil secretaries was accelerated by the adoption of indirect rule as the administrative philosophy of the Sudan Government after Stack's assassination. As the official responsible for implementing indirect rule, the civil secretary of the day, Sir Harold MacMichael, was able to gather all the threads of administration into his own hands, even taking over many functions that had previously been handled in the Palace Secretariat of the governors-general.[18]

Under MacMichael's successors, Sir Angus Gillan and Sir Douglas Newbold, the pattern of administration he had laid down remained essentially intact through the Second World War. Although Newbold began a process of change that would eventually transform the administration, by the time of his unexpected death in 1945 his successor, James Robertson, still controlled the entire internal administration of the Sudan, including such departments as Police, Prisons, Agriculture, Intelligence, Native Administration and Local Government, Aviation, Game Preservation, Forestry, Veterinary Services, and Personnel. He also shared responsibility with the financial secretary for the social and political aspects of economic schemes like the Gezira cotton plantations, the centerpiece of the country's export economy, and he generally oversaw labor matters in the condominium. He was a member of all major government committees and commissions, usually as chairman, and was the de facto head of the Governor-General's Council. Overshadowing all, perhaps, he was the acknowledged head of the Political Service itself, appointing (subject to the governor-general's approval) all administrative officers, from provincial governors to the lowliest assistant district commissioners and their Egyptian and Sudanese subordinates. Most important for this study, as civil secretary he was also the central figure responsible for "external" affairs, which primarily meant relations with the co-domini.[19]

Although he functioned theoretically only with the governor-general's authority, Robertson was himself probably the most important actor in the post-war drama of the Sudan, not only because of his policies but also because he remained at the helm of the Sudan Political Service from 1945 until the final demarche in 1953. Like Newbold, his predecessor and mentor, Robertson represented the second generation of the Sudan Political Service. Where Newbold had been molded by his experiences in the First World War, however, Robertson, a slightly younger man, had been spared both the romance of campaigning in the Libyan desert and the disillusionment of trench warfare on the Western Front. Neither a romantic nor an idealist, he seems always to have retained a sense of optimistic, almost boyish, innocence from the prewar era. One historian who knew Robertson has characterized him as "a Scot and a Balliol man in that order...intelligent but not an intellectual, gruff without pomposity, and kind

---

18. An implicit treatment of the shift in power from the governor-general to the civil secretary and the Political Service may be found in Daly's *British Administration*, as well as in his *Empire on the Nile*.

19. *Sudan Gazette*, 1945; Robertson, *Transition*, chapter 6.

without affectation." His temper was "titanic, matching his physique....He had to suffer fools, of course, but not gladly." He also had a sense of humor, slightly sardonic at times, often self-deprecating, and generally a bit ponderous. Robertson was above all the captain of the varsity, practicing the "art of the possible" with an air of dignity, certainly, but a dignity tempered generally by a sense of proportion and informed with a thoroughly pragmatic common sense.[20]

Robertson's plans as civil secretary for the internal development of the Sudan are beyond the scope of this book, but at the heart of them was a determination that the Sudan should be independent of Egypt and, if necessary, even from Britain. Since his own rather harrowing experience of the 1924 crisis as a solitary district officer in Blue Nile province, where he had marked Stack's assassination by hauling down the Egyptian flag, Robertson had come to see Egypt as the principal threat to all of the Political Service's work for the Sudanese. In September 1944, when Newbold was considering allowing the newly created Sudanese Advisory Council for the Northern Sudan to discuss the politically sensitive question of Sudanese nationality, Robertson, at the time deputy civil secretary, publicly responded to Egyptian charges that Khartoum was trying to separate the Sudan from Egypt. It was more than an official disclaimer, and it expressed his personal convictions about the status of the Sudan and the purpose of the Sudan Government.

The Sudan is constituted as a separate administrative entity by treaties; constitutionally it is a part neither of Egypt nor of Britain, and it is administered by the Sudan Government under the authority of a condominium of the Powers. . . . The Sudan Government is attempting to train the peoples of the Sudan for local self-government and the management of their own affairs . . . to develop institutions which exist in one form or another in all civilized countries.

As Egyptian pressure on Khartoum increased, so too did Robertson's conviction that the Sudanese must be protected at all costs from the "corrupt rule of the pashas." It was from this perspective that he prepared for Anglo-Egyptian re-negotiation of the 1936 treaty.[21]

In addition to Robertson, two other personalities stand out in the formulation and implementation of the Sudan's policy toward the co-domini in the postwar period: the Governors-General Sir Hubert Huddleston and Sir Robert Howe. Huddleston's role in particular was crucial in the years between 1945 and 1947, in defying both Egypt and Britain to preserve the Political Service vision of an eventually independent Sudan for the Sudanese. Huddleston was himself an old Sudan hand, having been first posted to the condominium in 1909. After a brief period doing administrative work in the Nuba mountains, he had joined the Xth Sudanese battalion of the Egyptian Army, eventually becoming the commander of the Camel Corps, and in 1916 he was instrumental in the campaign that

---

20. Collins, *Shadows*, 278.
21. The text of the statement was reported in *The Times*, 7 September 1944.

brought Darfur into the Sudan. In the early twenties Huddleston drew up the plans for disarming and evacuating all Egyptian troops in the condominium, and in 1924, at the time of the revolt, he executed the plans personally. Moreover, as acting sirdar after Stack's assassination, it was Huddleston Pasha who challenged the XIth Sudanese battalion as they marched to the Blue Nile bridge from their barracks, and it was Huddleston who ordered the Argyll and Sutherlands to open fire when the Sudanese refused to obey his orders. In the aftermath of the revolt, as all Egyptian troops were removed from the condominium, he was the principal architect of the Sudan Defence Force. After service outside the condominium, in 1940 Huddleston seemed a logical choice to take over as governor-general during the war.[22]

Huddleston's appointment to the Palace in Khartoum proved fateful not only for wartime morale in the Sudan but also for the peace which followed. He was a commanding personality, physically as well as psychologically. Staunchly moral, he had an unyielding sense of honor, as well as of responsibility, and refused to be bullied by anyone, least of all the Foreign Office—particularly one run by a Labour Government. Judging from his letters, Huddleston's worldview seems to have derived from the old Tory Party. He believed in the "values of the countryman" as he put it, by which he seems to have meant the paternalism of the landed gentry. Besides being an imperialist, he was essentially a Disraeli Conservative of the type that would have applauded the overthrow of Sir Robert Peel, and that, as Benjamin Disraeli himself put it, "has maintained at all times the territorial constitution of England as the only basis and security for local government." Huddleston would have agreed with Disraeli's conclusion in *Sybil* that "Loyalty is not a phrase, Faith not a delusion, and Popular Liberty something more diffusive and substantial than the profane exercise of the sacred rights of sovereignty by political classes." It is important here to remember that Huddleston's political views were shaped in the pre–First World War era, long

---

22. For an overview of Huddleston's career in the Sudan, see especially references in Collins, *Shadows*, passim. For evaluations of his early career that are considerably less flattering, see also Daly's *Empire on the Nile*, which characterizes Huddleston, at least in the twenties, as "trigger happy." For tributes from his colleagues and subordinates, see Robertson, *Transition*, 100-101, and especially Hugh Boustead, *The Wind of Morning* (London, 1971) 75-77, and 86-89. Huddleston evidently had a photographic memory, which may account for his vast repertoire of quotations, and an uncanny ability to give verbatim accounts, some twenty years later without benefit of notes, of despatches written at the time of Stack's assassination. According to Boustead, he was known among the Sudanese as "the hyena with the white feet," a reference (not necessarily flattering) to his penchant for night marches and his use of white spats to protect his ankles from thornbushes during his tenure as Kaid. For his role in the postwar negotiations, see especially W. Travis Hanes III, "Sir Hubert Huddleston and the Independence of the Sudan," *Journal of Imperial and Commonwealth History* 20, no. 2 (May 1992).

before Lloyd George and the Labour Party between them had destroyed the Liberals and forced the postwar transformation of the Conservative Party.[23]

As governor-general, Huddleston was largely content to leave the administration in the hands of the civil secretary, viewing his own role much like that of a constitutional monarch. Nevertheless, he was always thoroughly acquainted with the issues of the day, and frequently made shrewd policy suggestions that were welcomed by the Political Service. Above all, probably due to his experiences in 1924, Huddleston too was convinced that the Sudan must be defended at all costs against any Egyptian "infiltration" of the condominium. It was therefore with the governor-general's full support and considerable prestige behind him that Robertson formulated his policies toward the co-domini on the basis of a Sudan permanently independent from Egypt. As will be seen, Huddleston's unyielding commitment to an independent Sudan caused him to run afoul of both the Egyptian and the British governments. Where Robertson's position as a civil servant was essentially buffered from interference by the co-domini, as a political appointee Huddleston had no such cover. When his tenure was not renewed in 1947, Ernest Bevin handpicked his replacement, Sir Robert Howe, from among the Foreign Office career diplomats. Bevin certainly intended that Howe should be a more pliable tool than had been the crusty major general; with Robertson in the picture, however, it was not to be.[24]

Given Robertson's forceful personality, Howe, who seems to have been a mild-mannered character to say the least, probably had little chance for an independent policy of his own. The son of a train engineer, Howe had difficulty being accepted by the elitist Political Service and may actually have been rather intimidated by them. Moreover, as a career diplomat with little experience of the Sudan (he knew the country only through his post as British minister to Addis Ababa during the war), he had little impact on the actual administration of the

---

23. Disraeli, Benjamin, *Sybil* (London, 1985) 497.

24. Howe has not been the subject of any biographical study. For details of his life and career, see the *Dictionary of National Biography*. Varying assessments of his character may be found in Louis, *British Empire,* Daly, *Imperial Sudan*, and Collins, *Shadows*. Most in the Political Service seem to have found him aloof and a bit cold-blooded —at least there were loud complaints about the amount of time he spent away from Khartoum and the condominium, as well as his lack of sensitivity toward the departing staff in the transitional days before Sudanese independence. "There was no one even to shake us by the hand as we left and wish us good luck," was a not uncommon comment. On the other hand, some of his subordinates found him to be an uncommonly sensitive individual, "a mystic of great erudition" as Duncan put it in *The Sudan's Path*, 186. In retirement he seems to have become a rather bitter and lonely man (his wife died shortly after leaving the Sudan) and was apparently quite hurt by what he considered his shabby treatment at the hands of the Political Service. Such, at any rate, was the assessment of K.D.D. Henderson, former governor of Darfur, who visited Howe in his retirement in Wales (private communication, Henderson to the author).

condominium. Once beyond the reach of the foreign secretary, despite the circumstances of his appointment, he quickly adopted the Political Service position on Egyptian participation in the condominium. In his own words, within a fortnight of his arrival he was "heart and soul" with the Political Service and against any admission of Egyptian sovereignty over the Sudan. Even so, perhaps the greatest significance of Howe's tenure as governor-general between 1947 and 1953 was that he and Lady Howe suffered from the heat of Khartoum and consequently spent much time on leave or on tour. This left Robertson in virtual control of policy development as well as administration during critical periods of negotiation. To his credit, however, even after Robertson's departure in 1953, Howe continued staunchly to defend the Sudanese right to self-determination and independence in the face of continuing Egyptian efforts to prevent it. Like Huddleston, who had defied Labour Foreign Secretary, Ernest Bevin, Howe too refused to be bullied by the Foreign Office, particularly after it had been reoccuppied by Conservative Foreign Secretary Anthony Eden in late 1951. Eventually, Howe's diplomatic skills served both the Sudan and the British governments in good stead as he played the diplomatic game he knew best—conciliating the leading Sudanese politicians. In particular, his friendship with Isma'il al-Azhari, the future Sudanese prime minister, did much to smooth over the transition to independence. In the meantime, however, as will be seen, Howe proved as jealous of the Political Service plan for the Sudan and the rights of the Sudanese themselves to self-determination as Robertson and the Political Service could have wished.

1

The Politics of Condominium:
Winter and Spring 1946

In the Egyptian nationalist view, the original purpose of the 1899 Condominium Agreement, has, under one hypocritical pretext or another, been set aside, and an exclusively British Government on a colonial pattern installed in the Sudan. Egypt . . . and the Sudanese . . . have been treated as pawns on the chess-board of British imperialist strategy. Egyptian demands for the British evacuation of the Sudan are based on these false premises.
—Sir Stewart Symes, *The Times*, 13 March 1946

On 20 December 1945, the Royal Egyptian Government delivered an official note to the British Government asking for renegotiation of the Anglo-Egyptian Treaty of 1936, the principal diplomatic instrument that had governed Anglo-Egyptian relations for the previous ten years. The Egyptian note involved two primary questions: evacuation of British troops from Egypt; and the unity of the Nile Valley—in other words, the Egyptian question and the Sudan question. From the Egyptian perspective, the presence of British troops in the major cities of the land as well as in the vast Suez base constituted an intolerable infringement of Egyptian sovereignty and territorial integrity. The British, on the other hand, viewed their military presence as vital not only to the defense of Egypt but to the Western world in general. The prospect of war had not been banished by the defeat of the Axis Powers. It seemed to many in London, as also in Washington, to have taken root afresh in the growing hostility of the Soviet Union. As the cold war intensified, so did British efforts to ensure their military needs in the treaty revisions.[1]

---

1. A useful overview of the problems and background involved in this chapter can be found in George Kirk, *Survey of International Affairs: The Middle East, 1945-1950*, (Oxford, 1954), 116-29. For a more detailed analysis based on the relevant archival sources see especially W. R. Louis, *The British Empire*, part 2, chapter 6. The text of the Egyptian note, dated 20 December 1945, is in FO 371/45929, PRO.

For the British foreign secretary, Ernest Bevin, the primary concern in any treaty negotiations would be the question of regional Middle Eastern security and the retention of Britain's access to strategic military facilities in Egypt. The Sudan, at least initially, was of secondary importance to him. In fact, Bevin originally expected to reproduce the basic elements of the existing treaty, making only "cosmetic" changes to remove any appearance of continuing British "imperialism" in Egypt. In short, the foreign secretary hoped to salve the Egyptian *amour propre*, without jeopardizing Britain's dominant position in the Middle East. The ethos of the Labour Government had not changed British strategic interests or priorities: it simply dictated new methods for ensuring them.[2]

As for the Sudan question, unity of the Nile Valley meant considerably more to the Egyptians than the British ever believed. Egyptians viewed the territory of the condominium as an integral part of the Kingdom of Egypt, the administration of which had been "stolen" from them by British imperialism. For the British, on the other hand, apart from its strategic position commanding the Nile, the Sudan was inextricably linked with the name of Gordon, evoking images for the British people of the best and most altruistic achievements and self-sacrifice of Britain's "civilizing mission." Moreover, in the Sudan Political Service, the condominium had a well-organized and influential voice with which to assert the independent rights and well-being of the Sudanese, even if from a paternalistic viewpoint. More than one ex-member of the Service sat in the House of Commons. Despite Bevin's priorities, no negotiations between Egypt and Britain could be successfully concluded unless they dealt with the Sudan.

In Khartoum, both the governor-general, Sir Hubert Huddleston, and the civil secretary, James Robertson, had already anticipated the Egyptian note by reasserting the rights of the Sudanese people themselves. In November 1945, Robertson had promised the Advisory Council for the Northern Sudan that the Sudanese would be consulted should the future status of the condominium be raised in Anglo-Egyptian negotiations. At the same time, both he and Huddleston worked to obtain the endorsement of the British Government for the principle of consultation, and in December the Foreign Office too committed itself when the British under secretary of state for foreign affairs, Hector McNeil, virtually reproduced Robertson's pledge in the House of Commons. Angling for a British declaration guaranteeing to the Sudanese the eventual right of complete self-determination, in the first few months of 1946 Robertson pressed the question of how consultation should be effected and what Sudanese groups should be included in the process. Using the pledges to the Sudanese as leverage, both the civil secretary and the governor-general sought a comprehensive British policy statement that would repudiate once and for all any Egyptian claims to an equal share in the condominium administration, that would recognize and support

---

2. See especially Bevin's Memorandum for the Cabinet, C.P.(46)17, 18 January 1946, FO 371/53282, PRO.

the Sudan Government's development policies, and that would reinforce the Political Service's own hand with the Sudanese nationalists.[3]

OPENING GAMBITS

In early January 1946, Robertson gave an interview to a special correspondent of *Le Journal D'Egypte (Misri)* publicly reiterating the intention of the Sudan Government to consult the Sudanese on their future status. Although the civil secretary tried to reassure the Egyptians, denying that Sudan Government policy aimed at separating Egypt and the Sudan, his references to consultation alarmed the northern co-dominus. The "referendum" that would decide the future of the Sudanese, he declared, would take place when the co-domini had entered into consultations. A general plebiscite, however, would not be possible: there were still areas in the Sudan that did not understand Arabic and where the inhabitants had never heard of either Egypt or England. Instead, Robertson suggested, the Sudan Government would consult "certain bodies representing public opinion," such as the Advisory Council for the Northern Sudan, the province councils, and perhaps the chambers of commerce and certain individuals. Despite his efforts at reassurance, the civil secretary only emphasized Egyptian fears that the Sudan Government was pursuing a separatist policy.[4]

Robertson's interview irritated the Embassy. The ambassador, Lord Killearn, wrote to Huddleston complaining that the civil secretary's references to consultation of the Sudanese would be "unpalatable" to the Egyptians. Already, the ambassador reminded the governor-general, Egypt was charging that the British intended to consult the Sudanese only through organizations controlled by the Sudan Government—in effect by the British themselves. Robertson's statements about the impossibility of a general referendum would only tend to confirm the Egyptian view. Even more important, the ambassador wanted Khartoum to stop making waves for the Embassy unnecessarily. "May I ask once again," Killearn wrote, "that we may, without fail, receive previous

---

3. Robertson's Monthly Letter (hereafter cited as C.S. letter), no. 93, 5 January 1946, Perham Papers (hereafter MP) 571/2. For McNeil's statement see Great Britain, *Parliamentary Debates (Commons)*, vol. 418 cols. For Robertson's and Huddleston's efforts to obtain a British statement of policy, see above.

4. "Affaires Soudanaises," *Journal d'Egypte*, 10 January 1946. An extract of this article can also be found in FO 371/53249, PRO. Disingenuously, Robertson even insisted that the Sudan Government had no Sudanization policy; it simply appointed Sudanese to those positions where they were qualified. All positions were advertised in both Cairo and London—if Egyptians were rarely chosen, he suggested, "c'est que les détenteurs de diplômes supérieurs réclament de forts traitements, et, en général, n'aiment pas séjourner au Soudan." Concluding the interview, Robertson denied allegations that any obstacles were placed in the way of Egyptians wishing to enter the Sudan: after all, the Treaty of 1936 provided for free entry as soon as the health regulations had been complied with.

warning of pronouncements by the Sudan Government which . . . are bound to
have political repercussions in Egypt? The danger of such repercussions is now
greater than ever."[5]

Killearn's irritation with Khartoum stemmed partly from his own delicate
position. The British Government had not yet officially replied to the Egyptian
note of 20 December. Nor had it decided how the Sudan question should be
handled. Speculation in the Sudan itself during 1945 had included the possibility
that a trusteeship under the United Nations might be arranged. Some in the
Political Service believed that such an arrangement would at least guarantee the
eventual independence of the Sudan. Moreover, they expected that Britain would
be the trustee, with the administration remaining in the hands of the existing
Sudan Government. Such thoughts were anathema to the Embassy in Cairo. At
the end of January, Killearn telegraphed the Foreign Office, urging that the
British side should steer all commentary away from any suggestion that the
Sudan would be administered by the United Nations, that the Sudanese would be
prepared to accept "Egyptian tutelage," or that "it is now a bargaining match
between Great Britain and Egypt in promising the Sudanese self government."
Anxious to avoid further Sudanese complications, the Foreign Office agreed.[6]

The British response on 27 January 1946 to the Egyptian request for treaty
negotiations only increased the pressure on the Sudan Administration. Agreeing
to discuss revision, Bevin nevertheless publicly suggested that the 1936 treaty
should itself remain the basis for any further agreement. "The essential
soundness" of the treaty, he insisted, had been demonstrated during the war. As
for the Sudan, apart from acknowledging that Egypt wanted to include the issue
in the negotiations, the foreign secretary made no other comment, neither
agreeing to Egyptian claims nor refuting them. For many Egyptians, it was not
an auspicious beginning for negotiations. From Cairo's perspective, not even
the Labour Government seemed willing to deal with Egypt on an equal basis and
in good faith.[7]

The Egyptians were unpleasantly surprised at the length of time it took the
new Labour Government to respond to their request. Although having agreed to
negotiations in principle the Foreign Office did not name the negotiating team
until 30 March. Moreover, when it did, the names proved thoroughly
unacceptable to the Egyptians. Bevin had appointed the ambassador in Cairo as
the head of the British negotiating delegation, supported by his advisors in the
Embassy. It was a serious mistake, confirming the fears of Egyptian nationalists
that even the Labour Government was not really committed to any equitable
relationship between the two countries. After all, Lord Killearn had intervened on
at least four occasions during the war to determine the composition of the
Egyptian Cabinet. He and his advisors, particularly Oriental Secretary Sir Walter

---

5. Killearn to Huddleston, 19 January 1946, FO 371/53249, PRO.

6. Cairo to Foreign Office, no. 143, 31 January 1946, FO 371/53250, PRO.

7. For an evaluation of Bevin's statement and the Egyptian reaction, see especially
Kirk, *The Middle East*, 117-20.

Smart, were considered by most Egyptian nationalists as the principal architects of Britain's "imperialist" policy in Egypt. Bevin's response, therefore, offered little promise for an adequate redress of the Egyptian grievances over the 1936 treaty.[8]

While the Foreign Office seemed to vacillate over any far-reaching revision of Britain's relationship with Egypt, the Egyptians themselves took to the streets. Angered not only by the attitude of the British but also by the apparent acquiescence of the Egyptian Cabinet, on 9 February Egyptian nationalists and students rioted in Cairo and Alexandria. The prime minister, Mahmoud Fahmi al-Nuqrashi Pasha, banned public demonstrations, but with little effect. Moreover, the ban apparently annoyed King Farouk, who sympathized with the anti-British demonstrators. By the thirteenth, al-Nuqrashi Pasha had been replaced by Isma'il Sidqi Pasha, a wealthy, politically independent politician, a former prime minister who had dominated Egyptian politics in the early 1930s at the head of a corrupt and oppressive anti-Wafdist Government. Sidqi promptly rescinded the ban. Further demonstrations and a general strike lasting through the rest of March and into early April were accompanied by attacks on British personnel and the destruction of British property.[9]

Against this background of violence, in March, Lord Killearn retired as ambassador, to be replaced by Sir Ronald Campbell. After representations from Sidqi Pasha, on 2 April the British foreign secretary also changed his previous stand on the treaty delegation and announced that he himself would lead the British negotiating team. Furthermore, preliminary discussions would be handled by a Cabinet-level mission under the leadership of the minister for air, Lord Stansgate. Bevin's decision to handle negotiations personally and the appointment of the Stansgate delegation transformed the situation in Egypt; combined with Killearn's departure, it convinced many Egyptians that the British Labour Government was now prepared to negotiate in good faith.[10]

In Khartoum, both Robertson and Huddleston viewed the changes with considerable trepidation. Ironically perhaps, they lamented the disappearance of Lord Killearn from the scene. For all his faults from Khartoum's perspective, Killearn had been a tower of British strength on the Nile. Despite his inevitable preoccupation with Egypt, often at the expense of the Sudan, the Sudan officials appreciated Killearn's capacity to use force if necessary to preserve British interests in both countries. They were less sanguine about Campbell, not least because he had been appointed by Bevin. Stansgate too worried them. Sidqi Pasha had commended the air minister's appointment—"as Mr. Wedgwood Benn, he defended the Egyptian cause in and out of Parliament just after World War One, when few other Britons spoke favourably on behalf of my country"—but

---

8. Ibid. See also Louis, *British Empire*, part 2, chapter 6.

9. Louis, *British Empire*, part 2, chapter 6. See also C.S. letter nos. 95 and 96, March and April 1946, and Sudan Political Intelligence Summary no. 56, January-April 1946, MP 571/2.

10. Sudan Political Intelligence Summary no. 56, January-April 1946, MP 571/2.

this hardly constituted a recommendation to Sudan Political Service members who remembered the turmoil of the 1920s and the assassination of Sir Lee Stack. Eleven months later, after the failure of Stansgate's mission, Robertson wrote: "I hope Lord Stansgate will now pass gently out of our affairs, and not interfere any more. I have never been less impressed by anyone and I think he was a menace all through." Robertson was even more scathing about the new ambassador. "Campbell too is a featureless chap with no personality: the Embassy has now lost all power and prestige in Cairo, and the old Residency atmosphere has gone. When Killearn was there we had a big man, who counted in Egypt." As Anglo-Egyptian negotiations drew nearer, both Robertson and the rest of the Political Service braced for the coming ordeal.[11]

THE EGYPTIAN "COUNTEROFFENSIVE"

While the Embassy and the Foreign Office tried to downplay the Sudan issue in Anglo-Egyptian negotiations, the Egyptians did precisely the opposite. From the end of December 1945, the civil secretary's office complained of an impending Egyptian "counterattack" in the Sudan. In January 1946 King Farouk's name was reintroduced in the Friday prayers by the imam of the Khartoum mosque. About the same time, numerous Egyptian officials began to make the trek south, visiting both the Northern and the Southern Sudan. On 5 January Robertson warned the Political Service that within the next two months it could expect several Beys, a number of journalists, and some 180 students from Egyptian universities and secondary schools to tour the Sudan. A few days later the Egyptian minister of education, Dr. 'Abd al-Razzaq Sanhouri Bey, arrived in Khartoum to open a new Egyptian secondary school. Sanhouri Bey's visit proved to be the first major shot in the new Egyptian propaganda campaign.[12]

Although subsequently reporting that the Egyptian Minister had been personally "careful to preserve all the proprieties," Robertson complained that some members of Sanhouri's entourage were "less guarded." The attitude of Egyptian journalists in the party especially disgusted the civil secretary. They had obviously come south to sound out Sudanese opinion on the question of union with Egypt and "were merely out to get hold of material which they could use (or abuse) in the Egyptian political interest." Even more alarming from Robertson's perspective, Sanhouri Bey's visits seemed deliberately designed to publicize the pro-Egyptian faction among the Sudanese nationalists: he took great pains to be photographed with Sayyid 'Ali al-Mirghani, leader of the

11. Sidqi is quoted in Kirk, *The Middle East*, 119-20. For his full comment see *Times*, 22 April 1946. Robertson's assessment is in Robertson to Mayall, 18 February 1947, Robertson Papers, SAD (hereafter RP) 521/6/29.

12. C.S. letter no. 93, 5 January 1946, MP 571/2.

Khatmiyya, and Isma'il al-Azhari appeared prominently at receptions and social functions for the Egyptian entourage.[13]

Nor was Sanhouri Bey the only Egyptian visitor to cause difficulties for Sudan authorities. His visit was followed closely by that of Muhammad Mahmud Gelal Bey, a lawyer who was also a confirmed nationalist, an adherent of the Ikhwan al-Muslimin (Muslim Brotherhood), and a member of the Egyptian Parliament. Although ostensibly interested in cottonseed oil, Gelal Bey used his visit to indulge in propaganda for both the Muslim Brotherhood and the unity of the Nile Valley. Similar propaganda was spread by Egyptian students and their professors. As Robertson put it, Sanhouri Bey's visit had resulted in "a distinct rise in the political temperature" in the Sudan.[14]

While the visits of Egyptians might seem of little consequence to outside observers, the Sudan Political Service viewed them as potentially explosive. In terms reminiscent of the aftermath of 1924, Robertson and Huddleston saw the Egyptian campaign as a kind of airborne infection, against which they feared the unsophisticated Sudanese had no natural immunities. While their complaints to the Embassy and the Foreign Office frequently sounded petty and alarmist, as they bemoaned Egypt's seduction of the Sudanese, Robertson and Huddleston were responding in true Political Service fashion to an old nightmare. "Although each Egyptian visit may be innocuous and cannot be prevented on the grounds of public security," Robertson wrote in the first week of February 1946, "the series of visits one after another undoubtedly does raise the temperature and in the long run must affect public security." The civil secretary warned that there would be a "good deal of bother" before the new treaty was signed, including demonstrations and rioting in the larger towns if "riff-raff and corner-boys are excited and suitably financed by politically-minded agitators."[15]

Only a few days later, several incidents occurred involving Egyptian troops in the Sudan which the governor-general took even more seriously. On 11

---

13. Note on visit to Sudan of Dr. Abd El Razzaq Sanhuri Bey . . . January 1946, FO 371/53250, PRO. On the ninth al-Azhari hosted a tea in honor of the education minister and given by the Congress at the Omdurman Graduates Club. A Congress speaker, Mubarak Zarruq, reviewed the Congress's history since 1938 and concluded by reiterating Congress's claim to be the only legitimate and representative voice of the Sudanese people. Azhari closed the meeting by raising three cheers for King Farouk. It had been, in the government's estimation, "quite frankly a political meeting."

14. C.S. letter no. 94, 6 February 1946, MP 571/2; Annexure to Khartoum Despatch no. 24, 12 February 1946, FO 371/53250, PRO. One visitor in particular, Dr. Abd al-Moneim Sharqawi, a lecturer in law at Farouk University, delivered a lecture to about five hundred people at the Sudan Schools Club in Omdurman, a lecture that the Sudan Government found especially contentious. Sharqawi called arguments for separation "a very bogus claim. . . . the policy of the usurper . . . who seeks his own private aims . . . his cotton for the Cotton Companies, nothing else." Separation had resulted only in "tyranny, disease, poverty and ignorance."

15. C.S. letter no. 94, 6 February 1946, MP 571/2.

February, at a luncheon given by the Egyptian troops in Port Sudan in celebration of King Farouk's birthday, the Egyptian officer commanding, Bimbashi Dessouki, raised a cheer for "the King of Egypt and the Sudan." Despite the Egyptian monarch's intervention to retain him in the Sudan, Huddleston had Dessouki transferred back to Egypt. Several days later a similar incident occurred when a group of Egyptian soldiers were marched *en bloc* to a cinema where a picture of Farouk and Ibn Saud appeared. Once again the cry was raised, three cheers for Farouk, king of Egypt and the Sudan. This time the governor-general asked the chief staff officer of Egyptian troops in the Sudan to issue written orders making such actions liable to punishment. When the Egyptian minister of defence intervened, agreeing only to issue verbal orders, Huddleston vowed to carry his complaint to the Egyptian Cabinet.[16]

The incident of the Egyptian Bimbashi galvanized the governor-general. Huddleston had been observing developments with growing alarm. The day after the Port Sudan incident, he drafted a strongly worded despatch to Killearn outlining his concerns and advocating a stronger stance toward Egyptian propaganda. Although the administration had done its best to accommodate Egyptian visitors, even providing them with fare concessions on railways and steamers in the Sudan, Huddleston complained, "our hospitality has been grossly abused." Despite efforts to be fair to Egypt, Huddleston declared, the virulence of the propaganda campaign in the Sudan as well as the "Wafdist agitation already threatening to disturb the peace of Cairo" compelled him to take measures to prevent the spread of Egyptian disorders into the Sudan.[17]

Huddleston also blamed the British for the worsening atmosphere in the condominium. The older "stable elements" among the Sudanese, he warned, were worried that their voice, "the true voice of the country," would be "drowned in the irresponsible clamour of Ashiqqa youth." The uncertainty of British policy undermined their local authority as well as their faith in Britain and the Sudan Government. At best, these Sudanese leaders foresaw a further relegation of the Sudan question and an increasingly unstable condominium; at worst, they feared "a repetition of the events of 1924—a recurrence of disorders, in which Sudanese lives and Sudanese prospects will once again be sacrificed to Egyptian political intrigue." The time had finally arrived, Huddleston threatened, when the Sudan Government would be justified in exercising, "with a new severity," its power under the 1936 Treaty to deny entry to Egyptian visitors whose presence might threaten public order.[18]

The next day, Huddleston sent an even more alarming assessment of the deteriorating situation in the Sudan, where reports that Egypt would accept no less than total British evacuation of her territory, and the incorporation of the Sudan into the Egyptian kingdom, had caused "widespread anxiety" among the Sudanese. Huddleston was experiencing an intense feeling of déjà vu:

---

16. Ibid., no. 95, 12 March 1946.
17. Huddleston to Killearn, no. 24, 12 February 1946, FO 371/53250, PRO.
18. Ibid.

The position at the moment is in many ways similar to the early days of 1924, when the late Sir Lee Stack wrote in his Despatch No. 69 of May 25th 1924:

"Whatever the outcome of the forthcoming negotiations, in order to retain the confidence of the people and to maintain British authority it is essential that His Majesty's Government should give a clear pronouncement that British control will not be withdrawn from the Sudan."

Huddleston even provided a draft statement that he hoped the British Government would issue. Denying any intention to influence the Sudanese either for or against Egypt, London should nevertheless reassert that the object of the condominium must be the welfare of the Sudanese and that the Sudanese alone should decide their future status. In the meantime:

Their welfare cannot be secured unless a stable and disinterested administration is maintained in the Sudan. The objects of such an administration must be the establishment of the organs of self-government, the appointment of Sudanese to government posts as and when qualified, and the raising of the capacity of the mass of the people for effective citizenship. These are the objects of the present Sudan Government, and His Majesty's Government fully support them. . . . His Majesty's Government will agree to no change in the status of the Sudan as a result of Treaty Revision until the Sudanese have been consulted through constitutional channels.

Only such a declaration by the secretary of state, Huddleston declared, would rally those Sudanese "looking for a sign." Without it, he warned again, "the position may well deteriorate until trouble similar to that of 1924 occurs and . . . rioting and possible bloodshed put back the schemes of political, educational, medical and economic development now being planned, and alienate the affections of the people for years to come."[19]

Huddleston's argument failed to move the Embassy. Killearn agreed that the "abuses" of Egyptian propaganda should be taken up with the Egyptian Government, but he preferred to do this himself, informally, with the Egyptian prime minister—and anyway the coming hot weather would probably discourage further Egyptian junkets south. Instead of gratuitously denying visas or laying down public principles that might be contentious, it would be better for the Embassy and the Palace to consult as the need arose on an individual basis. On the most important question, a statement of British policy, Killearn was polite but firm: "Having weighed carefully the cogent arguments put forward by the Governor General in favor of such a statement, I nevertheless consider that at this moment it would be inopportune." It had been agreed to give Sidqi Pasha a chance, the ambassador pointed out, to produce an atmosphere conducive to successful treaty negotiations in Egypt. Only if Sidqi failed to restore and maintain order would there be a strong case for issuing Huddleston's statement.[20]

---

19. Ibid., no. 25, 13 February 1946.
20. Killearn to Bevin, no. 320, 4 March 1946, FO 371/53250, PRO.

Although Huddleston's despatches had not overly impressed Lord Killearn, repeated references to 1924 were not wasted on the Foreign Office. Patrick Scrivener had pricked up his ears in some alarm. The head of the Egyptian Department admitted to being considerably more impressed than the ambassador by Huddleston's "grave warning" concerning an outbreak of disorders. "No one knows better than the Governor-General," Scrivener minuted, "what happened in 1924, and I do not think we should run any risk of its happening again out of deference for the susceptibilities of the present Egyptian administration." Like moderate Sudanese, Foreign Office officials were slightly mystified by Khartoum's reluctance to put a halt to the Egyptian campaign. Why, one Egyptian Department official wondered, if the Sudanese were asking for steps to be taken denying entry to the Egyptians, did the governor-general not do so? Scrivener agreed that Huddleston's despatches made "unpleasant reading" and that "the Sudan Govt. have been rather too 'coulant' with these nefarious Egyptian propagandist activities in the Sudan."[21]

The answer to such questions was actually quite simple, though neither the Egyptians nor the Foreign Office would have credited it: the Sudan Government believed itself to be the agent of both co-domini. However much they preferred Britain, officials in Khartoum scrupulously attempted to maintain at least the appearance of a condominium. Huddleston and Robertson believed they could restrict Egyptian propaganda only when it directly threatened the constitutional foundations of the condominium itself. Indeed, it was for this reason that they so desperately wanted a British declaration to counter Egyptian claims. Despite all their efforts, Lord Killearn remained adamant—and in any contest between the Palace and the Embassy, the advantages lay with the latter. Yet as Douglas Newbold had once observed in 1944, with Britain and Egypt in disagreement, the Sudanese themselves became the leverage point in condominium politics. In the end, it was neither Palace nor Foreign Office that swayed the Embassy, but Sudanese nationalists.[22]

THE SUDANESE DELEGATION IN CAIRO

As Huddleston had feared, in early March the disturbances occurring in Egypt spilled over into the Sudan. On the fourth, while Egyptian students observed a "day of mourning" for the "victims" of the Cairo riots, students at Gordon Memorial College decided to march through the streets of Khartoum in sympathy. The procession, accompanied by police, was peaceful and lasted about an hour. The next morning about three hundred students from the King Farouk School and the Coptic Egyptian School, apparently with the acquiescence of

21. Minute by Scrivener, 17 March 1946, FO 371/53250, PRO.

22. Ibid.; see also Foreign Office to Cairo, no. 491, 18 March 1946, FO 371/53250, PRO. Killearn's replacement, Campbell, also resisted such a measure on the advice of his Embassy officials.

faculty members and the headmasters of the two schools, also carried out a peaceful two-hour demonstration in Khartoum.[23] On 6 March, the "infection," as the Sudan Political Intelligence Report put it, spread to Omdurman to government secondary and junior-secondary schools. Some two hundred students, accompanied by "corner-boys and riff-raff" marched through Omdurman market and then set out for Khartoum. Another procession was organized by a group of school boys from Omdurman. Accompanied by police, both groups eventually marched through Khartoum before being shepherded back to Omdurman, where they dispersed. Huddleston blamed the disturbances on Egyptian propaganda. The student demonstrations were soon followed by more serious actions from the nationalist parties themselves.[24]

After Bevin's agreement to renegotiate the 1936 treaty, all politically conscious Sudanese parties in the condominium determined that this time they would not be left out, as had happened at the time of the original treaty negotiations in 1936. First the Graduates' General Congress—dominated by Isma'il al-Azhari's pro-Egyptian Ashiqqa Party and supported by the adherents of Sayyid 'Ali al-Mirghani's Khatmiyya tariqa (or religious "brotherhood")—and subsequently the anti-Egyptian groups led by the Umma Party of the Mahdist leader, Sayyid 'Abd al-Rahman al-Mahdi (the posthumous son of the same Mahdi who had overthrown Gordon in 1885), announced their intentions to send their own representatives to Cairo for the negotiations. This announcement caught the Sudan Administration a bit off-guard and threw the new British ambassador in Cairo into conniptions.[25]

There had been a general interest in the idea of sending representatives to the treaty negotiations on the part of all the Sudanese parties for some time. The composition of a delegation, however, had been stalled as the various groups tried to form a united front under the auspices of the United Parties Committee. On 11 March, apparently tired of waiting, al-Azhari announced that he was booking passage for himself and a Congress delegation to go to Cairo on the twenty-second in order to represent their policy of "union under the Egyptian Crown." Alarmed, the other parties were anxious that Congress should not be

---

23. Sudan Political Intelligence Summary no. 56, January-April 1946, FO 371/53328, PRO; also Khartoum to Cairo, no. 41, 9 March 1946, conveying Civil Secretary's "Note on Students' Demonstrations . . . 4th-6th March 1946," in FO 371/53251, PRO.

24. Khartoum to Cairo, no. 41, 9 March 1946, conveying Civil Secretary's "Note on Students' Demonstrations . . . 4th-6th March 1946," in FO 371/53251, PRO. Students from the Ma'ahad had shown signs of "truculence" and "fanaticism" that worried the authorities. Although no injuries or damage was reported, Robertson had local councils, district commissioners, and the governor of Khartoum Province stop the processions altogether.

25. Dakhlia to Sudanology [Civil Secretary Khartoum to Sudan Agent London], no. 604, 23 March 1946, and Cairo to Foreign Office, no. 529, 23 March 1946, FO 371/53250, PRO.

the sole spokesman for the Sudan in Egypt.[26] Working furiously, the United Parties finally persuaded al-Azhari to participate in an all-party delegation. The price of agreement was a compromise formula, based on an all-party declaration that had been made the previous October, as the lowest common denominator on which all parties could agree. The program of the new united delegation was to ask the co-domini for a joint statement accepting the formation of "a free democratic Sudanese government in union with Egypt." This free government would then decide on the form of union and, against the background of that union, would "enter into alliance with Great Britain." The Congress "Egyptian Crown" formula was conspicuously lacking.[27]

From Robertson's perspective, the Sudanese delegation to Cairo proved to be the best of a bad job. He had worked assiduously to persuade Congress not to send representatives to the negotiations in Egypt. He had also done his best to cultivate and encourage the anti-Egyptian forces within the nationalist ranks. With Huddleston's approval, in March the civil secretary approached Sayyid 'Abd al-Rahman and suggested that he was prepared to consider favorably a request to rebuild the Mahdi's gubba, or tomb, in Omdurman. He also promised to "reconsider" official policy restricting the presence of Mahdist agents in certain parts of the Sudan. After decades of ambivalence toward the Mahdi's son, the Sudan Government was now wooing him as its natural "patriotic" nationalist ally against the Egyptian threat. In the meantime, however, despite the civil secretary's remonstrances, Isma'il al-Azhari remained determined to carry on with his own trip to Egypt; unwilling to leave his rival alone in the field, as well as sensing a potential political advantage in appealing directly to the co-domini, 'Abd al-Rahman too decided that there must be a united front for the Sudan in Cairo.[28]

As it became clear that the pro-Egyptian parties would attend, Robertson's next-best option was to encourage the "moderates" of the United Parties Committee, and the anti-Egyptian factions led by the Umma Party, to go along as a counterbalance to al-Azhari. Despite the all-party declaration, the Ashiqqa and the Umma still held opposing views on the question of unity with Egypt. With such internal disagreements, Robertson believed, the delegation would be unlikely to do any serious damage to the Sudan Government's own position; indeed, there was little doubt that the delegation would eventually break apart, thereby exposing publicly the differences among the Sudanese nationalists and

---

26. Ibid.; Sudan Agency Cairo to Embassy, 4 April 1946, FO 371/53252, PRO.

27. The agreement was a close-run affair: it was not reached until the twenty-first and even then details concerning the division of places in the delegation (seven representatives each from the pro- and anti-Egyptian groups) were not resolved until after al-Azhari's advance party had already departed. For a full description of the negotiations, see Sudan Political Intelligence Summary no. 56, January-April 1946, FO 371/53328, PRO.

28. Ibid.; see also C.S. letter no. 96, 8 April 1946, MP 571/2.

bolstering the Sudan Government's contention that even the "educated class" could not speak authoritatively for the Sudanese people.

Despite the apparent unity of the Sudanese delegation, both Robertson and the governor-general adamantly insisted that it did not truly represent the Sudan as a whole. Before the decision of the United Parties Committee to join the Ashiqqa in a united front, Huddleston had recommended that the Embassy should persuade the Egyptian Government to make it clear that the government did not want al-Azhari's group to come, and to "cold-shoulder it" if it did. Even after the joint delegation had been formed, Robertson telegraphed R. C. Mayall in London, stating that it should be "emphasised with as much publicity as possible that whatever the affiliations of the deputation may be and however it may describe itself it does not (repeat does not) represent the Sudan as a whole." The Congress, Robertson argued, did not even represent a substantial number of the actual Graduates, many of whom were to be found in the upper reaches of government service. Nor did they speak for the tribal nazirs and chiefs, who themselves represented over 90 percent of the Northern Sudanese. Furthermore, the South, with nearly two-fifths of the total population of the Sudan, was not represented at all. Despite these arguments, the Sudan Government soon confronted its stiffest challenge regarding the delegation not from the Egyptians or the Sudanese but from the British Embassy itself.[29]

In the short term, the Sudanese delegation to Cairo achieved what Robertson and Huddleston had failed to accomplish—a statement of British policy by the foreign secretary. Confronted by the imminent arrival of the Sudanese nationalists with their demands for a "free and independent Sudan in union with Egypt and alliance with Great Britain," the ambassador at last gave way. As Scrivener in the Foreign Office put it, "The Embassy's view has been changed by force of circumstances." Campbell resurrected the governor-general's draft statement, the Foreign Office agreed, and on 26 March Bevin duly proclaimed the British Government's official position to Parliament. It was Huddleston's text almost verbatim—with one significant addition: "The objects of . . . administration must be to establish organs of self-government *as a first step towards eventual independence*." The addition, which was Scrivener's, delighted Khartoum even as it alarmed the Embassy.[30]

The arrival of the Sudan delegation in Cairo caused the Embassy considerable anxiety. For Sir Ronald Campbell, newly ensconced in Lord Killearn's chair, the overriding concern was Anglo-Egyptian Treaty revision. Fearing that the Egyptians might woo the Sudanese to gain an advantage in the negotiations, Campbell proposed to counter such tactics first by receiving the Sudan

---

29. Cairo to Foreign Office, no. 529, 23 March 1946, and Dakhlia to Sudanology, no. 604, 23 March 1946, FO 371/53250, PRO.

30. Cairo to Foreign Office, nos. 529, 530 and 531, 23 March 1946; minute by Scrivener, 24 March 1946; and draft reply to Cairo telegram no. 530 with addition in Scrivener's hand, all in FO 371/53250, PRO. Bevin's statement is in Great Britain, *Parliamentary Debates (Commons)*, 26 March 1946, vol. 421.

delegation officially at the Embassy and second by announcing an immediate increase in the pace of Sudanization. Telegraphing his views to the Foreign Office on 2 April, the ambassador argued that despite al-Azhari's predominant position and strong personal links with Egypt, the united delegation was widely representative of the Northern Sudan and commanded "the general support of all the political class of the Sudan." He therefore proposed that if the delegation members contacted the Embassy, they should be received either by himself or by the British treaty delegation if it had arrived. If the Sudanese did not contact the Embassy, then the Embassy should make "unofficial" contact and do "everything possible . . . to prevent them falling completely under Egyptian influence." From Khartoum's perspective, the ambassador's views were alarmist and dangerous; they soon precipitated an open breach between the Embassy and the Palace.[31]

Campbell and the Embassy staff took the Sudanese delegation much more seriously than did the Sudan Government. Huddleston and Robertson considered the Sudan delegation to be outside the constitutional bounds within which they were pledged to consult the Sudanese. They had never recognized Congress, even before it had split into different factions, as representative of any but a small number of the Sudanese intelligentsia. Even with the addition of the Umma Party, they maintained, the delegation could hardly be considered representative of more than about 1 or 2 percent of the condominium's population. Objecting to Campbell's plan to court the Sudanese, on 4 April Huddleston telegraphed:

I am most strongly opposed to any official recognition being given to the deputation. . . . The Sudan Government have officially published that it does not recognise the deputation as representative and said: "While it is the alleged intention of the deputation to put their viewpoint before the negotiators there is nothing to show that the negotiators have agreed to see or are likely to see a deputation for which they have not asked and which is unrepresentative of any but a small section of the community."

To give the deputation any recognition, the governor-general concluded, "could not be done without seriously weakening the position of the Councils and prejudicing H.M.G.'s policy."[32]

Khartoum's attitude irritated Campbell. Breaking normal procedures, the ambassador did not immediately repeat Huddleston's telegram to London. The Foreign Office learned of the governor-general's attitude through the Sudan Agency in London. Taking the point, Scrivener nevertheless agreed with Robertson and Huddleston. Although the Embassy should receive the delegation if it contacted them, the head of the Egyptian Department also insisted that Embassy officials make it clear that they viewed the delegation as representative only of certain political groups and not of the Sudan as a whole. Moreover, if

---

31. Cairo to Foreign Office, no. 594, 2 April 1946, FO 371/53251, PRO.
32. Khartoum to Cairo, no. 39, 4 April 1946, Secret, FO 371/53251, PRO.

the Sudanese did not contact the Embassy, matters should be left in the hands of the Sudan agent in Cairo. "The Embassy," Scrivener minuted, "should not run after these people; who will merely convict themselves of political folly and gross discourtesy if they do not get in touch." Unconvinced, early in April the ambassador asked Huddleston to send Robertson north for consultations on both the Sudanese delegation and the Sudan Government's Sudanization policy. Stubbornly, Robertson insisted that the Sudan delegation had been doomed from the beginning.[33]

The program to which the United Parties had agreed in order to achieve unity had been a compromise proposal for a free democratic Sudan Government in "union" with Egypt and alliance with Great Britain. As Robertson pointed out, the original Congress "Egyptian Crown formula" had been dropped. Differences between Ashiqqa and Umma remained, however, embodied in the word "union," a rather loose translation of the Arabic word *'ittihad*.[34] Even before the Sudanese delegation had left for Cairo, Robertson's public relations officer, E. N. Corbyn, telegraphed from London warning that *'ittihad* did not necessarily mean "union" in the sense in which that word was understood in England. "In political language in this country," he wrote, "the word 'union' means governmental amalgamation, e.g. the union with Scotland, or the Union with Ireland (cancelled by the recognition of Eire), or the Union of South Africa. This is not what four of the Sudan Parties mean by the word, though they have been tricked by the Ashiqqa into using a word of double meaning." Corbyn suggested translating the word as "association." "If it is stated here," he concluded, "that every 'Party' in the Sudan desires 'union' with Egypt, immense mischief will be done in the way of misunderstanding . . . the real desires of the Sudan."[35]

While Corbyn worried about the effect of the term "union" on the British Government and people, Robertson had already seen the wider implications. The day after the delegation left for Cairo he telegraphed to Mayall, "Future cohesion of delegation under Egyptian pressure is problematical." It was an accurate assessment. As soon became apparent, the Egyptians interpreted the term "union" in the same fashion as the British. Nor would Cairo compromise on this interpretation. Al-Azhari was caught between the platform of his own party, intensified by Egyptian pressure in Cairo, and the less categorical interpretation of *'ittihad* accepted by the United Parties Committee in Khartoum. Even as Robertson tried to explain the situation to Campbell, the Sudanese delegation was falling apart.[36]

---

33. See minutes by Scrivener, 4 and 12 April 1946, FO 371/53251/J 1462, PRO; Cairo to Foreign Office, no. 662, 13 April 1946, FO 371/53251, PRO.

34. For Robertson's attitude, see especially C.S. letter, nos. 96 and 97, 8 April and 11 May 1946, MP 571/2. See also Dakhlia to Sudanology, no. 632, 27 March 1946, FO 371/53251, PRO.

35. Corbyn to Robertson, 24 March 1946, FO 371/53250, PRO. Mayall agreed "very strongly" with Corbyn's argument.

36. Dakhlia to Sudanology, no. M.213, 27 March 1946, FO 371/53251, PRO.

Robertson arrived in Cairo on 9 April. Before leaving Khartoum, he wrote to the Political Service that some in the Umma Party ranks were anxious that Azhari was "not playing fair." The Umma leaders had asked for a report from their representatives in Cairo. "If they are double-crossed," Robertson wrote, "they will secede and speak for themselves." On the day of his arrival in Cairo the civil secretary called on the Egyptian prime minister. He told Sidqi Pasha that the Sudanese delegation represented only about ten thousand out of eighteen thousand "literate Sudanese," a bit more than half. The following day, during his meeting with the ambassador, the civil secretary pursued the same line, insisting that the delegation was not truly representative.[37]

Despite Robertson's assurances, Campbell refused to do nothing to counter Egyptian influence with the Sudanese. Even if the delegation was not fully representative of the Sudan as a whole, he argued, it nevertheless spoke for a fairly large proportion of the educated and articulate elements. If indeed a rift had appeared between the Sudanese program and Egyptian aims, as Robertson suggested, then "it was obviously desirable that . . . we should exploit this rift for our own interests." Pressing the civil secretary, Campbell got Robertson to agree that the Embassy should contact the delegation informally.[38] With Robertson's acquiescence, on 12 April Dr. Eric Pridie, health counsellor at the Embassy and formerly head of the Sudan Medical Service and member of the Governor-General's Council, entertained the leading Sudanese delegates to tea to meet Sir Walter Smart, the Embassy oriental secretary.

As the civil secretary and the ambassador had arranged, Smart led the delegates out on their demands for participation in the forthcoming negotiations, pointing out "gently" the "practical difficulties" involved in such participation. The oriental secretary also played up the Sudan Government's Sudanization program, encouraging the Sudanese to express themselves directly to the administration in Khartoum. In return, the Sudanese only reinforced the Embassy's belief that the delegation was more representative than Robertson thought and that a major reason for its approach to Egypt was that "they deeply mistrusted the sincerity of the Sudan Government on Sudanisation."[39]

While the Embassy did its best to counter Egyptian influence with the Sudan delegation, the Egyptians themselves played both sides of the fence. In the press and in private, Egyptian statesmen of all factions insisted that the Sudanese delegation was proof that the Sudan wanted complete unity with Egypt. All suggestions that this "unity" might not necessarily be under the sovereignty of the Egyptian Crown were shouted down. At the same time, conversations with Lutfi al-Sayyid, the Egyptian minister for foreign affairs, and with Sidqi Pasha

---

37. C.S. letter no 96, 8 April 1946, MP 571/2; Campbell to Bevin, Confidential, no. 533, 18 April 1946, FO 371/53252, PRO. Robertson's version of the same meeting is in C.S. letter no. 97, 11 May 1946, MP 571/2.

38. Ibid.

39. Note on tea party for Sudanese delegates by E. D. Pridie, 13 April 1946, FO 371/53252, PRO.

convinced Campbell that the Egyptian Government viewed the Sudanese as an embarrassment and a hindrance to Anglo-Egyptian negotiations.

On 10 April, Lutfi al-Sayyid complained to the ambassador that *"ces messieurs du Sudan"* did not seem to know very clearly what they wanted, that in any case treaty revisions were solely a matter for decision between the British and Egyptian governments, and that for its part, the Egyptian Government "probably did not possess the necessary knowledge and information about the Sudan to form an opinion . . . on . . . whether the country was ripe for the self-government which . . . the delegation seemed to be demanding." Meeting with Sidqi Pasha the next day, Campbell mentioned that he intended to make contact shortly with Sir Hubert Huddleston at Wadi Halfa. "There was only one thing he wanted of the Governor-General," the prime minister told the ambassador, "namely that he should not for the moment do anything 'salient.'" In an obvious reference to the Wafd, Sidqi bemoaned that unfortunately in Egypt "there were 'statesmen'. . . who were unable to refrain from declarations" on the Sudan. Sidqi himself, Campbell reported to the Foreign Office, "wanted to keep everything to do with the Sudan quiet and first to get the Egyptian question settled."[40]

Whether or not the Egyptian Government really did not know what to do with the Sudanese delegation, the matter was soon academic. As it became clear that the Egyptians expected the Sudanese to conform to their interpretation of unity under the sovereignty of the Egyptian Crown, on 20 April the independence faction within the delegation referred matters back to the United Parties Committee in Khartoum. After consultation with Sayyid 'Abd al-Rahman and the moderates of the committee, they returned to Egypt with word that the All-Party Declaration remained the basis of the Sudanese position. The firmness of the independence group, combined with Egyptian intransigence on the sovereignty issue, soon forced the dissolution of the delegation. On 4 May the Umma representatives left Cairo and returned to the Sudan.[41]

As Robertson prosaically reported to the Political Service on 11 May, the delegation had found "that the Egyptians were not ready to agree to the Sudan idea of a free democratic government which on obtaining its independence would then decide its future relations with Egypt." The civil secretary elaborated in a more colorful vein:

Ismail el Azhari found himself on a very difficult wicket: he was faced with the fast bowling of the Egyptian Pashas on the one side, and an "Umma" wicket-keeper behind the stumps, who was ready to take advantage of any slip he might make. . . .

---

40. Campbell to Bevin, Confidential, no. 533, 18 April 1946, FO 371/53252, PRO.

41. For a full account of the Sudanese delegation, its friction with the Egyptians, and its eventual break-up, see especially Sudan Political Intelligence Summary no. 56, January-April 1946, in FO 371/53328, PRO, and Appendix D to the same report, "Events in Egypt—April 1946," in MP 571/2.

He therefore had to steer a course between being too pro-Egyptian, in which case he would lose the support of the Umma delegates, or adhering too closely to the Party memorandum, in which case the Egyptians would not play. After about a month in Cairo, and various indiscretions by Azhari, reference back to Omdurman was made and the United Parties stuck to their original policy. This resulted in the break-up of the delegation in Cairo, and the Umma and Ahrar returned here about a week ago.

With scarcely concealed satisfaction, Robertson reported that Azhari was now in an "unenviable" position: "The Egyptians have refused to accept his proposals, and his stock, and that of the remainder of the delegation, is now pretty low both in Cairo and in the Sudan."[42]

SUDANIZATION AND THE EMBASSY-PALACE RIFT

Although Robertson's evaluation of the Sudan delegation had been vindicated, the Embassy remained concerned about the pace of Sudanization, and especially about Robertson's decision not to include the Political Service in any precipitate dilution plan. Writing to the Foreign Office at the end of March, Campbell reported that there was "real and wide-spread dis-satisfaction" among representative Sudanese over the pace of Sudanization. The Sudan Government's "gradualist" policy was "out of step with the tempo of the post-war world." Egyptians offered the Sudanese "immediate self-government in union with Egypt."[43] "I am convinced," Campbell insisted, "that the only effective way of countering the present Egyptian political offensive in the Sudan is to give the Sudanese effective assurances on the question of their future administration of their country." It was not enough simply to declare that British policy aimed at self-administration and eventual self-determination; the situation called for deeds.

I would most strongly recommend that the Sudan Government should, immediately, and independently of treaty discussions in Cairo . . . draw up a detailed plan of Sudanisation in consultation with the Sudanese. . . . I would further recommend . . . an announcement of the intention of the Sudan Government, as an earnest of their good faith, to appoint a Sudanese Provincial Governor and two or three Sudanese District Commissioners in responsible political posts, or the Sudanisation of a Province.

Despite the potential threat to administrative efficiency, the ambassador concluded, a "bold and resolute gesture" was necessary "to hold our position in the Sudan . . . and . . . not to find the ground cut from under our feet . . . by the Egyptians."[44]

---

42. C.S. letter no. 97, 11 May 1946, MP 571/2.

43. Cairo to Foreign Office, no. 124, 26 March 1946, Top Secret, FO 371/53251, PRO.

44. Ibid.

Campbell reiterated his views during his conference with Robertson in April. As Robertson himself reported the encounter to the Political Service: "Sudanisation, in the eyes of the Embassy, was one of the most important cards to play in order to retain the support of the Sudanese for the present Sudan Government, and Bowker, Audsley, Pridie, Sir Walter Smart and Lord Kinross attacked me very hard on this and suggested that we make sweeping promotions, specially in the Political Service. . . . Pridie turned out his favourite proposal of a completely Sudanese province." Regardless of the pressure exerted by the Embassy, however, Robertson was not prepared to overthrow his plans for the Political Service. Drawing a distinction between the technical services and the administrative as opposed to the political aspects of the Political Service, the civil secretary refused to budge on the policy he had laid down at the Governor-General's Council in December. Four days later, the ambassador took the matter up personally with the governor-general at Wadi Halfa.[45]

Following Robertson's lead, Huddleston listened patiently to Campbell's arguments, and then made the Sudan Government case. There were Sudanese who could "hold down" responsible positions, but under the pressures of the new development program they would be unable to keep up. This in turn would throw more work on already overburdened British staff. Indeed, the whole development program would be held up "proportionately" with any increase in Sudanization. Drastic Sudanization, moreover, would undermine the "faith" of British personnel. Not least, the educational problem limited the number of qualified Sudanese that would be available in the next five years. In principle, the Sudan Government did not want to create a "Sudanese bureaucracy" but rather sought to build up the local authorities in an organic development of self-government from the bottom up. From a "political" angle, in fact, promoting qualified young Sudanese officials over the heads of older, more senior Sudanese "would do more harm than good and would create widespread grievances among the section of the population now most attached to the Sudan Government." In short, Huddleston believed, they had gone as quickly as was possible.[46]

This time the Foreign Office supported Campbell. On Bevin's personal approval, they telegraphed Khartoum, noting that in implementing a "bold program of Sudanisation," the Sudan Government would be "carrying out the wishes of H.M.G." Despite Whitehall's intervention, however, the Sudan Government resisted all efforts to force its hand. In fact there was serious miscommunication between the Embassy and the Palace. Campbell had come away from his meetings with Robertson and Huddleston convinced that he had made the case for more rapid Sudanization. Robertson, on the other hand, reported to the Political Service that he and Huddleston had "persuaded the Ambassador that a too rapid Sudanisation is impossible and that our present method and proposals, if speeded up a bit, are the most satisfactory way of obtaining reasonable progress." Thus, while Campbell believed that he had

---

45. C.S. letter no. 97, 11 May 1946, MP 571/2.
46. Campbell to Bevin, no. 546, 22 April 1946, FO 371/53252, PRO.

carried his point, the Sudan Government laid plans for an advance on its own lines.[47]

It was clear to both Robertson and Huddleston that Sudanization, as far as the Embassy was concerned, meant primarily Sudanization of the Political Service as a means of countering Egyptian promises for immediate Sudanese self-government. Yet the civil secretary insisted such a move would be "retrograde." While the Embassy was mainly concerned with keeping Egypt at bay and the Sudanese nationalists quiet during the treaty negotiations, the Sudan Government attempted to plan for Sudanese self-government. During their meeting at Wadi Halfa, Huddleston caught the ambassador off-guard by proposing to announce "forthwith" the formation of a committee to study the creation of a full-fledged representative Sudanese Legislative Council. Instead of creating a Sudanese bureaucracy to replace the British one, Huddleston and Robertson had decided to establish self-governing institutions that would forever prejudice Egyptian participation in the condominium.[48]

The institution of a Legislative Council seemed a perfectly logical step from Khartoum's point of view. The Embassy, on the other hand, dealt with Egyptian opinion, which would undoubtedly be seriously inflamed by such a constitutional advance in the Sudan. Recovering from his momentary discomfiture, on 20 April Campbell telegraphed London and Khartoum, opposing any announcement of plans for a Legislative Council in the Sudan. Sidqi Pasha, he reminded them, had asked that nothing "salient" should be done by the Sudan Government while negotiations were still under way. The ambassador endorsed this suggestion. Once again Campbell displayed his lack of understanding of the Sudan Government's position: "We can press ahead with Sudanisation but there should be no major constitutional change." Once again, the ambassador was backed up by the Foreign Office. Once again, Robertson and Huddleston followed their own policy.[49]

Four days after his meeting with Campbell, on the opening day of the fifth session of the Advisory Council for the Northern Sudan, Huddleston not only announced that he was calling an immediate conference to consider the next steps by which Sudanese could be associated more closely with their own government, but also stated his confidence "that in twenty years' time the Sudanese will be governing their own country assisted and advised by a certain number of non-Sudanese specialists and technicians." Going further, he defined his ultimate policy: "The Government is aiming at a free independent Sudan which will be able as soon as that independence has been achieved to define for itself its relations with Great Britain and Egypt." This was "reassurance" for the Sudanese,

---

47. See draft of Foreign Office to Cairo, no. 726, 18 April 1946, in Scrivener's hand with Bevin's initials, FO 371/53251, PRO; Cairo to Foreign Office, no. 702, 20 April 1946, FO 371/53252, PRO; C.S. letter no 97, 11 May 1946, MP 571/2.

48. Cairo to Foreign Office, no. 702, 20 April 1946, FO 371/53252, PRO; C.S. letter no. 93, 5 January 1946, MP 571/2.

49. C.S. letter no. 93, 5 January 1946, MP 571/2.

with a vengeance. Even Robertson was caught off-guard by Huddleston's timeframe for self-government. Having once stated a limit in this public fashion, Huddleston had virtually pledged not only the Sudan Government but also the co-domini, or at least the British, to carry through on his "promise" to the Sudanese. Adding teeth to his policy, he charged the Conference on Closer Association to produce a definite timetable for advances in self-government. So, far from doing "nothing salient," Huddleston had thrown his challenge directly at the feet of both Egypt and Great Britain.[50]

Huddleston's speech drew immediate fire from the Egyptians. While a violent ant-British outburst occurred in the Egyptian press, with virulent personal attacks on Huddleston himself, in London the Egyptian ambassador, Amr Pasha, presented an aidé-memoire emanating from Farouk, protesting that the governor-general had obviously overstepped his "administrative jurisdiction." Huddleston had "assumed for himself a grave political authority to the extent of planning the present and future of the Sudan without consulting the Egyptian Government." This had placed the Egyptian Government in a difficult position and had seriously aroused public opinion. In short, Huddleston had "disturbed" the atmosphere necessary for negotiations.[51] Sidqi Pasha himself was more restrained, preferring not to inflame the situation further. Sidqi clearly wanted a treaty; like Bevin, he hoped that if an atmosphere of calm could be preserved negotiations would not be prejudiced. His staff made clear to the Embassy, however, that the premier was annoyed. Eventually, driven by the exuberance of the press, Sidqi too publicly denounced Huddleston for overstepping his authority, observing that Huddleston might even be in trouble with London because he had acted without prior consultation of either co-dominus.[52]

Sidqi's statement and the Egyptian newspaper protests had repercussions in the Sudan. Early in May, Robertson submitted the minutes of the Advisory Council's fifth session to the Embassy. He insisted that the proceedings of the session had been "cheerful and buoyant," primarily as a result of the governor-general's opening speech. The confident mood thus engendered, however, had now begun to wear off "under the influence of Egyptian propaganda questioning my competence to make such a speech." What was needed, Robertson wrote, was

---

50. Governor-General's Opening Speech to Advisory Council for the Northern Sudan, 17 April 1946, and other enclosures in Mayall to Scrivener, 30 April 1946, FO 371/53252/J 1743, PRO. In his memoirs, Robertson admitted that pressure from the Embassy had affected his decision to increase the pace. It is clear, however, that he thought in terms of advancing Sudanese self-government, rather than simple Sudanization of the Political Service. See Robertson, *Transition*, 94.

51. There is a brief summary of the Egyptian press in FO 371/53252/J 1716, PRO; but see especially aide-mémoire by Amr Pasha, 26 April 1946, and British responses in FO 371/53252/J 1867, PRO. Referring to the Dessouki affair, Amr also complained that Huddleston had expelled the Egyptian officer from the Sudan despite requests that he be transferred within the condominium.

52. Cairo to Foreign Office, no. 161, 25 April 1946, FO 371/53252, PRO; Cairo to Foreign Office, no. 906, 20 May 1946, FO 371/53253, PRO.

an endorsement of the governor-general's statement by His Majesty's Government.[53]

In some respects, Huddleston's creation of the Administration Conference actually fell in line with Campbell's desire for a definite timetable for Sudanization, which would convince the Sudanese of British sincerity. At the same time, Khartoum's insistence on equating Sudanization with constitutional advances upset the ambassador. Responding to Robertson's request on 20 May, Campbell "sympathised" with the governor-general's position but pointed out the objections to a statement from His Majesty's Government. Huddleston's speech, Campbell asserted, "was largely instrumental in bringing UMMA political representatives into line with other Sudanese delegates." An endorsement now might bring the two factions, which had since parted company, back together. Moreover, the ambassador smugly observed, "The Governor-General's reference to self-government by the Sudanese in twenty years and not self-administration has given a certain specious justification to Egyptian assertion that he was over-stepping his powers. Naturally we should not admit this but expediency makes it desirable that we should if possible avoid argument." Not least, Campbell concluded, the British Government was about to tackle the Sudan issue in the treaty negotiations, and it would be better to do nothing that might further excite Egyptian opinion or annoy Sidqi Pasha and King Farouk.[54]

From the time of Huddleston's speech to the Advisory Council, relations between the Embassy and the Palace steadily deteriorated. Writing to James Bowker, the minister of state in the Embassy, Robertson disputed Campbell's interpretation. So far from having brought the two factions of the delegation together, he argued, Huddleston's speech had given the Umma delegates "just that solid 'something' for which they had been waiting to put in the balance against the Egyptian blandishments," thereby providing them an excuse to break with al-Azhari. In short, the governor-general's statement had actually caused the split in the Sudan delegation. The only "fly in the ointment," Robertson insisted, was Egypt's charge that the speech had been "unconstitutional." Consequently, if Khartoum could get backing from London, they would be on a "better wicket" than they had been for months. The Embassy was unimpressed. Within a week, Campbell made a concerted effort to reassert over Khartoum an authority dormant since 1926.[55]

Writing to Huddleston on 3 June, Campbell suggested that there "might be advantage in referring to the Egyptian Government certain of the proposed amendments to Sudan laws and ordinances which are passed from time to time by the Governor-General's Council and submitted to me for approval." Both the idea of submitting legislation to the Egyptians as well as Campbell's assertion that he "approved" laws and ordinances before they were passed by the Governor-

---

53. Robertson to Campbell, no. 72, 9 May 1946, FO 371/53253, PRO.
54. Cairo to Foreign Office, no. 906, 20 May 1946, FO 371/53253, PRO.
55. Robertson to Bowker, 22 May 1946, FO 371/53253, PRO.

General's Council were highly provocative from Khartoum's viewpoint. Although the Palace did regularly pass proposed laws to the Embassy for comment, it viewed this as a courtesy. Prior consent had not existed since Lord Cromer's day, although various ambassadors had periodically tried to revive the custom. Moreover, such communications had always been done "under the table," like the bulk of the Embassy's confidential dealings with the Sudan Government, to avoid any appearance of going behind the back of the Egyptian co-dominus. Indignant, Robertson and Huddleston viewed Campbell's suggestion as yet another indication of the Embassy's willingness to "appease" Egypt.[56]

This time Khartoum held the better hand. As even the Foreign Office realized, the Embassy's proposal did not conform to the 1899 Condominium Agreement, which only required the governor-general to notify both the British consul general and the President of the Egyptian Council of Ministers after legislation had been promulgated. Moreover, the Egyptian Department agreed, it smacked of "appeasement" and was "thoroughly misconceived." Even worse, it was dangerous: "The Egyptians . . . already . . . think they can ask us for anything and get it. Gratuitous concessions such as this will merely whet their appetite." Not least, Scrivener pointed out, such measures would "discourage" members of the Sudan Government, "who are not too happy as it is."[57]

While Campbell's suggestion was scotched, it nevertheless confirmed Khartoum's fears that the Embassy was nearly as dangerous to the Sudan as the Egyptian Government itself. As treaty negotiations progressed during the summer of 1946, the Sudan Government increasingly doubted its "allies" in Cairo and was reinforced in the conviction that it alone had the best interests of the Sudanese at heart. Moreover, as negotiations continued into the fall, all the old suspicions of Bevin and the Foreign Office also resurfaced. For many in the Sudan Political Service it seemed as if there was a conspiracy in the corridors of Whitehall and the conference rooms of the Embassy to sell the Sudan to Egypt in exchange for the new treaty. In October 1946, it would become clear that their fears were far from groundless.

56. Campbell to Huddleston, no. 133, 3 June 1946, and accompanying minutes in FO 371/53253, PRO.

57. Minute by Scrivener, 14 June 1946, and subsequent Foreign Office to Cairo, no. 1191, 16 June 1946, FO 371/53253, PRO.

2

Agreement and Failure: Anglo-Egyptian Negotiations and the Stonewall of the Sudan

> The King of Egypt said that he is convinced of the need of a Treaty, but not at any price (the price being the Sudan). Equally I cannot do what I believe to be wrong in order to get a quick Treaty of Alliance.
>
> —Ernest Bevin, August 1946

"Yesterday," Margery Perham wrote on 5 July 1946, "British troops marched out of the citadel at Cairo as a visible proof of our good faith. . . . in a few days Lord Stansgate will return to Egypt to resume negotiations on the Anglo-Egyptian treaty." "The future of the Sudan," she warned, "is perhaps the most difficult of all the questions still to be answered in these discussions." The problems involved in the defense of the Suez Canal were "controversial, but . . . not at bottom complex." Nor were the interests of the two countries in the Canal hard to reconcile. Commercial relations between Egypt and Britain too were complex but awoke "less passionate sentiments." The Sudan, however, presented a problem "at once complex and heavily charged with national sentiment, and at the root of it is the germ of a genuine and permanent conflict of interests, not so much between Britain and Egypt as between the Egyptians and the Sudanese."[1] It was a view shared and probably inspired by the Sudan Government in Khartoum.

The Egyptian demand for treaty negotiations had involved two primary nationalist goals. These goals were expressed in the twin slogans of "evacuation" and "Unity of the Nile Valley." From the British perspective, the two points were covered by the "Egyptian question" and the "Sudan question." The Egyptian question, as far as London was concerned, boiled down to one central problem— guaranteeing the defense of Egypt and the Suez Canal. Consequently, the Egyptian question was also generally referred to as the "military" side of Anglo-Egyptian relations and, for the British, represented by far the most important

---

1. *Manchester Guardian*, 5 July 1946.

aspect of the negotiations. The Sudan question was more problematical. Intent on the primary goal of obtaining an acceptable military treaty, the British Government never quite took Egyptian claims in the Sudan seriously. As Perham warned in the summer of 1946, however, the Sudan question was to prove crucial to any real Anglo-Egyptian understanding.

For the purposes of the present discussion, it is not necessary to go into the military negotiations of the Anglo-Egyptian treaty in detail. Briefly, they divided into two areas: the initial Egyptian demand for a complete British military withdrawal from Egyptian territory; and the British desire for a military alliance that would give them sufficient means to defend Egypt and the Canal in case of any threat—notably from the Soviet Union. The question of evacuation was a vexed one from the British perspective. It raised party animosities between Conservatives and Labourites to new levels of vituperation. The military alliance was less difficult and soon came to revolve around British suggestions for some form of regional Middle Eastern defence scheme. For the Egyptians, however, evacuation meant real freedom after seventy years of British domination. And any treaty of military alliance would have to take into account Egypt's deep-seated mistrust of British intentions: provisions for any British reentry into Egypt, or even for a commitment of Egypt to side with Britain in time of war, were bound to be viewed by the Egyptians with extreme suspicion. Throughout the negotiations, as the Egyptian negotiators told their British counterparts, the psychological factor would be crucial to any eventual agreement.

The psychological aspect of evacuation was quickly apprehended by the chief British negotiator, Lord Stansgate, who arrived with the British treaty delegation in Alexandria on 15 April 1946. Deluged immediately with the intensity of Egyptian emotions on the subject, Stansgate became convinced that negotiations would succeed only if the British Government announced forthwith its intentions to evacuate. Only such a bold and dramatic gesture, he argued, could create an atmosphere of goodwill in which Britain might quickly obtain the necessary military alliance and treaty of friendship. On Stansgate's recommendation, and after considerable discussion in the Cabinet, on 7 May the British prime minister, Clement Attlee, publicly offered to withdraw all British forces from Egypt "and to settle in negotiation the stages and date of completion of this withdrawal, and the arrangements to be made by the Egyptian Government to make possible mutual assistance in time of war or imminent threat of war in accordance with the alliance."[2]

Following acrimonious debates in Parliament, two weeks later the British foreign secretary, Ernest Bevin, offered the Egyptians a draft treaty of alliance based on evacuation but including strict, even ironclad, provisions for a British reentry in case of imminent war. Following through with Attlee's pledge, as Perham reported in the Guardian, on 4 July, not an auspicious day in the

---

2. *Parliamentary Debates (Commons)*, 7 May 1946. See Stansgate's telegrams to Foreign Office with accompanying minutes in FO 371/53292. For a useful evaluation of Stansgate and his mission, see also Louis, *The British Empire*, part 2, chapter 6.

imperial calendar, British troops finally left the Citadel in Cairo as a mark of the Labour Government's good faith, thereby ending an occupation that had begun in 1882. Despite the gesture, however, the military negotiations did not fall into place as the British hoped they would. Negotiations dragged on through the summer and into the fall of 1946.[3]

In face-to-face meetings in London at the end of October, Bevin and Sidqi Pasha, the Egyptian prime minister, finally agreed on the military terms of the new treaty. These terms included a British pledge to evacuate Cairo, Alexandria, and the Delta by the end of March 1947, and the rest of Egypt by September 1949; an Egyptian pledge to support Britain militarily in case of aggression against countries "adjacent to Egypt"; and the creation of a Joint Defence Board to coordinate and make recommendations in case of events that might "threaten the security of the Middle East." Financial matters were to be negotiated in a separate agreement. The Egyptian question appeared to have been settled at last on terms acceptable to both the British chiefs of staff and the Egyptian nationalists.[4]

Yet despite the apparent achievement of Anglo-Egyptian agreement, by the first week of December Sidqi Pasha had resigned, and Anglo-Egyptian relations had reached a new low. The stumbling block was not the military question, or even the complex economic issues, but, as Perham had foreseen, what Bevin himself called the "stonewall" of the Sudan. And the stonewall was not primarily a construction of the Sudanese themselves but rather of the Sudan Administration, acting in what it maintained were the best interests of the Sudanese. A defeat for both the British and the Egyptian governments, the final breakdown of treaty negotiations represented not so much a victory for the Sudanese nationalists as a victory of the Sudan Political Service over the Embassy, the Foreign Office, and the Egyptian Government.

TREATY NEGOTIATIONS AND THE SUDAN: SPRING AND SUMMER 1946

Early in 1946, the Foreign Office developed its first draft of a potential Sudan clause for the new treaty. This draft repeated, almost verbatim, the old article 11 of the 1936 treaty—with an important exception. Where the old treaty acknowledged simply that the aim of the condominium administration was the "welfare of the Sudanese," the new version seemed to apply the tenets of the Atlantic Charter and spirit of the United Nations to the Sudan. "The High Contracting Parties," began article 8 of the draft treaty, "are agreed that the

---

3. For a full overview of the treaty negotiations from the British perspective, see the printed memorandum, Anglo-Egyptian Treaty Negotiations, 1945-47, marked Secret, 12 March 1947, FO 371/62962, PRO.

4. Ibid. For a fuller treatment of the military side of the negotiations and the question of evacuation, see Louis, *The British Empire*, part 2 chapter 6.

primary object of their administration is the training of the Sudanese for self-government, and that, so soon as this objective is attained, the Sudanese peoples shall be free to decide their future relationship with the High Contracting Parties." This elaboration on the earlier theme of Sudanese welfare underlay Ernest Bevin's pledge of 26 March to encourage the development of a self-governing and eventually independent Sudan.[5]

During his April meeting with Ambassador Campbell at Wadi Halfa, Huddleston admitted that the new Sudan clause, from the perspective of the Sudan Government, was "ideal." At the same time, however, the governor-general also warned that it would disappoint the Sudanese because it contained no provision for consulting them. The Foreign Secretary, Huddleston explained, had promised during his statement to the House of Commons in March that the Sudanese would be consulted if there was to be any change in their status. While it was true that this implied no obligation to consult them if no change in status was effected (as was clearly intended by the British draft treaty), the governor-general pointed out that "the Sudanese mind was . . . not logical enough to appreciate this point." In effect, the Sudan Government's commitment to consultation of the Sudanese had begun to take on a life of its own.[6]

Khartoum had begun planning for consultation as early as January, even before the foreign secretary had been goaded into his March "pledge." It was a logical step following Robertson's assurances to the Advisory Council of the Northern Sudan the previous December. Moreover, the Foreign Office itself, as well as the Embassy, had realized that in the postwar atmosphere of world opinion, the principle of consulting the Sudanese must be observed. Nevertheless, there was general agreement among the British officials that, as Lord Killearn had suggested in January, the Sudan question should not be raised until the military issues had been settled. Campbell reiterated the point to Bevin in March: "It would clearly be undesirable to start consulting the Sudanese if the negotiations are subsequently to break down on the evacuation question without touching on the Sudan at all." Consultation of the Sudanese, the new ambassador suggested, should not begin until there was a "good prospect of a favourable outcome" to the military negotiations.[7]

Both Huddleston and Robertson seem to have taken the consultation issue very seriously. They had originally hoped that the Sudanese might be consulted before negotiations were held between the co-domini, so that their wishes might form the basis for Anglo-Egyptian consideration of the Sudan. At the same time, the Sudan officials themselves hoped to define the parameters of consultation. Late in February Huddleston submitted a draft memorandum which he proposed to use at the appropriate moment as the basis for consultation. Although he and Robertson saw their primary responsibility as consultation of the "constitutional

5. For the new Article 8 and proposed Annex dated 22 March 1946 see FO 371/53251/J 1414, PRO.

6. Campbell to Bevin, no. 546, 22 April 1946, FO 371/53252, PRO.

7. Bowker to Bevin, no. 354, 11 March 1946, FO 371/53250/J 1195, PRO.

organs" of the Sudanese, the provincial councils and the Advisory Council of the Northern Sudan, they also planned to invite comment on the memorandum from the Graduates' General Congress, the two Sayyids, and the Khartoum Chamber of Commerce. In addition, and of particular importance in the Southern Sudan, provincial governors would also be asked to estimate "popular opinion" in their territories and the likely results of any change. Displaying the continuing paternalism of the Political Service, Huddleston insisted that without the sort of "guidance" provided in his memorandum, true consultation of the diverse body of Sudanese opinion would be "impossible."[8]

Huddleston's memorandum on the future of the Sudan was an almost classic statement of the Political Service mythology. Beginning with a recitation of the achievements and high moral purpose of the condominium administration, it outlined all that the Political Service had done for the Sudan since 1898, "when no school, hospital or wealth existed in the country." Moreover, it repeated the administration's public policy that its aim for the Sudan was "gradual evolution to complete internal self-government." Yet bound by the views of the Political Service, the memorandum did not contemplate any speedy transfer of real power to the Sudanese. Instead it concentrated on the need for completing development of a "homogeneous entity" in the Sudan—in short, the full development of a proper nation-state able to "stand firmly on its own feet." Within this framework, the governor-general wanted the Sudanese to consider "(a) the final objective to be aimed at, and (b) the constitution and organisation to be maintained during the immediate training period, and especially the question of who is to guide and train the Sudanese." It was a polite way of asking whether they wanted to be ruled for the foreseeable future by Britain or Egypt.[9]

Huddleston also provided "guidance" on what the ultimate objective should be, suggesting four possibilities: a completely independent Sudan; a Sudan completely incorporated into Egypt as an Egyptian province; a self-governing Sudan in some form of union with Egypt "under the Egyptian Crown"; or a self-governing Sudan in some form of association with the British Commonwealth. As for the immediate future, Huddleston wrote, there seemed to be three alternatives: the progressive development of the current policy of the Condominium Government, that is, creation of a self-governing and economically self-dependent Sudan, with gradual Sudanization of all government posts according to availability of qualified Sudanese; continuation of the condominium regime, but with substitution of a "considerable number" of Egyptians for British in all ranks of the administration—in short, a true "condominium" government; or finally, substitution of Egypt as the dominant partner in the condominium, with a concomitant substitution of Egyptians in the highest government posts in place of British Political Service officers. Disingenuously disclaiming any endorsement of a particular choice, the

---

8. Khartoum to Cairo, no. 31, 23 February 1946, FO 371/53250, PRO.

9. Annexure to Khartoum Despatch no. 31, 23 February 1946, Memorandum on the Future of the Sudan, Secret, FO 371/53250, PRO.

memorandum concluded pointedly: "Attention should be paid . . . to the immediate advantages and disadvantages of any change at a time when schemes of development are being initiated and . . . modification of the present regime might delay their implementation."[10]

For once, the Embassy was in general agreement with Khartoum's suggestions for consultation. Commenting on the governor-general's draft memorandum early in March, the minister of state in Cairo, James Bowker, made only minor criticisms of detail. At the same time, he pointed out that the Egyptians would inevitably consider the process of consultation proposed by the Sudan Administration as "artificial." Indeed, the Embassy official admitted, "Any consultation of a primitive country is bound to be unreal." The unreality in the case of the Sudan was compounded by the "impossibility" of serious consultation with tribesmen in the Southern Sudan. The alternative to consultation directed by Khartoum, however, would be "consultation by less direct methods from the Egyptian side." Consequently, although consultation must obviously remain under British control, this fact should be kept as much in the background as possible.[11]

There is considerable evidence in the documents to suggest that Robertson and Huddleston wanted to "internationalize" the Sudan question. Both men were clearly proud of the administration's record. They honestly, if somewhat naively, believed that if the Sudan question was ever examined by an international body like the United Nations, the Egyptians would be put quickly out of court. Thinking in terms of trusteeship, the Sudan Government gently worked its way toward some sort of international recognition, both for the Sudan as a unique state, separate from both co-domini, and for the achievements of the Political Service. From this perspective, the question of consulting the Sudanese soon took on another dimension.[12]

During their April meeting at Wadi Halfa, Huddleston admitted to Campbell that he, like Bowker, worried that any form of inquiry carried out by the Sudan Government alone would be highly suspect to the Egyptians. He suggested, therefore, that a commission from outside the Sudan should investigate the attitude of the Sudanese, perhaps something along the lines of the Mandatory Commission which had visited Iraq. Campbell agreed that Egypt would oppose any method of consultation that rested solely in the hands of the Sudan

---

10. Annexure to Khartoum Despatch no. 31, 23 February 1946, Memorandum on the Future of the Sudan, Secret, FO 371/53250, PRO.

11. Bowker to Bevin, no. 354, 11 March 1946, FO 371/53250, PRO.

12. As early as August 1945 E. N. Corbyn had written a memorandum for the Sudan Government on the potential position of the Sudan as a trusteeship under the United Nations Charter, pointing out that it would be a direct step toward independence. For earlier views on the subject, see also the many references to trusteeship and Sudanese independence throughout Sir Douglas Newbold's correspondence, reproduced in K.D.D. Henderson, *The Making of the Modern Sudan* (London, 1953). Corbyn's memorandum is in FO 371/53252, PRO.

Government or of the British, but he was not entirely sanguine about the chances of a wholly neutral committee. Egypt, he pointed out, would probably insist on appointing its own member to any commission of inquiry on the Sudan. When Huddleston did not demur, the two agreed that procedure for consultation would have to be worked out "in concert" with the Egyptians.[13]

In mid-April, Lord Stansgate endorsed the governor-general's suggestion for a commission to carry out consultation of the Sudanese. Anxious to placate the Egyptians, the minister for air suggested that the British-draft Sudan clause should actually include a reference to the proposed commission. After conversations with the Egyptians, who seemed interested in the proposals, by early May the composition of the commission and its terms of reference had become the major topic of discussion on the Sudan question. From London to Khartoum, consideration of Huddleston's suggestion took on the appearance of a series of ethnic jokes, as British officials weighed the comparative advantages and shortcomings of having a Belgian, a Portuguese, or a Turk on the commission. "The Dutch suggest themselves," Scrivener minuted at one point, "but they lack experience of African administration (except in their South African form!)." "A good Belgian would be easier to find than a good Portuguese," Sir Orme Sargent, the permanent under secretary, summed up for Bevin, "while a Frenchman might have preconceived views as regards British methods of administration."[14]

While the Foreign Office and the Embassy initially planned for a three-member commission, modeled on the Nile Waters Commission of the 1920s, Robertson and Huddleston had in mind a five-man body. Moreover, they wanted the terms of reference to be so written that they would allow a minimum of interference into administrative matters. Anxious that "consultation" should not be turned into a referendum on the specific policies of the administration, or the intricacies of administrative detail, they proposed that the commission should be appointed "for the purpose of making recommendations for the future of the Sudan." In addition to a British and an Egyptian member, they suggested, there should also be three "independent members," one of whom would be the chairman of the committee. A three-man body, with only the chairman independent, would throw the "whole onus of decision" onto him.[15]

In June, Robertson elaborated, explaining that the main concern was to have a commission with a fairly broad basis, and hence more authority, "whose recommendations will command the respect of the Sudanese." He also explained the advantages of a commission from Khartoum's perspective. Even if the co-

---

13. Campbell to Bevin, no. 546, 22 April 1946, FO 371/53252, PRO. The Iraq Commission had consisted of "Lord Lugard, a Belgian, a Turk and one other member."

14. Cairo to Foreign Office, tels. nos. 750 and 751, 27 April 1946, with accompanying minutes, esp. Scrivener, 29 April 1946, and memorandum by Sargent, Sudan, 9 May 1946, FO 371/53252, PRO.

15. Cairo to Foreign Office, no. 754, 13 May 1946, repeating Khartoum to Cairo, no. 57, 2 May 1946, FO 371/53252, PRO.

domini did not agree to the recommendations a commission might make, he wrote, "we should at least have had an independent opinion and the Sudan Government might obtain some useful recommendations about knotty problems, such as the South; the future of the Advisory Council, and how fast we can go ahead with Sudanisation." Not least, the civil secretary expected an impartial commission would give the Political Service a boost: "The Commission might well emphasise the work which has been done in the past—which many people seem now to forget—and remark on the strides which the country has made. This would be useful to the Sudan Government."[16]

While the British thus considered their own proposals for a commission, the Egyptians too began to formulate views on the Sudan. Like the British, the Egyptians also had more than one voice. As head of a minority government dependent largely on King Farouk, Sidqi Pasha walked a narrow line in the treaty negotiations. Whatever his own policies, he could not afford to offend either the king or the other parties in his coalition. Even with the opposition Wafd Party he had to tread warily, especially in the single most important area of Egyptian politics, the renegotiation of the treaty with Britain. Largely for this reason, Sidqi had invited all elements of Egyptian politics to form a united negotiating delegation. While the Wafd remained aloof, others did join, but the result was a body that the Egyptian prime minister did not fully control. During the summer of 1946, considerable disagreement developed within Egyptian ranks on the relative importance of the Sudan in the treaty negotiations.[17]

Sidqi Pasha clearly wanted a treaty. Moreover, he was probably willing personally to leave the Sudan question as it had been in 1936. The Egyptian treaty delegation, however, took a more nationalistic stance, insisting that the new treaty should include a separate protocol on the Sudan, with a specific admission of Egyptian sovereignty over the territory. Outside the negotiations, the Wafd too demanded not only recognition of Egyptian sovereignty but also complete British evacuation from the condominium as well as Egypt. Despite 'Amr Pasha's assurances that the Egyptian monarch would raise no difficulties over the Sudan, as the position of the delegation became clear Farouk himself became unwilling to compromise on sovereignty.[18]

---

16. Robertson to Bowker, CS/SCR/97.H.1., 15 June 1946, FO 371/53253, PRO.

17. Sidqi's position and the composition of the Egyptian treaty delegation are dealt with extensively in Cairo to Foreign Office, nos. 437 and 438, 8 March 1946, FO 371/53287/J 1043 and J 1059, PRO. See also minute by Riches, 11 March 1946, on Egyptian political parties that "differ from one another as the result of differences of personalities rather than principles."

18. It was commonly reported at the time that the obstructive element in the delegation was led by Makram Pasha, an old Wafdist who had broken with Nahas Pasha, the Wafdist leader, in 1942. See, for example Kirk, *The Middle East*, 124. According to Hafez Afifi Pasha, one of Egypt's representatives to the United Nations, at least three other delegates—Sharif Sabry, Hussein Sirry, and 'Ali Shamsi—were also committed to "chauvinistic ideas of the most extreme nature." Sirry had actually admitted that a group within the delegation "had decided from the start to prevent the

The first exchange of draft treaties occurred on 19 May. Lord Stansgate found the Egyptian text to be "a childish effort so limited in scope as to be quite hopeless from our point of view." Sidqi Pasha responded in kind averring that the British draft would "make a bad impression on the Egyptian Delegation." On the Sudan question, the Egyptians made their position perfectly clear. "The high contracting parties," their Sudan clause stated, "undertake to enter into negotiations immediately in order to determine the status of the Sudan within the framework of the interests of the Sudanese peoples on the basis of the Unity of the Nile Valley under the Egyptian Crown." The British submitted the draft article already approved by the governor-general, calling for self-government, the freedom of the Sudanese to decide their future relations with the co-domini, and the appointment of a joint commission to make recommendations for effecting these principles.[19]

While negotiations on the Egyptian question continued through May and into June, Sidqi Pasha made no comment at all on the British Sudan proposals. Early in June an impasse occurred when the Egyptian delegation rejected the British draft treaty with its proposed military convention. Stansgate was recalled to London for discussions, but after continuing conversations between the British ambassador and Sidqi in Cairo, and 'Amr Pasha and the Foreign Office in London, early in July negotiations resumed. In the meantime, the Defence Committee of the British Cabinet, which was ultimately responsible for overseeing the negotiations, agreed to announce a complete British evacuation of the Nile Delta by 31 March 1947. In a new atmosphere, during the early part of July, the two sides came closer to agreement on the military aspects of the treaty. The primary objects of dispute became the length of time the chiefs of staff insisted was necessary for a complete withdrawal from Egyptian territory (five years) and the terms under which Britain might reenter the country in case of an "aggression" against neighboring territories. Full agreement remained elusive, however, and desultory talks continued throughout the summer.[20]

While the military negotiations thus progressed slowly, in July Sidqi Pasha and his foreign minister, Lutfi Al-Sayyid, finally raised again the question of the Sudan. There could be no doubt, they insisted, about the sovereignty of the Egyptian Crown over the Sudan. Nor was this a matter on which the Sudanese could be consulted. Although expressing interest in the proposed commission,

---

conclusion of any treaty with Sidki." Afifi also believed that the "wrecking tactics" of the delegates could not have been sustained for so long against Farouk's wishes. Bowker agreed with this analysis. In a minute of 19 October 1946, Scrivener too registered his conviction that Farouk was "playing a double game on the Treaty." See Cecil Campbell to Bowker, 13 October 1946, FO 371/53315, PRO.

19. Anglo-Egyptian Treaty Negotiations, 1945-47, Secret, 12 March 1947, FO 371/62962, PRO.

20. Ibid. For the British internal debate over evacuation see also Louis, *The British Empire*, part 2 chapter 6.

the Egyptian premier made it clear that the basis of its investigations must be the unity of the Nile Valley under Egyptian sovereignty. On 1 August, the Egyptian delegation as a whole presented a note going even further. Not only must Egypt have "all rights without exception" in the Sudan, but the Sudan itself should be a part of the Egyptian administrative system. Moreover, the Sudanese had no right to dispute such a status. As Lord Stansgate reported to Bevin, the point had been reached when even if agreement was achieved on the other aspects of the treaty, the Sudan would constitute a "major obstacle" to a successful conclusion. "I can conceive a situation arising," the minister for air gloomily predicted, "in which the Egyptians . . . would break on the sole question of . . . sovereignty."[21]

The Foreign Office found the Egyptian claims preposterous. At the same time, they saw the Egyptian note as a potentially useful opportunity to score points in the international arena as well as in the Sudan itself. "The best that can be said of these impudent claims by the Egyptians," Scrivener minuted, "is that our publicity services ought, if necessary, to be able to run a splendid campaign against Egyptian imperialism." The Egyptian delegation, Scrivener believed, unlike the warier Sidqi, had "overreached themselves." Eric Beckett suggested that the Egyptian note was "quite unacceptable." Moreover, by leaking it to the Sudan, "we could blow the Egyptians right off this perch." With this kind of support from his officials, Bevin drafted for the British delegation new instructions that, in Scrivener's words, "foresee no compromise on the Sudan issue." Even as the Foreign Office thus resisted the Egyptian claims, however, it also began examining the whole question of sovereignty to see just how far it might compromise if necessary.[22]

From the presentation of the Egyptian note on the Sudan in August, the status of the condominium increasingly became the focal point of Anglo-Egyptian disagreement. Anxious to accommodate the Egyptians, and clearly aware of the extent to which they were committed to their demand for sovereignty, Stansgate and the British delegation in Alexandria pressed the Foreign Office to compromise. Even before the August note, after his discussions with Sidqi in July, Stansgate realized that the entire negotiations might hinge on the Sudan. Robertson later remembered visiting the slightly haggard peer about this time at the Montaza Palace in Alexandria. "I found Lord Stansgate in his dressing gown with a bad cold. It was very hot and the delegation was wilting. Lord Stansgate appeared far from sympathetic towards my views about the Sudan, but I hoped he was only irritable because of his cold." With Egyptian demands on one hand, and Robertson's own strident views concerning British pledges to the Sudanese on

21. Louis, *The British Empire*, part 2 chapter 6; Alexandria to Foreign Office, no. 43, 1 August 1946, and accompanying minutes, FO 371/53254/J 3385, PRO.

22. Alexandria to Foreign Office, no. 43, 1 August 1946, and accompanying minutes, FO 371/53254/J 3385, PRO.

the other, Stansgate undoubtedly suffered from more than a cold—he was trying to reconcile the irreconcilable.[23]

While Stansgate sweltered in the heat of an Alexandrian summer, in London the British Cabinet began to feel frustrated. Treaty negotiations seemed to be going nowhere, and despite what the Cabinet considered substantial British concessions, the anti-British campaign in the Egyptian press was becoming even more violent. On 5 August the head of the Foreign Office conveyed his colleagues' dissatisfaction to the secretary of state for air:

We seem to be placed in the position that, unless we give way on all points to the Egyptians, we get no Treaty. His Majesty's Government cannot conscientiously give way all round. They consider that Sidki should be faced bluntly with the outstanding feature of these negotiations, namely, the fact that since they started we have met the Egyptians on practically every issue they have raised, whereas their own response to our requests has been both slight and grudging.

As for Egyptian claims in the Sudan, "the Cabinet stands absolutely firm. His Majesty's Government cannot compromise on this. . . . The Egyptian Government can of course make a unilateral declaration on this matter; but we can accept no form of words in the protocol which admits the sovereignty of the Egyptian Crown." Even as the Cabinet thus sought to stiffen Stansgate's backbone, however, officials in the Foreign Office were beginning seriously to consider the very concession the Cabinet itself had just categorically refused to endorse—a recognition of Egyptian sovereignty over the Sudan.[24]

THE PROBLEM OF SOVEREIGNTY AND THE SUDAN QUESTION

The question of sovereignty over the Sudan provided the "legal" minds in the Foreign Office a splendid opportunity to let themselves go. In a lengthy minute summing up the basis of the British position, the head of the Treaty Department, Eric Beckett, observed that sovereignty as it related to the Sudan was a "legal and theoretical" question. "Though sovereignty is an everyday term in international law, international lawyers seldom agree exactly on the definition of sovereignty itself."[25] There were two schools of thought: "school A which regards the sovereign as being the owner of the ultimate title as opposed to the owner of the immediate rights of administration and a school B which holds that the sovereign is the person internationally responsible at the moment." School B would suggest that sovereignty in the Sudan was divided, since administration

---

23. Robertson, *Transition*, 95.

24. Foreign Office to Alexandria, no. 30, 5 August 1946, FO 371/53308, PRO.

25. Minute by Beckett, 7 August 1946. That Beckett's analysis was accepted as Foreign Office policy can be seen in Foreign Office to Alexandria, no. 45, 10 August 1946, FO 371/53254, PRO.

was (theoretically) divided. School A was more complicated and hinged on two points: whether Egypt had ever lost sovereignty over the Sudan, as a result of the Mahdist rising; and if so, whether the "reconquest" had merely restored Egyptian sovereignty or created a new "joint sovereignty." It was with a certain relief that the Foreign Office eventually decided to avoid such "theoretical questions." "Our task," Bevin eventually summed up for Stansgate, "is to deal with practical matters viz. what should be put in the treaty about the future of the Sudan. . . . the governing factors must be (a) the interests of the Sudanese and (b) the wishes of the Sudanese. . . . The facts of the situation and modern international doctrine render academic . . . any prior discussion of the vexed question of sovereignty over the Sudan."[26]

As the Egyptians remained adamant on the sovereignty issue, however, the British negotiators began looking for ways to accommodate them. In mid-August Lord Stansgate suggested moving toward United Nations trusteeship in the Sudan Protocol. The foreign secretary reacted sharply to the suggestion, even as a tactical move. "I am not enamoured of the idea of introducing into the Sudan protocol a reference to the principle of United Nations trusteeship," he cabled Stansgate. "It is not (repeat not) my intention that the Sudan should come under the trusteeship system." The specter of Molotov still haunted the corridors of Whitehall, and Bevin would consider nothing that might allow the Soviet Union to gain a foothold in the Anglo-Egyptian dispute. At the same time, he finally rejected the suggestions for a joint commission to investigate the future of the Sudan. With "internationalization" out of the question, at the end of August Sir Orme Sargent submitted a memorandum outlining two possible alternatives: a compromise formula in which the Egyptians could maintain their sovereignty while the British Government refused to comment on it; or an unqualified British recognition of Egyptian sovereignty.[27]

Confronted with a complete breakdown of negotiations, for the first time the foreign secretary began to consider fully the implications of the Sudan question. On 29 August, while in Paris at the Peace Conference, Pierson Dixon, his personal secretary, prepared a note on the Sudan for his chief's consideration. This note, along with the alternatives suggested by Sargent, marked the beginning of a volte-face in Bevin's Sudan policy.

Dixon reminded Bevin that from the British perspective it would be better to leave the sovereignty question in abeyance "as it has deliberately been left by successive British Governments during the past 50 years." This would force the Egyptians, "or the Russians," into a position of having to prove Egyptian sovereignty. While it might be possible to prove the "theoretical sovereignty" of

---

26. Foreign Office to Alexandria, no. 30, 5 August 1946, FO 371/53308, PRO.

27. Paris to Alexandria, no. 5, 18 August 1946, FO 371/53254. See also Minute on Sudan by Sargent, 29 August 1946, and Paris to Foreign Office, no. 608, 30 August 1946. In a memorandum written for the Cabinet, Bevin was more explicit: "I am not in favor of making the Sudan a trusteeship because of the risks of letting Russia into Africa" (FO 371/53255, PRO).

the Egyptian monarch, Dixon believed, "it seems inconceivable that any international body or tribunal would find that Egypt has the right to administer the Sudan by herself." On the other hand, a positive affirmation of Egyptian sovereignty by the British, after having left the question vague for so many years, would certainly "mean something." British recognition was not simply a matter of "prestige," as King Farouk had argued, Dixon maintained, but was considerably more significant: "The main effect would be to waive the future status of the Sudan in favour of union with Egypt. It might also weaken our position if challenged internationally about the Condominium." The argument was clearly against admitting Egyptian sovereignty, he told Bevin, "unless we wish to weight the scales in favour of the ultimate union of Egypt and the Sudan."[28]

For Dixon the crux of the matter was not whether Britain should acknowledge Farouk's sovereignty over the Sudan, but what future the British envisioned for the condominium. "Before we turn down the Egyptian request, ought we not to make up our minds what we wish the future status of the Sudan to be. Do we think that independence is the best solution or are we prepared to accept union with Egypt. On the long view the latter might be the right solution. It is difficult to see how the Sudan could stand alone." Bevin was impressed by his secretary's analysis. The next day he telegraphed to Sargent in London, adopting many of Dixon's arguments; he stopped short, however, of agreeing to an unqualified recognition of Egyptian sovereignty.[29]

There were three important consequences, the foreign secretary reasoned, that might result from an unqualified recognition of Egyptian sovereignty: serious unsettlement in the Sudan "involving difficulties to our administration during the interim period"; a considerable loss of British "face"; and a weighting of the future status of the Sudan "in favour of union with Egypt." The latter possibility was not necessarily a problem, Bevin wrote, echoing Dixon: "I am not . . . convinced that independence is the best solution. It seems to me that the Sudan will have difficulty in standing alone. Provided our defence interests in Egypt are sufficiently secured and the Defence Board is working effectively, I am not sure that our interests would not best be served by the Union of the Sudan with Egypt." Even so, given the difficulties involved in a loss of face and disorders in the Sudan, the foreign secretary preferred a middle course: "I have been considering whether it would be possible to have a form of words which would acknowledge the sovereignty of Egypt while also acknowledging the position of Great Britain as co-administrator." In short, Bevin now proposed to admit an existing Egyptian sovereignty, but without defining its nature and without undermining Britain's own "rights" in the Sudan.[30]

The position toward which the foreign secretary was moving was anathema to the Sudan Government. Both Robertson and Huddleston were on leave in Britain

---

28. Note by Dixon, Sudan, 29 August 1946, FO 371/53255, PRO.
29. Ibid.
30. Paris to Foreign Office, no. 608, 29 August 1946, FO 371/53255, PRO.

when the Egyptian delegation presented their note on the Sudan. In the middle of August the Foreign Office finally asked the governor-general to come in for consultations on the deteriorating negotiations. Huddleston was appalled by the alternatives in Sargent's note. Agreeing reluctantly to the first alternative of an Egyptian declaration on sovereignty and a British reservation, he refused categorically to accept an unqualified British recognition of Egyptian sovereignty. He made it clear that such a resolution would result in his resignation in protest. Summoned from Scotland, early in September Robertson too joined the discussions, reinforcing the governor-general's objections to any recognition of Egyptian sovereignty. A three-way consultation now took place between London, Paris, and Alexandria as the British sought a compromise formula acceptable to the Sudanese, as represented by Robertson and Huddleston, and the Egyptians.[31]

There is a hint in the documents at this point that Bevin was playing a less than straight game with both the Cabinet and the Sudan Government. In the Cabinet he came down forcefully against any admission of Egyptian sovereignty as a matter of principle considering his pledges to the Sudanese. Outside the Cabinet, however, he seemed fully prepared to admit, at least privately, that the Egyptian claim was valid. Moreover, all his efforts to find a "formula of words" come across as little more than sophistry. There was too much at stake, as far as Bevin was concerned, to break negotiations on the Sudan issue. Egypt was the linchpin of British defense of the Middle East. The Russian threat crops up regularly in the foreign secretary's telegrams to the British delegation in Alexandria. If an admission of sovereignty was the only way to get an acceptable treaty, then why should a country like the Sudan, which probably could not survive on its own anyway, stand in the way of Anglo-Egyptian friendship and agreement? This was the scenario that the Sudan Government had long dreaded—it was on them at last.[32]

Huddleston and Robertson remained in London throughout September and into October as the negotiations continued. Under Scrivener's wing, they participated

---

31. For Huddleston's reaction see Foreign Office to Paris, no. 1199, 29 August 1946, FO 371/53255, PRO.

32. See telegrams, memoranda, and minutes from mid-August to mid-September in FO 371/53255, PRO. On the same day that he began to reconsider his policy toward the Sudan along Dixon's line, Bevin approved a memorandum for Cabinet distribution opposing any recognition of Egyptian sovereignty in the treaty. Given American attitudes and the principles of the United Nations Charter, he argued, such a step would be regarded as "retrograde" and would expose Britain to charges of "Imperial behaviour and . . . overlooking the fundamental modern concept that the people themselves should be heard before a change in their status is made." The Sudanese would regard an admission of Egyptian sovereignty as a change in their status. In the Cabinet, Bevin's stance fairly reeked of moral rectitude: "I cannot do what I believe to be wrong in order to get a quick Treaty of Alliance." Yet at that very moment, the foreign secretary had already begun to convince himself that a compromise with Egypt's demands might not be "wrong."

in efforts to draft an acceptable compromise formula. In the process, Robertson managed to suggest changes that had the effect of reinforcing the position of the Sudan Government, much to Stansgate's distress. After considering Dixon's suggestions, the foreign secretary had drafted a new "formula of words" that might satisfy the Egyptians without undercutting his own position.

The high contracting parties agree that their primary policy in the Sudan shall continue to be the welfare of the Sudanese and the active preparation of the Sudanese for self-government.

As soon as this latter objective is attained the Sudanese people shall be free to decide their future. . . . If the Sudanese should decide in favour of independence, suitable agreements shall be made with regard to the development and utilisation of the waters of the Nile Valley for the greatest benefit of the Egyptian and Sudanese peoples and with regard to the other material interests of Egypt in the Nile Valley.

Meanwhile, the administration of the Sudan shall continue to be exercised jointly by the United Kingdom and Egypt in accordance with the Condominium agreements of 1899 and Article 11 of the Treaty of 1936.

The Egyptian Government declare that the preceding provisions of this Protocol do not prejudice the claim of His Majesty the King of Egypt to be the Sovereign of the Sudan. The Government of the United Kingdom, while pointing out that it will be for the Sudanese people to decide upon their future in accordance with paragraph (2) above and declining to make any pronouncement on the question of sovereignty, declare that nothing in the preceding Protocol prejudices that question.

Under pressure from the Foreign Office, Robertson and Huddleston eventually agreed to this draft, but doubted that the Sudanese would understand the last paragraph: they still hoped for the joint commission.[33]

On 5 September Bevin cabled an additional paragraph through the Foreign Office to Alexandria for Stansgate to present to the Egyptians. The opening sentence was Robertson's, and the paragraph reintroduced the role of both the Sudan Government and the joint commission:

The high contracting parties shall from time to time secure reports from the Governor-General on the progress of the Sudanese people towards the goal of self-government. At a suitable time they will appoint a joint commission to report on the question whether the Sudanese are prepared for full self-government and in a position to decide on the future of the Sudan and if so, to recommend suitable arrangements for ascertaining what are the wishes of the Sudanese people and for giving effect thereto.

From the Egyptian point of view, this new version of the joint commission, and particularly the emphasis on the governor-general's role, represented a significant move backward.[34]

---

33. Paris to Alexandria, no. 17, 31 August 1946, Secret, and Foreign Office to Alexandria, no. 87, 2 September 1946, FO 371/53255, PRO.

34. Paris to Alexandria, no. 21, 5 September 1946, FO 371/53255, PRO.

Ten days after receiving Bevin's new draft, Stansgate telegraphed his objections to London. The most obvious difficulty, Stansgate pointed out, was that the Egyptian draft protocol stipulated "immediate negotiations" to determine the status of the Sudan. The original British draft, calling for the immediate appointment and convening of a joint commission, had largely answered this demand, although not of course within the context of unity of the Nile Valley and Egyptian sovereignty. The new draft, delegating to the governor-general responsibility for the initial report on Sudanese progress, effectively rejected the Egyptian call for immediate negotiations. Moreover, "Egyptian reaction must be that a British Governor-General is a biased agent and that further serious Egyptian participation in examination of the Sudanese question is indefinitely postponed." Stansgate also complained that he had been given no reason for these modifications to the original idea, "which Governor-General strongly favoured." The overall effect of the new draft, he concluded, was "more uncompromising and provides less material for meeting Egyptian oft repeated wish for negotiation."[35]

By mid-September, however, both Bevin and the Foreign Office had become thoroughly exasperated with the attitude of their negotiator in Egypt. Stansgate had shown a tendency throughout the summer to play devil's advocate to all of their instructions and suggestions for conducting the negotiations. Anxious to deal on an equal basis with the Egyptians, the minister for air had bent over backward to see his opponents' point of view, even anticipating their objections to his proposals. It was too much for officials in London. "This is really terrible," Scrivener minuted. "The whole of the Delegation's energies are once more concentrated on modifying our proposals instead of on putting them across the Egyptians. And be it noted that those proposals are largely based on Egyptian (albeit royal) ideas."[36] Bevin too had lost patience. "I am not prepared to consider any change in the proposals," he telegraphed Stansgate, "at least until I have heard what the Egyptian reception of them is. . . . So please stick to my proposals until you get some authoritative reaction to them." In his own staccato scrawl, the foreign secretary improved on Scrivener's draft telegram: "Please get to grips with the Egyptians. It seems as if all the argument is with me. I must know where I stand and with firm action the issue will be narrowed. This delay is playing into the hands of Russia."[37]

Whatever Stansgate may have thought about the new draft, his perception of the Egyptian state of mind proved all too acute. The time had passed when "firmness" would win the day for the British delegation. The efforts of King Farouk and 'Amr Pasha in August to force a settlement on the treaty, including their suggestions that the Sudan issue might be dealt with outside the treaty

---

35. Alexandria to Foreign Office, no. 126, 15 September 1946, FO 371/53255, PRO.

36. Minute by Scrivener, 15 September 1946, FO 371/53255, PRO.

37. See draft telegram by Scrivener with Bevin's addition, Foreign Office to Alexandria, no. 111, 16 September 1946, FO 371/53255, PRO.

altogether, backfired both in the Egyptian delegation and Cabinet and in the country at large. Even if they had not, early in September an unexpected bombshell exploded in Anglo-Egyptian negotiations, bringing all Egypt's suspicion and frustration to a head. This new debacle came not from the British, however, but from the Sudan, indeed from Robertson himself. Once again the Sudan Administration, refusing to "hold down" the Sudanese to facilitate Anglo-Egyptian relations, had done something "salient."[38]

COMPLICATIONS IN THE SUDAN

While negotiations had continued from July through September in London and Alexandria, in Khartoum the Sudan Political Service was becoming increasingly nervous about the course of events. So too were members of the Umma Party and the adherents of independence. As Anglo-Egyptian talks dragged on, the independence groups in the Sudan worried that their own position might be bargained away by the British in exchange for the Anglo-Egyptian military alliance. In July, Abdullah Khalil, secretary general of the Umma, wrote again to the civil secretary, demanding an end to the condominium and the creation of an independent Sudanese state.[39]

Reminding the administration of the governor-general's speech to the Advisory Council the previous April, the Umma secretary quoted Huddleston's pledge: "The object of the Sudan Government [is] to build the organs of self-government with the aim of eventual independence." To this end, the governor-general had called the Sudan Administration Conference to recommend ways of associating the Sudanese more closely with their own government. "We understood from all this," Abdullah Khalil observed, "that the conference will be for devising means for eventual independence." Now it appeared that even the twenty-year timetable which the governor-general had mentioned, and which the Umma had assumed applied to independence, referred only to the establishment of self-government. Such a policy, Abdullah Khalil warned, "will urge this party to double its efforts for independence of the Sudan in any way it thinks fit."[40]

---

38. Farouk and 'Amr Pasha apparently agreed to consider the idea of having each side make a statement on sovereignty outside the treaty negotiations, postponing discussions on the Sudan until after the treaty itself had been signed. The Egyptian treaty delegation rejected this plan. See account in Anglo-Egyptian Treaty Negotiations, 1945-47, Secret, FO 371/62962, PRO.

39. Abdullah Khalil had initially written to the civil secretary on 9 May 1946. The Umma Party tried to get the Sudan Government to state unequivocally that "Self Governing Sudan" meant a "fully independent Sudan with complete Sovereignty" covering "the whole of the Northern and Southern Sudan within its geographical limits." See note by the Umma Party to the Sudan Government, 9 May 1946, and Robertson's response on 14 July 1946, FO 371/53257, PRO.

40. Umma to Civil Secretary, 23 July 1946, FO 371/53257, PRO. On 19 July 1946 the Umma also wrote directly to the co-domini through the governor-general,

Late in August the Umma Party wrote again, deprecating once more the suggestion that only self-government and not full independence would be reached in twenty years. In a less than subtle threat, it reemphasized that its participation in the Sudan Administration Conference had been "with the aim of eventual independence." Moreover it demanded that the whole matter should be referred to the United Nations if Britain and Egypt could not agree on this. In fact, although the Umma Party secretary complained about the actual reasons behind the Administration Conference, early in September he had good reason to appreciate its work.[41]

Convened almost immediately after its creation by the governor-general the previous April, the conference had worked steadily into the summer. Dividing itself into two subcommittees, one to examine local government and the other central government, by mid-July, before Robertson went on leave, both subcommittees had presented their reports and recommendations. These were, however, only preliminary reports. Robertson held a joint meeting of the subcommittees on 16 and 17 July, with as many members of the full conference as could attend, and made minor adjustments to the wording "for the sake of lucidity." With many members unavailable during the summer months and with the governor-general himself on leave in England, the civil secretary did not intend a full examination to take place until the following October, after which the final report would be presented to Huddleston. Meanwhile, Robertson intended to circulate copies to the senior members of the Political Service, as well as among Sudanese notables and party leaders, to get feedback before the full conference reconvened in the fall.[42]

Robertson well understood the implications of the subcommittee reports and the risk he ran of premature publication. Moreover, he was fully aware of the possible implications of a leakage for the treaty negotiations. Conveying copies of the reports to Mayall at the Sudan Agency in London, on 17 July he outlined his plans:

I also intend to issue these reports fairly widely to Heads of Departments, Governors and District Commissioners and to prominent Sudanese and I have no doubt that their recommendations will get into the press. This may easily cause alarm and excitement in Egypt and we shall be shot at again by the Embassy for doing something "salient" and putting the fat into the fire. I don't see very well how this can be avoided and we must give the Sudanese their head a bit, or we simply play into the hands of the Egyptians.

---

formally asking for cancellation of the condominium. Secretary, Umma Party, to Prime Ministers, Egypt and Great Britain, 19 July 1946, FO 371/53254, PRO.

41. A summary of this letter, dated 23 August 1946, is in Sudan Political Intelligence Summary no. 59 (New Series), August-September 1946, FO 371/53328, PRO.

42. Robertson to Mayall, 17 July 1946, CS/SCR/1.A.9/2, FO 371/53255, PRO.

Instructing Mayall to pass copies of the reports along to both the Foreign Office and the Embassy in Cairo, as well as to Huddleston, Robertson warned that the reports were not yet official. They were reports of subcommittees of a Conference that had yet to report to the governor-general, and had neither been accepted by the full conference itself, nor even been considered, much less accepted, by the Sudan Government. If they were eventually approved, and were found to entail "an alteration" of the Sudan's constitution, then they would have to be submitted to the condominium powers. In effect, the civil secretary had knowingly set the fuse on a time bomb in Anglo-Egyptian relations.[43]

On 9 September, in the midst of Bevin's new Sudan initiative, Robertson's bomb went off with a bang. Picking up the story from local Sudanese papers, the Egyptian press published the main recommendations of the two subcommittees of the Sudan Administration Conference. At the same time, the press reported that the conference reports had been taken to Britain by the civil secretary during July, for the prior approval of the Foreign Office, before an official copy had been communicated to the Egyptian Government. The charge was true: although Robertson did not take copies with him, he had already sent them through Mayall to the Foreign Office. The leakage had caught him, reporting to one of the co-domini without equally informing the other. Worse yet, from an Egyptian point of view, were the contents of the reports. As Scrivener in the Foreign Office put it, "The proceedings of the Committee on Local Government are unspectacular, but those of the Committee on the closer association of the Sudanese with the Central Government were nicely calculated to create alarm and despondency in Egypt . . . they certainly should not have been published before being communicated to the Egyptian Government." Khartoum quickly sent copies to Sidqi Pasha, but the damage had been done.[44]

As Robertson had foreseen, premature leakage of the conference reports seriously upset Anglo-Egyptian negotiations. With Bevin's new draft in front of them, members of the Egyptian delegation became even more uncompromising than before. Not only did they demand again that the sovereignty issue must be dealt with in the treaty, but now they even insisted that the Egyptian Government must take an "effective part" in "elaborating the democratic regime towards which the Sudan should be moving." "Egyptian sovereignty," they declared, "does not need to be claimed. It exists: it has never been possible to contest it." Taking a page out of Khartoum's book, even before they communicated this response officially to London, members of the delegation leaked it and the text of the draft protocol to the Egyptian press—with predictable effect on the Egyptian public. As the Cairo mob took to the streets,

43. Ibid.

44. See Alexandria to Khartoum, no. 2, 9 September 1946, repeated to Foreign Office, no. 119, and Khartoum to Foreign Office, no. 23, 12 September 1946, FO 371/53255; See also Minute by Scrivener, 25 September 1946, FO 371/53255/J 3927.

and the Wafd expressed its outrage, treaty negotiations came to an abrupt standstill.[45]

"SELLING THE PASS": CONCEDING EGYPTIAN SOVEREIGNTY

While the Wafd demonstrated, and the delegation expressed its indignation with the British stand on the Sudan, the Egyptian prime minister himself was furious. Sidqi Pasha viewed the conclusion of a successful treaty with Britain and the negotiation of a complete withdrawal of British troops from Egypt as the potential capstone to his own political career. Despite the leak from the Sudan, what most angered the Egyptian premier was the unauthorized response of his own treaty delegation. Thoroughly disgusted at last with their backbiting and stalling tactics, on 28 September Sidqi submitted his resignation in protest to King Farouk. The king himself appeared alarmed by the delegation's obstructionist attitude. After a brief interval, however, and an unsuccessful attempt to form a new Cabinet, Farouk turned once more to Sidqi and on 2 October prevailed on the aging statesman to continue in office. Still determined to achieve his goal, Sidqi accepted, proposing that he should visit Bevin in London personally, without the Egyptian delegation, in a final effort to resolve outstanding differences on the treaty.[46]

On the fourth and fifth of October, the leaders of the British treaty delegation met with Bevin in Paris to discuss the situation. At this point there were three outstanding difficulties on the military side of negotiations: article 2 of the draft treaty, dealing with mutual defense obligations in case of war; the period required for evacuation of British forces from Egyptian territory; and Britain's desire to retain British personnel after evacuation to maintain transit facilities for the Royal Air Force. The single greatest obstacle to agreement, however, was the Sudan question. The minutes show that even on the military side, the Sudan had become the major bargaining chip.[47] Stansgate and Campbell "emphasized" to Bevin that although Egypt had become more intransigent on article 2, if they "received satisfaction over the Sudan," they would probably agree to the British proposals. Agreement on the evacuation period, which Egypt insisted should be

45. Anglo-Egyptian Treaty Negotiations, 1945-47, Secret, FO 371/62962. Also see articles in *The Times*, 30 September and 1 October 1946, and especially telegrams between Foreign Office, Khartoum, and Alexandria, 9-30 September 1946 in FO 371/53255 and 53256, PRO.

46. Telegrams between Foreign Office, Khartoum, and Alexandria, 9-30 September 1946 in FO 371/53255 and 53256, PRO. Sidqi had suggested face-to-face negotiations with Bevin earlier, but the foreign secretary had declined, fearful that even if he reached agreement with Sidqi, the terms would be either repudiated by the delegation or made the basis of further Egyptian demands.

47. Records of meetings held in Paris on 4 and 5 October 1946 concerning Anglo-Egyptian Treaty Negotiations, FO 371/53314, PRO.

one year and the British five, also depended on the Sudan: "It was considered likely that provided the Egyptians received satisfaction over the Sudan they would agree to three years from the date of ratification." Thus the stage was set for what the Sudan Government would call the British "betrayal" of the Sudan.[48]

Although it is clear that he had already accepted the inevitable in his own mind, Bevin opened discussions on the Sudan by referring to his pledge the previous March to consult the Sudanese before making any change in the status of the Sudan. The foreign secretary apparently had an uneasy conscience. Going over all the possibilities that had already been discussed, he reiterated that he "distrusted" the idea of a trusteeship. Nor did he like the idea of a joint commission to be sent out in a year's time. Instead, Bevin suggested that the two questions of sovereignty and administration should be separated. "If sovereignty were conceded," he went on, "the Egyptians might agree to the maintenance of the present administration and to a stipulation that the Governor-General should always be a Briton." In five years' time, perhaps, a "Joint Council" composed of equal numbers of British and Egyptians, possibly with an American chair, might be established to act as a "watch-dog" on the development of self-government.[49]

The British negotiators agreed that "in order to obtain a Treaty at all it was necessary that sovereignty should be conceded to the Egyptians in some form." Stansgate remarked, "In their minds the Foreign Office had always acknowledged Egyptian sovereignty, though they had prevented the Egyptians from exercising it." Bevin concurred, observing that this previous position was of doubtful validity. No one made the case for dual sovereignty, which had been the foundation of the Sudan Government's argument since 1924. In the midst of these ruminations, three telegrams arrived from Alexandria conveying Sidqi Pasha's offer to come personally to London for face-to-face discussions. The military and evacuation questions, Sidqi had told the British chargé in Cairo, could be settled "in a quarter of an hour's conversation round the table." The only real disagreement was on the Sudan. "It would be a tragedy," the Egyptian premier lamented, "if negotiations were to founder on a British failure to accede to Egypt's demand for recognition of what was nothing more than a symbol of Egyptian sovereignty."[50]

With Sidqi's offer in hand, and general agreement on a concession of sovereignty, Bevin ordered Campbell and Sir Walter Smart, the Oriental secretary at the Embassy, to draft a new Sudan protocol. The new draft should make a distinction between administration and sovereignty: "thus the preamble should re-affirm both the historical position of the King of Egypt in the Sudan, and the administrative position of His Majesty's Government." In addition, the

---

48. Ibid., especially meeting on 4 October 1946.
49. Ibid.
50. Ibid.; Alexandria to Foreign Office, tels. nos. 162, 163 and 164, 3 and 4 October 1946. See also Anglo-Egyptian Treaty Negotiations, 1945-47, Secret, FO 371/62962, PRO.

ambassador was to reply to Sidqi and ask for an elaboration of the term "symbolic sovereignty." Finally, the meeting agreed that Sidqi's offer to come to London should be accepted. Working quickly, by 6 October Stansgate and Campbell had completed the new draft protocol and sent it to the Foreign Office for discussion with the Egyptian Department and the governor-general of the Sudan. Waiting with Huddleston at the Sudan Agency in London, on 7 October Robertson wrote in his diary, "It was on this day that we first heard that Mr. Bevin intended to do what he knew to be wrong: to sell the Sudan to Egypt to buy his Treaty."[51]

<hr>

51. Anglo-Egyptian Treaty Negotiations, 1945-47, Secret, FO 371/62962, PRO. Robertson, *Transition,* 95-96. There is some confusion about the chronology. Robertson states that it was on this date that he and Huddleston learned of the "still secret Bevin-Sidki Protocol." But the protocol was not developed until Sidqi's visit to London the following week. Robertson probably refers to the prior briefing he and Huddleston were given on the decision to concede Egyptian sovereignty if necessary. See for example Robertson to Hancock, 9 October 1946, in FO 371/53257, PRO, in which he states that they learned of the sovereignty decision "yesterday." Woodward cites the same quotation and reference in *Condominium,* but gives the date as 18 October.

3

The Bevin-Sidqi Protocol

We have lived on bluff for the last twenty-four years and now our bluff has been called—why should the Sudanese be punished for believing that we were honest men and not bluffers?

—Sir Hubert Huddleston, 1946

The decision of the British Foreign Office in September 1946 to concede sovereignty of the Sudan to Egypt came as a severe blow to the Sudan Government. Both the governor-general, Sir Hubert Huddleston, and his civil secretary, James Robertson, were alternately morose and outraged. Nevertheless, as they soon realized, things might have been worse. As the leading officials of the condominium administration, they were still being consulted by the Foreign Office on the best way to put the sovereignty issue across to the Sudanese. Moreover, although decided in principle, the deed had not yet been done. The Egyptian prime minister, Isma'il Sidqi Pasha, expected momentarily in London for private negotiations with the foreign secretary on outstanding differences in the Anglo-Egyptian treaty, had not yet arrived. For the moment, the decision to concede sovereignty remained secret. In the brief interval allowed them, the two Sudan Government officials carried on a last-ditch defense of the Sudan against the Anglo-Egyptian onslaught. With Robertson's full support, Huddleston waged a campaign designed to minimize the damage of any eventual Anglo-Egyptian agreement on the Sudan and to preserve at least the continuance of the British administration unchanged, as well as the ultimate right of the Sudanese to determine their own future status.

REARGUARD ACTION:
LONDON AND KHARTOUM, OCTOBER 1946

On 8 October, Robertson and Huddleston went to the Foreign Office to discuss the new Sudan Protocol with the permanent officials and the leaders of the British treaty delegation. The new formula was not as bad as they had feared it might be. The first two clauses still maintained that the aim of the condominium was the welfare of the Sudanese and their "active preparation for self-government," as well as reaffirming their right to choose the future status of the Sudan. In addition, article 4 guaranteed the continuance unchanged of the "existing system of administration" which had resulted from the 1899 agreements and the 1936 treaty. The real problem from the Sudan Government's viewpoint lay in the preamble, which referred to "the historic Sovereign rights of the King of Egypt over the Sudan" while mentioning only Britain's "administrative rights and responsibilities in the Sudan."[1]

Admitting that the central clauses of the protocol contained a "fair and reasonable" statement of the Sudan Government's aims, Huddleston nevertheless warned that reference to Egypt's sovereign rights would make the administration's position in the Sudan extremely difficult. There would be "rejoicing" in the pro-Egyptian Ashiqqa press and a corresponding discomfiture of "our own friends," the advocates of independence. Moreover, there might well be a swing of the moderates to Egypt, which must inevitably appear to be the winning side. Although, as Sir Orme Sargent pointed out, over time the impact might lessen, when it became clear that British control remained unchanged, it was equally probable that the Egyptians would not leave the Sudan Government alone. They would intensify their propaganda and "infiltration" into the Sudan, in order to make sure that when the Sudanese did finally choose their future, it would be with Egypt.[2] Sargent agreed that Huddleston's objections were valid, but he baldly stated the ultimate Foreign Office case: "No one liked this formula but the benefit of a treaty with Egypt was so great from the general world viewpoint, that the Secretary of State wished to get one if possible."[3]

Egyptian sovereignty over the Sudan, Sargent tried to reassure Huddleston, would be no more a reality than that of the Ottoman sultan over Egypt in Lord Cromer's time. "The Foreign Office's idea," Robertson wrote to his deputy in Khartoum, "is apparently that some symbolic sovereignty of this sort will satisfy the Egyptians and that they will be content once they have this. We doubt it and we are also sure that it will not be easy to explain this to the Sudanese." Later that day, the Sudan officials returned to the Foreign Office, this time to meet with Lord Stansgate and Ambassador Campbell, who had just flown in from meeting with Bevin in Paris. Again Huddleston explained his dislike of the protocol. The "sting" lay in the words "sovereign rights." The

---

1. Robertson to Hancock, 9 October 1946, Top Secret, FO 371/53257, PRO.
2. Ibid.
3. Ibid.

governor-general did not mince words. "We were asking the Egyptians and the Sudanese to read the word 'historic' in different ways," he observed, clearly skeptical of the ethical position, "the Egyptians as meaning 'historic and continuing,' the Sudanese as 'historic and obsolete.'" Avoiding the implication, Sargent replied that in exchange for sovereignty, the Egyptians would have to commit themselves to maintaining the present administration, to active preparation of the Sudanese for self-government and their eventual right of self-determination.[4]

Robertson then raised the question of Bevin's pledge to consult the Sudanese. Surely the protocol must be regarded as "changing the status" of the Sudan? Beckett quickly replied that if asked, both Robertson and the governor-general "must and can say that it does not affect the status. . . . it does not affect the existing status, though it will certainly affect the future status of the Sudan." "I must say," Robertson wrote to his deputy G. M. Hancock, "that this answer does not satisfy me, and that I think it does alter the status, in that H.M.G. thereby admit what they have never admitted before." When asked by the ambassador how the Sudanese currently envisaged the existence of partial British sovereignty, the civil secretary replied, that they "saw the British flag and the British administration everywhere. They had no interest in the theoretical aspects of sovereignty."[5]

Huddleston also worried that incidents like that of the Egyptian Bimbashi toasting the "King of Egypt and the Sudan" would become more frequent. If so, he complained, such incidents would constitute "a recurrent irritant which would be very provocative and disturbing." The British negotiators were blunt in their admission that in such cases Huddleston would be unable to protest. Stansgate commented that the Egyptians would immediately amend Farouk's title to "King of Egypt and the Sudan." Beckett chimed in, observing that there would also be no way of preventing the king from placing this title on his stamps and coinage. Like Robertson, Huddleston had little faith in the "symbolic" nature of such gestures. To the Sudanese, he remarked acerbically, "a King was not a symbol, but an oriental despot." The Foreign Office's answer to these arguments was that the Sudan Government should simply step up its own propaganda efforts. By playing down the sovereignty issue, "and stressing . . . that it was merely an empty symbol," the Sudan Administration could emphasize that the Egyptians were now bound by the other articles of the Protocol. Both the governor-general and the civil secretary remained skeptical.[6]

In spite of Huddleston's "unfavourable" reaction, the permanent officials themselves were inclined to like the new draft. Indeed, Sargent telegraphed to

---

4. Ibid.; Anglo-Egyptian Treaty. Record of meeting held on 8 October, Draft Minutes, FO 371/53257, PRO. Stansgate was interested in the Protocol's effect on the administrators. Would it really undermine the administration completely? The Sudanese, Huddleston replied, were all "anxious to be on the right side of the hedge."

5. Record of meeting held on 8 October, Draft Minutes, FO 371/53257, PRO.

6. Ibid.

Bevin in Paris, they would be lucky if the Egyptians accepted it. "They may well consider," he pointed out, "that they are being asked to pay too high a price for a symbolic sovereignty seeing that they will have to subscribe in a more definite form than ever before to the continuance of British administration in the Soudan until the Soudanese people decide their own fate." Even the governor-general, the permanent under secretary reported, had admitted that the "stabilisation of the administration under British aegis" was an important aspect of the new draft and had finally "reluctantly" agreed to accept the protocol as a whole if it was necessary to obtain a treaty even at this price. Events in both Egypt and the Sudan, however, soon vindicated and reinforced Huddleston's reluctance.[7]

Reading his morning paper on 10 October, Huddleston was alarmed by a Reuters report that Sidqi Pasha, announcing his forthcoming trip to London, had told journalists he would bring back Egyptian sovereignty over the Sudan. The governor-general quickly sought out Sir Walter Smart, to press once again the case against the sovereignty clause. Repeating all that he had said previously, now Huddleston went further, warning of the serious repercussions to be expected in the Sudan as soon as the concession of sovereignty became public. There would be much excitement, he told the Oriental secretary, and perhaps a considerable "landslide" from the Umma Party to the pro-Egyptian Ashiqqa as people scrambled to get in on the winning side. Alternatively, the Umma Party, which would undoubtedly be "much provoked" by the announcement, might well attack the Ashiqqa. "The result," Huddleston complained, "would be that the Sudan Government, in the interest of law and order, would have to strafe the Umma Party, who would be the assailants. In other words we would have to jump on our friends and alienate them." Sudan Government officials, Huddleston insisted, "were very anxious to avoid serious repressive measures which they had succeeded in avoiding ever since 1924."[8]

In his anxiety to convince the Foreign Office of the dangers involved in the new protocol, the governor-general overplayed his hand. Smart suggested it was simply a matter of maintaining order for a short time, severely if necessary, until the Sudanese were able to see that nothing had changed. Huddleston warned that neither the Sudanese in the administration itself nor those in the Sudan Defence Force could be counted on. Seeming to contradict his own position that the bulk of the Sudanese preferred the British to the Egyptians, the governor-general told Smart that with most of the Sudanese intellectuals in the administration," about 50% of the officials could not be regarded as loyal." Moreover, poor prospects

---

7. Draft telegram, Sargent to Bevin, 9 October 1946, FO 371/53257, PRO.

8. Minute by Sir Walter Smart, 10 October 1946. Reporting the conversation to Bevin on the fourteenth, Sargent quoted an observation by Ambassador Campbell: "We should perhaps qualify the epithet of 'our friends' as applied to the Umma Party. In fact, they seek to get rid of us as much as of the Egyptians." Sargent to Bevin, 14 October 1946, Top Secret, FO 371/53257, PRO.

for promotion in the Defence Force, compared with those of an expanding Egyptian army, also made the attitude of Sudanese officers "doubtful."[9]

Even worse, Huddleston argued that there were considerable elements in the Sudan, not only among the intellectuals, who would not be unfavorable to the Sudanese being put under Egypt—"for instance, the tribal Nazirs, who were restrained by us from committing grosser injustices towards their tribesmen and were inclined to think that an Egyptian Viceroy, with very few Egyptian subordinates, would give the Nazirs a free hand to do what they liked in the tribes." Ambassador Campbell pointed out the obvious flaw in these arguments: "I am always rather shaken by being told that 50% of the Sudanese intellectuals in the administration are not loyal and that there are considerable elements, not only among the intellectuals, who would not be unfavourable to the Sudan being under Egypt. It complicates our task in persuading the world that the Sudanese must not be exposed to the risk of going under Egypt because their wishes must prevail."[10]

While Campbell tended to dismiss the governor-general as an alarmist, Smart was inclined to be more sympathetic, especially regarding Huddleston's fear of disorders. The Oriental secretary in many ways represented the old school of British imperialism in Egypt. He recognized the growing tendency in both London and the Embassy to shy away from using force to protect British interests. Huddleston, he now suggested, should be given a definite assurance that he would not be "hamstrung in any repressive action which he has to take." There might well be trouble in the Sudan over the protocol, but firm action would resolve the issue:

There would undoubtedly be a difficult period, perhaps for a year or two, but I think we could get over this difficult period provided the governor-general had a free hand and his repressive action was not made impossible owing to representations made to him by us in Cairo in view of Egyptian reactions or owing to instructions from London in view of reactions in England. We must remember that this is an immense African country with an hysterical people, and once they get out of hand, the results might be very grave. A little firmness at once would get us over the difficult period.

Pace Lords Kitchener, Cromer and Killearn. "Firmness" might be out of date in Anglo-Egyptian relations, but for Smart at least, it was clearly a matter of political expediency, not principle.[11]

---

9. Sargent to Bevin, 14 October 1946, Top Secret, FO 371/53257, PRO.

10. Sargent to Bevin, 14 October 1946, Top Secret, FO 371/53257, PRO.; Campbell's observations on Smart's conversation with Huddleston, 11 October 1946. Campbell was always skeptical of what he regarded as Huddleston's "alarmist" attitude.

11. Minute by Smart, 10 October 1946, FO 371/53257, PRO. The Oriental secretary paid more attention to Huddleston's views perhaps because he, like the governor-general, had experienced the potential for violence in Arab politics first-

Although the governor-general was undoubtedly grateful for Smart's support, the Oriental secretary had misunderstood the whole point of the conversation. Neither Huddleston nor anyone else in the Political Service wanted to be forced to shoot the Sudanese in order to uphold Egyptian sovereignty. Smart's outlook was not only anachronistic but constituted a threat to all that the Sudan Administration had come to stand for. Although Huddleston subsequently insisted he would need two additional brigades in Khartoum before any hint of the sovereignty clause leaked, his entire effort in London was geared to making such reinforcements unnecessary. He soon received help toward this goal from the Sudan itself, both from the Political Service and from the Sudanese independence parties.

The fears of the independence groups in the Sudan had become intense with the Egyptian delegation's rejection of Bevin's Sudan protocol in mid-September, particularly after the text of the protocol itself had been leaked to the press. The new British position seemed to be a "retrogression" from Huddleston's and Bevin's promises of independence. Like Huddleston, Sayyid 'Abd al-Rahman reacted in alarm to Sidqi's pledge to acquire sovereignty over the Sudan. When further press reports indicated that Isma'il al-Azhari, the head of the pro-Egyptian Ashiqqa, would fly to London with Sidqi, in a secret meeting the Umma Party decided to send Abdullah Bey Khalil as well, to make their case for independence. As leaks continued to filter into the press about the new attitude of the British Government, on 19 October, the day after Sidqi's arrival in London, 'Abd al-Rahman sent a telegram to Bevin publicly protesting any British admission of Egyptian sovereignty over the Sudan. Agreeing with the Umma position, the Sudan Political Service too began to protest vigorously and suspended their efforts to "restrain" the tribal Nazirs from sending telegrams in support of 'Abd al-Rahman's message.[12]

---

hand. Also, he and Huddleston had served together in Egypt and the Sudan for many years.

12. Khartoum to Cairo, no. 107, 13 October 1946, FO 371/53257, PRO. Robertson specifically requested Foreign Office help in "giving publicity" to Abdullah Khalil. To the consternation of Sudan Government officials, the BBC persistently referred to Azhari as "the Sudanese leader." See telegrams and correspondence in J 4353, FO 371/53257, PRO. For the actions of the Political Service, see Khartoum to Foreign Office (Creed to Huddleston), no. 37, 21 October 1946. Creed, the legal secretary and acting governor-general in Huddleston's absence, was one of the most outspoken opponents of Bevin's policy in the Sudan. The Nazirs, he told Huddleston, had kept quiet during the summer "under our instructions," but he could no longer prevent them from expressing their feelings. Khartoum also worried that Egyptian propaganda was drowning out the independence parties. "The Umma case is going by default," Hancock cabled Robertson at the end of September, "since none of their press articles are repeated in the Egyptian Press and they have no delegates on the spot." Despite Creed's disingenuous assertion that he disapproved of the subsequent telegram campaign by the Nazirs supporting 'Abd al-

After a private letter arrived from Robertson to Henderson, complaining about the Foreign Office's *volte-face*, the senior members of the Sudan Political Service in Khartoum became nearly frantic. Horrified by the turn of events, Sir Thomas Creed, the legal secretary and acting governor-general in Huddleston's absence, immediately wired Robertson:

I am uncertain what new proposals are but if they involve any form of recognition of Egyptian sovereignty by His Majesty's Government I must point out urgently that this will be regarded in Sudan as a breach of faith, will destroy irretrievably all confidence in British and Sudan Governments, will shock and alienate loyal majority of Sudanese, undermine public security throughout the country and almost certainly involve resignations by British officials.

Confronted by this "betrayal" in Whitehall, the Political Service would even prefer an end to the condominium: "Alternatives of early or immediate consultation or reference to U.N.O. both infinitely preferable. All shades of Sudanese opinion would welcome latter course."[13]

As both legal secretary and acting governor-general, Creed's reaction to the British position epitomized the general feelings of the Political Service as a whole. Moreover, as the oldest and most senior of the three secretaries, he carried considerable weight with both Huddleston and Robertson. A staunchly moral man, with sharply cut views of right and wrong, the legal secretary was perhaps the most outspoken critic in Khartoum of any effort to placate Egypt at the expense of the Sudanese. During the period of the Anglo-Egyptian negotiations, Creed helped to set the tone of moral indignation that characterized Khartoum's response to Bevin's Sudan policy.

After receiving another letter from Robertson explaining the new protocol, on the day Sidqi Pasha arrived in London for his first meeting with Bevin, Creed fired off a barrage of telegrams—appealing to Robertson, Huddleston, Scrivener, and anyone who might listen—to stop the "betrayal." Asking that all negotiations with Sidqi be held up until he had had a chance to make his case, the acting governor-general worked desperately to salvage the situation. The new British position was about to make liars out of the Sudan Government. As recently as the day before, Creed reported, the director of Education in the Sudan, expressing the view "which we constantly express to responsible Sudanese," had once again assured Sayyid 'Abd al-Rahman that His Majesty's Government would never yield on the question of sovereignty, especially after Bevin's March pledge. The Umma leader, Creed warned, had said that "all is lost" if the British actually conceded Egyptian sovereignty, since this would destroy all confidence

Rahman, it seems clear that the Political Service was doing nothing to prevent it and may even have facilitated it. See correspondence in FO 371/53256, PRO.
13. Creed to Robertson, no. 68, 16 October 1946, FO 371/53257, PRO. The following paragraphs are drawn from Creed's subsequent telegrams to Huddleston, nos. 33, 34, and 35, 18 October 1946, *Most Immediate*, FO 371/53257, PRO.

in both the British and the Sudan governments. When 'Abd al-Rahman offered to go to London personally to state the case against Egyptian sovereignty, the acting governor-general made plain his own sense of moral outrage at the new British position: "I am not prepared to stand by and see Sayed deluded into inactivity by assurances of trusted British officials which are now in danger of being falsified. . . . I am having him indirectly informed . . . that this Government will place no obstacle in the way of his immediate departure if he wishes to go." Although Robertson warned Creed off this tack, it was clear that the Khartoum officials were as distraught by the turn of events as the Mahdist leader.

As for the new position on sovereignty, Creed argued that the British Government would be reversing a long-standing legal position and undermining the credibility of the Sudan Administration itself: "The Sudan Government with consistent and recent support from the Foreign Office has for years maintained that joint sovereignty lies in Britain and Egypt and the position hitherto taken up by His Majesty's Government is well known to educated Sudanese and big tribal and territorial leaders." Uneducated Sudanese, Creed observed, "take for granted" that Britain had sovereignty in the Sudan: any statement of sole Egyptian sovereignty would convince them that Britain was "giving up control." To suggest now that an admission of Egyptian sovereignty involved no change of status because the previous British position had suddenly been found to be "mistaken," the legal secretary indignantly insisted, "is merely legal sophistry which will convince no Sudanese and which almost all British officials will be ashamed to admit." After Bevin's March pledge and the governor-general's statement to the Advisory Council for the Northern Sudan in April, such action would be interpreted by British and Sudanese alike as "a direct breach of faith . . . and we shall have Ashigga and Umma alike denouncing our duplicity."

Legal and moral issues aside, the acting governor-general was also scathing in his criticism of the Foreign Office's credulousness in believing that a concession of sovereignty might be balanced by safeguards for continued British control of the administration. "It is folly," he expostulated, "to suppose that Egypt will not exploit to the full every legitimate and illegitimate advantage resulting from recognition of its sovereignty to the detriment of administration." The Foreign Office analogy between Egyptian sovereignty over the Sudan and Turkish sovereignty over Egypt bore "no relation to reality." Implicitly, Creed accused the Foreign Office of having forgotten its true responsibility. Adopting what was virtually the position of the Umma Party, the legal secretary made it clear that the Political Service itself no longer trusted either co-dominus to safeguard the future of the Sudan. In the event of negotiations breaking down, he concluded, "it is hoped that a unilateral statement will be made by His Majesty's Government that their policy is that the Sudan should be granted sovereignty and independence on a certain fixed date."

Despite Creed's impassioned arguments, it was too late. By the time his last telegram arrived in London, Bevin had already held his first meeting with the Egyptian prime minister. And in any case, the foreign secretary had already made his decision: the fears of the Sudan Administration were not to interfere with the conclusion of an Anglo-Egyptian treaty.[14]

THE BEVIN-SIDQI PROTOCOL

Between 18 and 24 October, Bevin and Sidqi held four meetings to discuss the treaty negotiations. Bevin did not in fact immediately give away his position. Opening the conversations on the afternoon of the eighteenth, the British foreign secretary expressed his surprise and regret that the Sudan seemed to be causing so much trouble. He had been under the impression, he told Sidqi, that evacuation was more important to the Egyptians. The Egyptian premier replied that while evacuation was indeed the first priority, the Sudan question was also one of vital interest to Egypt. After all, Egypt was the Nile, and therefore the Nile Valley must always be in the minds of Egyptians. Moreover, he asserted, Egypt had always had bonds with the valley of the Nile. Egypt and the Sudan had such common interests that "separation of the two could not be envisaged." The Egyptian prime minister cited the example of Britain and Canada as a parallel for Egypt and the Sudan.[15]

Moving on to discuss military matters, at the close of the meeting Bevin returned to the Sudan question, asking Sidqi for a clarification of his term "symbolic." Sidqi replied that this indicated the nature of the role Egypt expected to play in the Sudan. Egyptians did not seek to exploit the Sudan, he asserted, nor did they look for "material and moral profit." At the same time, he insisted that there was "unity with the crown of Egypt and a unity of bond which had always existed between the two countries." Seeming to contradict his promise that Egypt did not expect to interfere with the current administration of the territory, Sidqi told Bevin that Egypt needed an outlet for its university graduates: Egypt wanted to offer the Sudan "experts and professors in an 'elder brother' relationship." Despite equal treaty rights in the country, he reminded Bevin, Egypt had been "completely excluded . . . almost disregarded" in the administration of the Sudan. Egyptian influence, he continued, "had been consciously brushed aside." But Egypt, Sidqi concluded, "must at all times have the loyalty of the Sudan as it is from that country that her prosperity originates."[16]

---

14. Creed's last telegram was not received in the Foreign Office until 5:10 P.M. Bevin's meeting with Sidqi had begun at 3:30 that afternoon.

15. For an overview of the entire negotiations, see memorandum titled Anglo-Egyptian Treaty Negotiations, 1945-47, Secret, 12 March 1947, FO 371/62962. The minutes of the first meeting, 18 October 1946, marked Top Secret, are in FO 371/53315, PRO.

16. Anglo-Egyptian Treaty Negotiations, 1945-47, Secret, 12 March 1947, FO 371/62962. The minutes of the first meeting, 18 October 1946, marked Top Secret, are in FO 371/53315, PRO.

The British foreign secretary responded that he had tried to understand the Egyptian point of view but had failed. Moreover, he had been alarmed by statements in the Egyptian press suggesting that Egypt might be determined at a later date to secure British evacuation from the Sudan as well as Egypt. Deprecatingly, Sidqi asked Bevin to "disregard the views of the extremists in the service of the Opposition." Egypt, he insisted, sought a union with the Sudan based only on the interests of the Sudanese. As soon as the union had been recognized, he suggested, "the critics of Great Britain would disappear." At their second meeting the next day, Sidqi handed Bevin a personal note, explaining his own view of the Sudan question.

The heart of the Egyptian prime minister's argument concerning Egyptian sovereignty in the Sudan was legal: "Egyptian sovereignty is a historical and juridical fact which has been solemnly recognised by the British Government both before and after the 1899 agreement." The sole purpose of the 1899 arrangement had been to regulate the administration of the territory: it had never been intended to affect the principle of Egyptian sovereignty. Indeed, Sidqi pointed out, Britain had itself on numerous occasions reaffirmed Egyptian sovereignty in dealing with other powers and had always declared that Britain was in the Sudan solely to establish the authority of the Egyptian Sovereign. Moreover, Egyptian sovereignty did not threaten the rights of the Sudanese. Again Sidqi compared Egyptian-Sudanese relations to those of Britain and its dominions: allegiance to the same crown was in "perfect accord" with the principle of full independence in internal affairs. Finally, unconsciously echoing arguments that Bevin and Dixon had already considered, Sidqi observed that the Sudan "does not by itself form a political entity and it is clearly in the interests of the Sudanese to continue to be joined to an organised State."[17]

In considering Sidqi's arguments on sovereignty, Bevin expressed two primary concerns: first, that a concession of sovereignty would not involve any change in the present administration of the Sudan; and second, that the Sudanese should be able, after having attained self-government, to opt even for complete independence should they so desire. As far as the administration was concerned, Sidqi seemed to agree categorically: the agreement of 1899 would remain intact, as would article 11 of the 1936 treaty (excepting the last sentence in which Britain reserved judgment on Egypt's claim to sovereignty). "The normal relationship between the Egyptian Prime Minister and the governor-general would continue," Sidqi promised. "Egypt had no wish to meddle in the affairs of the Sudan." In response to Bevin's other concern, however, that of independence, Sidqi was more circumspect—and it was on this point that the entire treaty negotiations would eventually fall apart.[18]

---

17. *Note personnelle de Sedky Pacha sur la question du Soudan*, and translation made in the Foreign Office, 19 October 1946, FO 371/53257, PRO.

18. Anglo-Egyptian Treaty, Minutes of Second Meeting held at the Foreign Office, 19 October 1946, Top Secret, FO 371/53257, PRO.

If the Sudanese should ultimately decide on independence, Bevin pointed out to Sidqi, then Egyptian sovereignty "must necessarily go." Did Egypt claim that its sovereignty would remain even after the Sudanese had attained self-government? Did Egypt recognize that the decision would rest with the Sudanese? Prevaricating, Sidqi replied that it would be "many years before self-government was attained." Egypt, he continued, "could not envisage a hostile country on her borders and the Sudan must always remain a friendly neighbour." Bevin responded that Britain had always insisted on the right of a dependent nation, once it had reached the status of self-government, to secede if it chose to—as recently in India. Sidqi agreed with the basic premise but insisted that the right of secession "would be a voluntary action on the part of Egypt." Furthermore, the prime minister continued, it was too early to discuss these matters, "as one could not foresee the distant future."[19]

Bevin refused to let the matter go. The situation must be made "perfectly clear." Were the Sudanese being given a chance to be free, or did Egypt seek a "lasting settlement of sovereignty"? "It must be quite clear," the foreign secretary said, "that the Sudanese were free to renounce the sovereignty of Egypt if they so wished." Again Sidqi stalled. It was impossible to speak of the sovereignty question in these terms, he reiterated, for no one knew what developments might take place "over the next half-century." The question Bevin was asking him to answer "was a matter for our children to decide." The foreign secretary repeated that he could not countenance a situation in which "the Sudan, struggling for independence, would forever be under Egypt." Nothing must prejudice the right of self-determination.[20]

Backed into a corner, the Egyptian prime minister at last gave Bevin what he wanted—but in less than categorical terms. "If the Sudanese reached a certain point of development," Sidqi asserted, "they would surely become independent. Nothing on paper could prejudice the right of independence nor could it bind a people in search of liberty. It was a universal principle and not a matter for incorporation in a treaty." But since the new treaty was to be based upon the United Nations Charter, Sidqi continued, "which affirms independence of nations," it was unnecessary to repeat what the charter already specified. Pushed to the last extremity, the Egyptian prime minister had given his final word on the matter: though the idea of Sudanese independence might be a universal principle, no Egyptian statesman at this stage in Anglo-Egyptian relations would admit such a possibility in the written terms of a treaty.[21]

Sidqi Pasha's views of Egyptian sovereignty were upheld by the lord chancellor. Bevin had requested a legal opinion on the status of British sovereignty in the Sudan after receiving Sidqi's personal note. The crux of the chancellor's argument was that the Mahdist regime had not affected the status of the Sudan as a province of Egypt. A British claim based on conquest could be

---

19. Ibid.
20. Ibid.
21. Ibid.

legitimate only if it was accepted that the Mahdist regime had been sovereign. But, the lord chancellor found, "it is the fact that the operations undertaken were taken against rebels." Moreover, both the cost and the bulk of the troops in the reconquest had been Egyptian, and under the command of Kitchener, who was himself the sirdar, an officer of the Khedive. To base a claim on conquest in this case, the chancellor suggested, would be like asserting British sovereignty over Belgium after its recent liberation. The Agreement of 1899, he argued, could be read only as dealing with a system of administration; it left the "juristic sovereignty" where it had been before—in Egypt under Turkish suzerainty. In short, preferring the position that juridical sovereignty could rest in only one power, the legal officer of the British Crown concluded that in the Sudan, "we are not the sovereign."[22]

Despite the expert legal opinions, Bevin had apparently been impressed by Creed's urgent warnings from the Sudan. Huddleston too had seen Bevin personally to reinforce the acting governor-general's arguments. Even in the Foreign Office, Scrivener minuted that while juridically it was true that the best advice conceded Egyptian claims, and accepted that no change in status was implied in the draft protocol, he himself agreed with Creed that "*in practice* it does change that status." He added, "In the rather simple—though sharp—eyes of the ordinary Sudanese it will certainly change it." The head of the Egyptian Department noted that while the proposed solution was not "intrinsically bad—it has for example such powerful support as that of Sir Reginald Wingate"—as a change in practical status, "it ought to be put to the Sudanese . . . the Sudanese should be consulted before such a solution were announced." Meeting with Sidqi

---

22. Bevin also had the advice of Sir Reginald Wingate, second governor-general of the Sudan and former high commissioner in Egypt. In his eighties, Wingate still followed Sudan affairs. Writing to Bevin on 11 October, "Master," as he was still called by the Political Service, encouraged the foreign secretary to acknowledge Egyptian sovereignty openly: "I myself have always regarded the sovereignty of Egypt over the Sudan, as modified by the Condominium of 1899, as undoubted . . . it was I who, during the Fashoda Incident when Kitchener and myself met Marchand, persuaded Kitchener to fly only the Turkish (Egyptian) flag and to use the argument that we had reconquered the Sudan on behalf of the Khedive and not of the British Government." The best way to protect the Sudanese, Wingate believed, was not to exclude Egypt, which would only resort to clandestine propaganda, but to allow it to come into the open: "Egypt given an assured status in the Sudan is controllable there. It will depend largely upon the personality of the governor-general. She will doubtless try to influence the Sudanese to opt for her, but she will do it openly, and it is then up to the Sudanese." Such views represented a complete *volte-face* from Wingate's own strenuous efforts as governor-general to separate the Sudan from Egypt before 1922. Wingate to Bevin, Secret and Personal, 11 October 1946, FO 371/53257, PRO. For the lord chancellor's analysis, see printed Memorandum, Egypt and the Sudan, Secret, 24 October 1946, Minute by the Lord Chancellor to the Secretary of State, FO 371/53316, PRO.

again on the morning of ¨23 October, the foreign secretary remained cautious about admitting Egyptian sovereignty.[23]

With only the dry documents as witness, it is difficult to tell what motivated Ernest Bevin in his negotiations with Sidqi over the Sudan. Even before discussions began, the foreign secretary had decided to concede sovereignty if necessary to obtain the treaty. Yet in his conversations with the Egyptian premier, Bevin consistently argued that accepting Egyptian sovereignty would make things extremely difficult both for the Sudan Government and for the British position in the Sudan, as well as prejudicing the future of the Sudanese themselves. Perhaps this was a real concern. Or it may have been simply a diplomatic maneuver to get the maximum amount of leverage out of the Sudan concession, a final "carrot" with which to ensure agreement on the other points in dispute. If the latter, Bevin's tactic was successful. During talks on the twenty-third Sidqi expansively asserted that the Sudan question was "the synthesis" of the whole treaty. "If Egypt undertook great responsibilities in war in Egypt or in neighbouring countries, thus making great sacrifices and freeing British troops," he argued, "it was not a great thing to ask in return that their point of view on the Sudan should be accepted." Then Bevin suggested that the Sudanese "might be consulted on the question of sovereignty." If the Sudanese were "ripe" to decide on sovereignty, the Egyptian replied, then they were ripe to decide their whole future; "but we all agreed that they were not yet ready for such a decision."[24]

Under pressure from the Sudan Government, as well as from the Cabinet, the foreign secretary continued to press Sidqi Pasha on the meaning of the Sudan Protocol. Accepting Sidqi's basic argument that sovereignty belonged to Egypt, in exchange for assurances that there would be no interference in the existing administration of the Sudan, Bevin was still concerned about the Sudanese right of self-determination. His own pledge the previous March had come to haunt the foreign secretary. With charges from Khartoum that admitting sovereignty would constitute a "breach of faith," Bevin stressed again and again the Sudan clause in his conversations with the Egyptian premier. It is clear from the record that the hard-bargaining former trades union leader was never able fully to pin down the canny Egyptian. Every time Bevin sought concrete assurances, Sidqi Pasha talked around the central issue. The Sudanese were simply not yet in any position to decide what they wanted, Sidqi argued; therefore any discussion of "independence" was premature—and since there had always been Egyptian sovereignty, acknowledging it changed nothing.[25]

---

23. Minute by Scrivener, 19 October 1946, FO 371/53257, PRO.

24. Anglo-Egyptian Treaty, Minutes of Third Meeting, 23 October 1946, Top Secret, FO 371/53318. Sidqi was prepared to sign the documents at this session, but Bevin wanted another meeting.

25. Reading the transcripts of these meetings, one finds it difficult not to conclude that Sidqi astutely outmaneuvered Bevin.

Accompanied by Stansgate and Campbell, at eight o'clock on the evening of 24 October, Bevin called on Sidqi Pasha in his suite at Claridge's for one final personal discussion to clear up the outstanding points in the treaty—especially the Sudan. It was essential, Bevin told Sidqi, that he should able to explain both to Parliament and to the Sudanese that nothing now agreed in the treaty changed the status of the Sudan. Of course, replied the Egyptians, but nothing had changed. The foreign secretary then referred to his discussions with the governor-general and asked that the Egyptian formula, "within the framework of the unity between the Sudan and Egypt under a common Crown," be amended to read "the historic unity." As Huddleston had earlier objected, so now Sidqi pointed out that this would suggest that the unity was "a thing of the past." Bevin gave way.[26]

Bevin then raised the problem of the future. It was essential, he told Sidqi, to make clear that the Sudanese, once they had reached a stage in which they might choose the future status of their country, could opt for independence. Moreover, it should also be made clear that the Sudanese would be consulted "when the time came for the two High Contracting Parties to realise" the objectives stated in the first sentence of the protocol. After assuring himself that the decision would still rest with Britain and Egypt, but not with the Sudanese, Sidqi agreed to include a reference in the protocol to consultation. He made no comment at all, however, on Bevin's assertion that the Sudanese must be free to choose independence. Confronted with Sidqi's impassivity, the foreign secretary did not press the point. Nor did he protest when Sidqi asked for a deletion of the last paragraph of the draft, calling for the Joint Commission and periodic reports from the governor-general on Sudanese progress toward self-government. The foreign secretary himself had never liked the proposal, which he viewed as an ill-conceived gambit by the Sudan Political Service. Having now given way on virtually every point disputed by the Egyptians, Bevin had at last cleared the stage for Anglo-Egyptian agreement.[27]

With the final text agreed, Bevin asked for and received an oral assurance that Egypt would recognize Britain's right to retain any troops it liked in the Sudan. Still worried about the obvious disagreement in interpretation of the Sudan Protocol, Bevin made one last effort, suggesting that there should be an exchange of letters setting forth an agreed interpretation. As the Egyptian prime minister was well aware, however, it might be worth his life in Egypt to agree on paper that the Sudanese could opt for independence. An exchange of letters would therefore immediately cause an impasse in the negotiations. When Sidqi declined the British proposal, Bevin too understood that no more could be done if a treaty was to be signed. The foreign secretary did not insist. On 25 October, Bevin and Sidqi Pasha, with their advisors, initialed the draft Anglo-Egyptian treaty, an evacuation protocol and the Sudan Protocol and pledged that each

---

26. Anglo-Egyptian Treaty, Understandings Reached between the Secretary of State and Sidki and Hadi Pashas, 24 October 1946 (Fourth Meeting), Top Secret, FO 371/53316, PRO.

27. Ibid.

would recommend full ratification to their respective governments. Both the Sudan question and the Egyptian question appeared to have been brought to successful conclusions at long last. The basis for this long-hoped-for agreement, however, as Creed later wrote from the Palace in Khartoum, was no more than "wishful thinking."[28]

The Egyptian prime minister returned from London to Egypt on 26 October 1946. Even before his aircraft had touched down in Cairo, the Egyptian press began reporting that he had succeeded at last in "bringing the Sudan to Egypt." Late that night, stumbling exhausted from his plane at the Cairo airdrome, Sidqi bombarded with questions from waiting journalists, again referred to his success. Although his precise words later became a subject of controversy, the aging prime minister was quoted in the Egyptian press as claiming: "It has definitely been decided to achieve unity between Egypt and the Sudan under the Egyptian Crown." There was no mention of the provisions for self-government or, above all, of the right of the Sudanese to choose their own future status. Over the next several days, further reports of a British admission of Egyptian "sovereignty" over the Sudan were broadcast in the Sudan itself. The worst fears of both the Political Service and the independence groups in the Sudan had come to pass.[29]

REPERCUSSIONS IN THE SUDAN

While Bevin and Sidqi negotiated in London, the Political Service leaders and the adherents of Sudanese independence waited anxiously in the Sudan. As Sayyid 'Abd al-Rahman and leading nazirs of the Northern Sudan telegraphed Bevin protesting any concession of sovereignty, and as Creed argued the position of the Sudan Government, rumors of a British "sellout" abounded. On 23 October, Reuter's reported from London that Sidqi Pasha "is understood to oppose the British suggestion of consulting the Sudanese . . . until a period of Egyptian sovereignty has done something to offset British influence." Confirming Creed in his assessment of Egyptian motives, this report actually reassured the Mahdists—surely, they believed, the British would not allow such a blatant challenge to their authority in the condominium.[30]

On 27 October, reassurance turned again to incredulity and dismay when Sidqi's claim to have brought Egyptian sovereignty over the Sudan back to Cairo was announced in morning broadcasts of the BBC. Exacerbating matters, Egyptian press and broadcast accounts consistently translated "sovereignty" with the Arabic word *siyada*, which in the colloquial Arabic of the Northern Sudan

28. Ibid.

29. For the controversy surrounding Sidqi's exact words, see the *Round Table*, March 1951. For British reaction, see Anglo-Egyptian Treaty Negotiations, 1945-47, Secret, 12 March 1947, FO 371/62962, PRO.

30. Diary of Events since October 12th, compiled by Robertson after his return to Khartoum, FO 371/53259, PRO.

carried the connotation of a master-slave relationship. Immediately, Umma leaders waited on the acting governor-general and civil secretary, seeking an official denial of Sidqi's statement. Caught off-guard, however, and fearing that the report was all too true, Creed and Hancock could only state that while they believed the press reports were misleading, they had no information from London. They advised the Sudanese leaders to await further news. Ignoring the advice, in an emergency meeting the Umma executive decided to suspend its participation in the Sudan Administration Conference, to announce a boycott of the Advisory Council for the Northern Sudan, to cable a protest immediately to Prime Minister Attlee, and most provocative of all, to summon their supporters from outside Khartoum while scheduling a demonstration that night in Omdurman.[31]

That evening some three thousand independence supporters assembled at the Umma Club in Omdurman. After speeches denouncing the British for "having sold the Sudan to Egypt," they marched to the headquarters of the Congress in the Graduates' Club. Prevented from entering by police, the crowd then marched to the Mahdi's tomb. Eventually, after sporadic stone throwing, and after inflicting minor injuries on several Ashiqqa leaders, the Mahdists dispersed. As the Sudan Intelligence summary put it, "the Ashigga remained quiet." The next day, however, some two hundred boys from the Farouk School also marched, this time in celebration of the Unity of the Nile Valley. That night the Umma Party was joined by others of the independence groups, and a new Independence Front was formed to oppose the Unionist Front sponsored by the Ashiqqa under the auspices of the Graduates' General Congress. Meanwhile, Sayyid 'Abd al-Rahman's supporters from the provinces gradually began to fill up the three towns.[32]

While the Umma took to the streets in protest, in London the Foreign Office too was appalled by reports of Sidqi's "indiscretions." Bevin himself had already left for a meeting of the United Nations in New York. It remained to his officials to try to pick up the pieces. On the evening of the twenty-seventh, Scrivener drafted a stiff telegram instructing the ambassador in Cairo to take the Egyptian prime minister to task. "It was agreed at outset of discussions," the head of the Egyptian Department reminded Campbell, "that nothing should be said to the press apart from statements agreed between Sidki and the Foreign Secretary." Now it seemed that Sidqi himself had jumped the gun, claiming to have achieved unity between Egypt and the Sudan under the Egyptian Crown, "without one word about the administration, the future status of the Sudan, or the right of the Sudanese to choose their future." The "extremely tendentious nature of Sidki's

---

31. Ibid. Sudan Government officials harped on the devastating effects of the term *siyada*. See Sudan Intelligence Summary no. 60 (New Series), September-October 1946, FO 371/53328, PRO, especially Khartoum to Foreign Office, no.39, 28 October 1946, FO 371/53258, PRO.

32. Sudan Intelligence Summary no. 60 (New Series), September-October 1946, with appendices, FO 371/53328, PRO.

disclosures" not only might cause His Majesty's Government serious embarrassment but also could have "grave results" in the Sudan. Anticipating a private notice question in Parliament, the Foreign Office moved quickly to salvage the situation by denying that there had even been any negotiations between Bevin and Sidqi—there had been only "exploratory talks . . . without commitment by His Majesty's Government."[33]

In Bevin's absence, on 28 October the prime minister, Clement Attlee, personally responded in the House of Commons to press reports of Sidqi Pasha's statements. Following a Foreign Office brief, Attlee denied that Bevin and Sidqi had engaged in formal negotiations. These were "conversations on a personal and exploratory basis . . . conducted on the understanding that they did not commit either Government, and that they were . . . confidential." Attlee regretted that "incomplete reports" had appeared in the newspapers. Pressed by the Conservative Party opposition, he assured the House that he contemplated "no change in the existing status and administration of the Sudan . . . and no impairment of the right of the Sudanese people ultimately to decide their own future." Nothing, Attlee concluded, had been "finally negotiated."[34]

The prime minister's statement reassured no one. In Egypt the anti-government Wafdist press used his description of Sidqi's statements as "partial and misleading" to lambast the Egyptian premier. In Khartoum, on the other hand, Attlee's explanation was first not heard by most Sudanese until the morning of the twenty-ninth, and then did not seem to deny that a concession of sovereignty had actually been made. Indeed, the British prime minister could not deny it, for the charge was true. Despite British efforts to gloss over the problem, no amount of sophistry, as Creed had once put it, could hide the fact that Bevin had tacitly, even openly, acknowledged Egyptian sovereignty over the Sudan in the draft protocol. And although the Foreign Office and the Embassy might talk all they liked about continuity of administration, it was precisely the question of sovereignty that had come to obsess the independence faction among the Sudanese nationalists. Even as Attlee made his statement in the House of Commons, in the Palace in Khartoum the acting governor-general of the Sudan was dictating a report for the Foreign Office on the disastrous effects of Sidqi's statement in the Sudan.[35]

Creed was in no mood to be diplomatic or to spare the feelings of anyone connected with the British Foreign Office. Sidqi's claims, he telegraphed to London, had caused "bewilderment . . . which is fast developing into bitter accusations of duplicity against His Majesty's and this Government." The

33. Foreign Office to Cairo, no. 1862, 27 October 1946, FO 371/53258, PRO.
34. Great Britain, *Parliamentary Debates (Commons)*, 28 October 1946.
35. For reactions in both Egypt and the Sudan to Attlee's statement see Sudan Intelligence Summary no. 60 (New Series), FO 371/53328, PRO. Also see an Aide Memoire by Robertson, 5 November 1946, FO 371/53259, PRO. For a summary of Egyptian Press reactions to Attlee's statement, see Cairo to Foreign Office, no. 1612, 29 October 1946, FO 371/53258, PRO.

British Government, Creed went on, was regarded as having made "a deliberate breach of a pledge deliberately made to consult the Sudanese." No diplomatic or legal argument would convince the Sudanese that a concession of sovereignty did not involve a change in their status. There had already been violent speeches and a large-scale demonstration involving several thousand people. "If these disorders increase, as they inevitably will if negotiations continue in their present direction," Creed remarked caustically, "I cannot believe that His Majesty's Government view with equanimity the possibility of this Government being forced to call in the military to quell disturbances caused by alleged breach of faith of his Majesty's Government."[36]

Creed agreed with the Sudanese about London's breach of faith. He was furious that a solid foundation of goodwill and efficient administration, built up over the years by the Political Service, was now being squandered by Whitehall diplomats for a treaty with the Egyptians. The reaction of British officials themselves, he reported, "has been one of incredulous amazement." Bevin's diplomacy was about to cost the Sudan Government the loyalty of the Sudanese, thereby jeopardizing the entire achievement of the condominium administration. If the British Government insisted on making a concession of sovereignty to Egypt without first consulting the Sudanese, Creed warned, "it would not in my view be possible for the existing administration to function reasonably in the absence of active Sudanese cooperation and . . . whole progress of Sudanese towards self-government would be irretrievably obstructed." He concluded: "I cannot believe His Majesty's Government appreciates the extent to which the administration of this vast country depends on confidence between British and Sudanese. His Majesty's Government proposes to wrench out that confidence by its very roots."[37]

Late on the night of 29 October, Huddleston and Robertson arrived back in Khartoum by air. While Creed managed to prevent the Umma leaders from holding any demonstrations at either the airfield or the Palace, during the afternoon tension between independence supporters and adherents of unity with Egypt, notably among students at Gordon College, increased. Although a serious clash was avoided, and there were no attempts to waylay the governor-general and the civil secretary, large meetings of Umma supporters were held again that evening in Omdurman. The following night, with permission from the authorities, between three and four thousand people marched under the red, green, and black tricolor banners of the Mahdiyya to Gordon's Statue in front of the governor-general's Palace, where they presented Huddleston's representative with a written protest "against the decision taken by Great Britain and Egypt regarding the sovereignty over the Sudan." Still under control by the Umma leadership, the crowds then dispersed without incident.[38]

36. Khartoum to Foreign Office, no. 39, 28 October 1946, FO 371/53258, PRO.
37. Ibid.
38. Ibid.; see also Robertson's Diary of Events since October 12th, FO 371/53259, PRO.

On the morning of 31 October, Huddleston issued an appeal to both sides for moderation. At the same time, Robertson asked the Independence Front leaders to meet with him to discuss the situation. They refused, noting that nothing had yet been said by either the governor-general or Prime Minister Attlee to deny the Egyptian claims of sovereignty. At Gordon College, students left classes to hold yet another meeting in support of unity of the Nile Valley—college authorities closed the institution entirely. Tired of leaving the field to the Umma, that afternoon al-Azhari's supporters in the Congress and the Ashiqqa asked for permission to hold their own demonstration the next day. Since the Umma had been given free rein to express their dissatisfaction, Robertson felt compelled to allow the unionists their fair chance. When he asked the Independence Front for an assurance that they would not interfere, however, he received only an evasive reply. Sayyid 'Abd al-Rahman's supporters from the countryside, many of them Baggara tribesmen whose fathers and grandfathers had been the staunchest fighters of the Mahdi and the Khalifa, continued to infiltrate the three towns.[39]

On 1 November, the supporters of unity of the Nile Valley staged their counterdemonstration beginning in Abbas Square, Omdurman. After an initial clash between the two sides, in which a vehicle was overturned and fifteen passengers were attacked, none fatally, by spear-wielding Mahdists, the unionist procession passed without further major incident. After the demonstrators had returned to Abbas Square and begun to disperse, however, the offices of two independence newspapers, guarded by large Mahdist contingents, were attacked by unionists throwing stones and bottles. In retaliation, a party of Mahdists marched on the Graduates' Club and wrecked it. The Omdurman police, busy trying to keep the demonstration under control, were unable to prevent either attack. Meanwhile, a company of the Sudan Defence Force Camel Corps was standing by in Khartoum. Although they had not intervened in the attack on the newspapers, after the wrecking of the Graduates' Club they were rushed to Omdurman to help the overstretched police restore order. By evening the Camel Corps and the Omdurman police had put a stop to the violence.[40]

The next day Robertson summoned the secretaries of the political parties to his office. This time it was not an invitation. Exercising his full authority, the civil secretary directed the Sudanese leaders to disband their followers and send them home. Furthermore, he ordered them to abstain from all public political meetings and to pass this word along to their branches in the provinces. At the same time, Robertson issued a directive to provincial governors banning all public meetings throughout the Sudan until further notice. Meanwhile, the governor-general himself interviewed Sayyid 'Abd al-Rahman, who had prudently remained outside the city during the demonstrations, arriving in Khartoum only that morning. Although Huddleston asked the Sayyid to join him in issuing a call for restraint, the Mahdist leader declined. Unwilling to associate himself with the government at this point, 'Abd al-Rahman preferred instead to issue his

---

39. Robertson's Diary of Events since October 12th, FO 371/53259, PRO.
40. Ibid.

own separate appeal to his followers to be patient and return to their homes. Over the next several days, the Sudan Government worked diligently to get the thousands of Ansar tribesmen, who had flocked in over the previous week, out of the three towns and back to their own territories.[41]

The outbreak of disorders was no more than both Robertson and Huddleston had warned the Foreign Office might happen. Huddleston had told officials in London that if the sovereignty clause went through, he would need at least two brigades of British troops in the Sudan before any hint of the agreement leaked out. With one brigade already in Khartoum, this meant that another would have to be flown in immediately from Palestine. Although Sidqi's statement had caught everyone by surprise, including British military authorities in the Middle East command, within days of the violence in Omdurman the second brigade was airlifted to Khartoum. Even before the troops arrived, however, Huddleston had begun to alter his position. The final straw was not simply the position of the Sudanese independents, but that of the Sudan Political Service itself. In the face of Sidqi's statement, its repercussions among the Sudanese, and finally the advice of the three secretaries, the governor-general became unwilling to impose the Bevin-Sidqi protocol upon the Sudanese without a final effort to dissuade the British Government from its present course.[42]

41. Ibid. Also see Khartoum to Cairo, no. 123, 1 November 1946, no. 126, 3 November 1946, FO 371/53258, PRO, and Khartoum to Foreign Office, no. 46, 3 November 1946, FO 371/53259, PRO. Huddleston reported that Abd al-Rahman had relied on Bevin's personal message of reassurance of 26 October in framing his appeal for restraint to his followers.

42. Khartoum to Foreign Office, no. 46, 3 November 1946, FO 371/53259, PRO. For Huddleston's military assessment and request, see correspondence in J 4514, FO 371/53258, PRO.

4

The "Revolt" of the Sudan Political Service and the Failure of Anglo-Egyptian Negotiations

It has been suggested that the British negotiators have forgotten verse 21 from the 2nd Book of Kings, Chapter 18: "Now behold thou trustest upon the staff of this broken reed even upon Egypt, on which if a man lean it will go into his hand and pierce it. So is Pharaoh King of Egypt unto all that trust on him." I hope we shall not have to read Farouk for Pharaoh.
                                                          —Sir James Robertson, December 1946

In the eyes of the Sudan Political Service, the Bevin-Sidqi Protocol of 1946, formally acknowledging Egyptian sovereignty over the Sudan, represented the nadir of Anglo-Sudanese relations. Viewed by Sudanese nationalists and British officials alike as a "betrayal," it marked the end of an era of relative trust and collaboration between the Sudan Government and those Sudanese who hoped for complete independence from both Britain and Egypt. For Sir James Robertson nearly thirty years later, its memory still brought echoes of the sense of shame and embarrassment he had felt at the time as civil secretary of the Sudan Government "Huddleston and I went back to the Sudan, arriving late in the evening of 29 October. . . . My British colleagues were polite and sympathetic, but I felt that they thought we had sold the pass and let them down; and the Sudanese, who usually came to meet me on my return from leave, were silent and unwelcoming." The reason was not hard to discover. "Sidky Pasha had returned to Cairo a few hours earlier and on landing had announced that he had brought back *seyada*—sovereignty—over the Sudan. In Arabic *seyada* can mean the authority of a master over a slave . . . this was what the Governor-General and I were thought to have agreed to."[1]

As the independence faction within the Sudan, led by the Umma Party of Sayyid 'Abd al-Rahman al-Mahdi, reacted violently, and as the Political Service began seriously to consider having to use real force to impose the new Protocol,

---

1. Robertson, *Transition*, 151.

both Robertson and his two senior colleagues, Edington Miller, the financial secretary, and Sir Thomas Creed, the legal secretary, decided that they could not accept the policy of the British Government without a fight. They had persistently opposed the Protocol and now saw the violence of the Umma's opposition as an opportunity to sink it once and for all. In an unprecedented move, the three secretaries composed a joint memorandum, addressed to Huddleston but aimed at the British Foreign Office, openly challenging the British position on sovereignty and accusing the British Government of a breach of faith to the Sudanese people. The lurid scenario they now depicted as the probable outcome was a British colonial nightmare:

If the protocol goes through . . . resignations will occur from government and local government services; there will be widespread non-cooperation from both parties, e.g. the independents who believe themselves betrayed and the "Unionists" (Wadi el Nil front) who wish to see the present administration ended. There may be risings among the tribes resulting in the loss of British lives . . . a relapse to a police state and . . . postponement of all the benefits to the Sudanese which it is claimed the protocol safeguards.

"We recommend most strongly," the secretaries advised the governor-general, "that Your Excellency should personally see the Prime Minister so that H.M.G. may reconsider the position."[2]

Huddleston agreed completely with his advisors. Since the initial Egyptian request for treaty negotiations, he had done his best to bind the British Government as well as his own Sudan Government to consult the Sudanese should any change in their status be contemplated. Horrified by the course of the treaty negotiations, he had submitted to the Bevin-Sidqi Protocol only under extreme pressure from the Foreign Office and only with an assurance that Egyptian sovereignty would be purely "symbolic"—nothing else would change in the actual administration of the condominium, nor would the Sudan Protocol prevent the Sudanese, after achieving self-government, from opting for complete independence. Sidqi Pasha's statements, however, and especially the play they received in the Egyptian nationalist press, completely altered the situation from the governor-general's point of view. After a stormy interview with Sayyid 'Abd al-Rahman, Huddleston decided that nothing would restore Sudanese faith in either the British or the Sudan Governments so long as the Sudan Protocol

---

2. "We did not think," Robertson later wrote, "that we could possibly remain in the Sudan to force a Treaty on these terms upon the Sudanese. In this I think we were voicing the opinions of the entire British staff of the Sudan Government, on whom the orderly running of the country chiefly depended." (Ibid.). Actually, though still remarkable as a direct challenge to the authority of the Foreign Office, the terms of the memorandum were rather less categorical than Robertson remembered. See copy of letter from Creed, Miller and Robertson to Huddleston, 6 November 1946, in FO 371/53260, PRO.

continued to admit Egyptian sovereignty. On 3 November he cabled Prime Minister Attlee, proposing to return to London to explain how Sidqi's statements had destroyed any chance of implementing the Protocol without serious violence.[3]

The Foreign Office was not enthusiastic about Huddleston's proposed visit. They had already experienced his moral indignation and opposition to the Protocol and saw no point in disputing it again. Moreover, with Bevin still at the United Nations, Huddleston would be appealing over the foreign secretary's head directly to the prime minister and the British Cabinet. Drafted by the Foreign Office, Attlee's response to Huddleston therefore contained a rebuke as well as a not-too-subtle hint that he should remain at his post: "I am disappointed and disturbed by your admission of failure to persuade Sudanese leaders of the very real advantages of the Sudan Protocol, such as maintenance of the administration in its present form, self-government and free choice of their future status which more than counter-balance the symbolic and face-saving concession implied in the words 'within the framework of the unity between the Sudan and Egypt under the common crown of Egypt.'" The prime minister argued that "even taking into account an admittedly excitable race such as the Sudanese," surely the advantages of the protocol, "if well and truly pressed home to the Sudanese leaders," should have offset the Egyptian disclosures. Huddleston's return at the present moment might stir up Egyptian suspicions. With British reinforcements due in Khartoum on the seventh to provide extra security, perhaps the Sudan Government should simply improve its "propaganda machine" and step up publicity efforts to put the Protocol across effectively. If, despite all these arguments, the governor-general still insisted on coming home, Attlee concluded, "then I agree that you should do so." Huddleston arrived in London on 9 November.[4]

Huddleston's visit proved even more troublesome than the Foreign Office expected. In an official letter, Huddleston told Attlee that he and his principal advisors were convinced that it was now impossible to convince the Sudanese Independent Front, "which has the support of the majority," of any advantages in the Protocol that would outweigh the concession of sovereignty. The terms of the Protocol could only be carried out by force—but this, Huddleston insisted, "would be so complete a reversal of all that the Sudan Government has worked for for the past half century, and would so completely destroy Sudanese faith in the good intentions of His Majesty's Government, that I have returned . . . to explain in person the basic change that has taken place in the situation. . . . If the protocol has to be implemented by force all the confidence engendered by fifty years of cooperation between British and Sudanese will vanish overnight."

---

3. Khartoum to Foreign Office, no. 46, Top Secret, Personal from Huddleston for Attlee and Bevin, 3 November 1946, FO 371/53259, PRO.
4. Sargent to Attlee, 4 November 1946, and draft telegram no. 52, Foreign Office to Khartoum, 5 November 1946, FO 371/53259, PRO.

Huddleston demanded that the British Cabinet itself should give "full consideration" to the altered circumstances before making a final decision on the Protocol. If it still chose to continue with the policy, he warned, "I must record that I can no longer be in agreement with the sovereignty clause." On 11 November, he met informally with Cabinet ministers and Foreign Office officials at No. 10 Downing Street to make his case in person.[5]

As the Political Service had hoped, Huddleston's trip provided a useful "corrective" to the British Government's misconceptions about the situation in the Sudan. "The Governor General," Attlee cabled Bevin after the meeting on the eleventh, "explained that up till 1924 there was a true condominium but in that year we turned out all Egyptian troops. . . . The fact is that the Sudanese have for the last twenty-two years shut their eyes to any Egyptian connexion and nothing was ever done to open them to the true state of affairs." Despite a tardy lesson in the history of the condominium by Sir Orme Sargent, both Attlee and Bevin seemed taken aback with this information. "I had no knowledge," the foreign secretary replied, in a remarkable admission of ignorance about the state of Sudanese affairs, "that we had been acting since 1924 in the manner indicated." Attlee himself found the Sudanese attitude incomprehensible. "Even admitting the extreme parochial outlook of the Sudanese," he cabled Bevin, "I find it very difficult to understand their line. In this country we have always understood that Egyptian sovereignty over the Sudan existed though not explicitly stated." The prime minister reflected the general ignorance of Sudanese matters that prevailed in Whitehall outside the Egyptian Department of the Foreign Office.[6]

Despite Huddleston's arguments, Attlee wanted to press on with the protocol. "If we go back now on the Sudan Protocol," he cabled Bevin, "there is no doubt in my mind that we lose the Treaty, for Sidky's Government could no longer stand. Our relations with Egypt and all our defence arrangements in the Middle East would once more be thrown into the melting pot. We should probably be taken to the United Nations Organisation by the Egyptians on the whole issue and certainly to the International Court on the sovereignty aspect and we are advised that the Court would confirm the Egyptian case." Neither referral to the United Nations nor referral to the International Court would help Britain's position in the Sudan. Indeed, if the court upheld Egypt's claim to sovereignty, Attlee pointed out, the British position would be infinitely worse. Moreover, it

---

5. Huddleston to Attlee, 10 November 1946, FO 371/53260, PRO. It was not quite the governor-general's final bolt: "Nevertheless, if His Majesty's Government wish me to continue as Governor-General I am ready to do so and to carry out the terms of the protocol . . . believing that my personal influence might possibly reduce the amount of force required."

6. Foreign Office to New York, no. 2079, 12 November 1946, Top Secret, Personal from Prime Minister to Foreign Secretary, FO 371/53260, PRO.

would not even help to placate the Sudanese, "who already know that we have admitted Egyptian sovereignty."[7]

Bevin agreed: he was beginning to believe that the real problem in the Sudan was not the Sudanese independents but the Political Service itself. When Attlee telegraphed Khartoum's objections to using force and the institution of "a police state with censorship" to impose the Protocol, the foreign secretary responded sharply:

This really does seem to be painting our activities in the blackest light. If we had to use force it would only be to maintain law and order nor do I see why we should be called upon to set up a "police state with censorship." As for the disappearance overnight of all the confidence in the British built up over fifty years that could only come about as a result of either malicious interpretation of the draft protocol or excessively bad presentation on our part.

Bevin had no doubts about his course of action. In spite of Sidqi's leaks and threats of trouble in the Sudan, he telegraphed Attlee, they must stick to their agreement with the Egyptian prime minister: "Vacillation under the threat of force would be the worst thing for our position not only in the Sudan but throughout the Arab world."[8]

Nor, despite an impassioned plea against recognition of Egyptian sovereignty, had Huddleston convinced the rest of his audience either. Meeting on 12 November with Hector McNeil, Bevin's parliamentary under secretary, the governor-general learned that he had "frankly . . . failed to convince the members of the Cabinet . . . that the Sudan Independence group were . . . completely unmoveable on the sovereignty clause." Stung, Huddleston replied with the disdain of the expert for the uninitiated: "This is wishful thinking, and like all wishful thinking, at base dishonest. If you don't believe me, produce only one other person with knowledge of the Sudan comparable to mine who disagrees with me; otherwise you MUST believe me." Huddleston now believed that the problem was not simply a case of Whitehall's lack of knowledge about the situation in the Sudan, but rather one of choosing political expediency over what was morally right. "Say to me," he told McNeil, "as I said to you yesterday—'It is meet that one man die for the people' and I will agree with you." He added: "It may be necessary for the Sudan to pay the price of the mistake of His Majesty's Government in the past. That is honest and logical. Don't avoid the issue by saying that if the Sudanese were sensible there would be no price to pay; the whole essence of our trouble is that on this particular point the Sudanese are not 'sensible'. The situation is then clear and I can decide whether I can be their executioner or not." Describing Huddleston to Attlee, McNeil noted: "He is in a

---

7. Ibid.
8. New York to Foreign Office, no. 1613, 12 November 1946, FO 371/53260, PRO.

Messianic frame of mind, and I think he is going to resign." Although McNeil
was wrong in this assessment, the governor-general stubbornly refused to return
to his post without a written reply to his letter, containing an assurance that the
Cabinet as a whole had given "full consideration" to the changed circumstances
in the Sudan.[9]

On 14 November Attlee read Huddleston's letter and explained the situation to
the full Cabinet. Despite the governor-general's warnings, the prime minister
argued against withdrawing from the Sudan Protocol. At the same time, he
proposed to ask Huddleston to continue in office and to give him a letter to be
shown to leading Sudanese, explaining the British Government's determination
that no Egyptian interference would be allowed in the Sudan despite the
sovereignty clause. With both the foreign secretary and the prime minister in
agreement, the Cabinet once more endorsed the Bevin-Sidqi Protocol.
Disappointed, Huddleston nevertheless accepted the Cabinet's decision and their
invitation that he should continue in office but made no immediate plans to
return to the Sudan.[10]

The governor-general was no longer concerned solely with the issue of
sovereignty. After his initial interview with Attlee, he had called on the
Egyptian Ambassador in London. 'Amr Pasha only reinforced his suspicion that
Egypt intended to use the new Protocol as a cover for increased interference in
the Sudan. "It is not only Water Security that the Egyptians want in the Sudan,"
Huddleston subsequently reported to Sir Orme Sargent, "they want much more—
'Imperial Sovereignty.'" Citing an article in *The Times* by Azzam Pasha, the
Egyptian secretary general of the Arab League, Huddleston warned of a "strong
build-up of Egypt's historical mission in Africa." It was a picaresque scene that
he painted for the permanent under secretary:

Ismail is the central figure—the sands of the Sudan are stained with the blood of
Egyptians, etc., etc.

---

9. Huddleston to McNeil, 13 November 1946, Secret; Note by Huddleston, 12
November 1946; and note by McNeil, 12 November 1946, all in FO 371/53260,
PRO. McNeil suggested calling a Sudanese conference in London, representative of
both sides, administrative and political. This would serve the dual purpose of
providing Huddleston a "straw" to which he could cling, thereby "stalling" his
resignation, while at the same time ensuring that the Sudanese leaders would be in
England immediately after the signing of the Anglo-Egyptian treaty, thus making
any immediate explosion in the Sudan itself unlikely.

10. Cabinet Conclusions 96 (46), 14 November 1946, and Attlee to Huddleston,
Confidential, 14 November 1946, FO 371/53260, PRO. The Cabinet also agreed that
a further letter should be given to Huddleston to be shown to British officials in the
Sudan, explaining the reasons for the British Government's recognition of the
Egyptian claim and "stating that the position and prospects of British officials would
not be jeopardised."

If you have not a glorious victory, a glorious defeat is almost as good an agent for exciting the people—cf. Majuba in our own history.

Cromer's regime is looked upon as a period of foreign domination and shame. . . . Egypt is going through a Rudyard Kipling imperialist phase, with the Sudan in the role of India and Ismail in that of Queen Victoria—a 50-years time lag is nothing in world history.

"Must we pander to such a fantastic distortion of facts?" Huddleston demanded. "However much Sidki Pasha and Co. for tactical reasons harp . . . on the 'symbolic' sovereignty, the real intention is Imperial expansion and the absolute absorption of the Sudan."[11]

On 15 November, Huddleston wrote yet again to the Foreign Office, this time complaining to Hector McNeil about recent references in King Farouk's speech to the "ancient ties binding Egypt and the Sudan" as yet further proof of Egypt's true intentions: "What are the ancient ties binding Egypt and the Sudan? Conquest, oppression, slavery, maladministration? There are no others. This is a good example of the build-up of an Egyptian imperialist tradition to which I have referred on various occasions." By now, however, Huddleston had made himself a thorough nuisance to the British Government. In spite of their appreciation of his expert opinion, McNeil replied, the Foreign Office and the Cabinet "cannot hope otherwise than that the upshot of our negotiations will not be as serious in the Sudan as you anticipate." There was simply no alternative to the government's present course of action. "I hope you will now . . . go back to your post," McNeil wrote with scarcely concealed exasperation. "That seems to me of supreme importance, both to His Majesty's Government and to the Sudanese."[12]

Having failed to get the Bevin-Sidqi Protocol shelved, Huddleston now confronted the problem of actually persuading the Sudanese to accept it with a minimum use of force. "My first and principal objective," he outlined his plan for the Foreign Office, "will be to recover . . . the confidence of the Sudanese . . . and to find some way of attracting their co-operation during the period of their training for self-government." The price of Sudanese confidence, he believed, would be "an immediate and really substantial first instalment of self-governing institutions, something much more rapid and drastic than . . . hitherto

---

11. Huddleston to Sargent, Secret, 13 November 1946, FO 371/53260, PRO.

12. Huddleston to McNeil, Secret, 15 November 1946, and McNeil to Huddleston, 15 November 1946, FO 371/53260, PRO. Even Patrick Scrivener, head of the Egyptian Department and normally sympathetic to the Sudan Government, thought this interpretation a bit extreme. "I do not think we need take Egyptian imperialism too tragically," he minuted. "The social problems which (once the more exciting treaty issue is out of the way) will arise in Egypt will absorb more than all Egyptian energy and capability. Sir H. Huddleston—who is pardonably depressed—forgets the old question 'what will the other man be doing all this time?'" Minute by Scrivener, 13 November 1946, FO 371/53260, PRO.

contemplated for the immediate future." Huddleston insisted that both co-domini should authorize him to invite representative Sudanese, including the leaders of all political parties, to formulate proposals for the "immediate establishment of such political and administrative institutions as they may consider necessary during the period of their training for self-government." Only rapid movement toward self-government could offset the danger of increased Egyptian infiltration into the Sudan and reassure the Sudanese that they would soon be able to determine their own future. Speed was essential. "If there is any delay after my return to Khartoum, riots may compel me to use force and . . . there would be no hope of co-operation."[13]

While the Foreign Office was willing to go along with the governor-general's requirements, events in Egypt soon confirmed Huddleston's fears of Egyptian plans for a more forward involvement in the condominium. As Sidqi returned to Cairo to place the new treaty with its protocols before the Egyptian treaty delegation and Parliament, it became clear that on the Sudan Protocol at least, there were irreconcilable differences of interpretation—differences which the governor-general and the Political Service refused to allow the British Government to ignore. "Having been driven out of his first line of defence," Robertson subsequently described Huddleston's dilemma to the Political Service, "His Excellency . . . now found he had to defend a second line." The point at issue was one which Bevin had allowed Sidqi to gloss over during their discussions—the right of the Sudanese to secede from the Egyptian Crown should they want to.[14]

COMPLICATIONS IN EGYPT AND THE SUDAN

Despite the apparent success of Sidqi Pasha's talks with Bevin in London, the Egyptian prime minister soon ran into stiff opposition in Egypt itself. Violent demonstrations in the Sudan, following his statement at the Cairo airdrome, were followed by further reports in the Egyptian press emphasizing that the new Sudan Protocol meant a "change of regime" in the condominium. As his opposition focused on the Sudan issue, Sidqi too began to insist that he had provided for a more effective Egyptian participation in the Sudan Administration. The Sudan Protocol, along with Sidqi's explanation of it to the Egyptian treaty delegation, "leaked" to the press. All Egypt now learned that Sidqi had told the

---

13. Note by Huddleston, 15 November 1946, FO 371/53260, PRO.

14. For the Foreign Office attitude, see minute by Scrivener, 14 November 1946, FO 371/53259. "I gather that the Governor-General will seek authority to enter into consultation with all parties immediately on his return to the Sudan. I think he should get it . . . and that he should urge this course on Sidky on his return to Cairo. It might forestall the shooting which the Governor-General fears." For Robertson's assessment, see C.S. no. 104, Secret, 3 December 1946, MP 571/2.

delegation that the Protocol did not provide for any right of Sudanese secession from the Egyptian Crown. On 16 November, as the opposition continued its attacks, all of the Bevin-Sidqi draft documents were published in the Cairo papers. The same day, the Egyptian treaty delegation met for over three hours to discuss the situation. Despite Sidqi's explanations, it soon became apparent that his enemies in the delegation were determined to prevent any agreement from being concluded on Sidqi's terms. Bypassing the delegation, he decided to lay the draft treaty and protocols before the Chamber of Deputies in camera.[15]

While Sidqi Pasha struggled to obtain approval for his agreements with Bevin, in London Huddleston himself began to demand reassurances about the firmness of the British interpretation of the Bevin-Sidqi Protocol. As it became clear that Sidqi's interpretation was diametrically opposed to that explained to him by both Bevin and Attlee, Huddleston now insisted that the letter he was to be given should state the British interpretation unequivocally and that he should be able to "stand firm" on it. Attlee agreed to give Huddleston his guarantees. Apparently without consulting Bevin on the exact wording, the prime minister wrote formally to the governor-general, "expressly stat[ing] that the Sudanese people would eventually have the right to separate themselves from the Egyptian crown should they wish to do so." With this letter in hand, Huddleston finally made his arrangements to return to Khartoum.[16]

Huddleston's extraction of ironclad guarantees for the Sudanese from Attlee soon forced an Anglo-Egyptian showdown. The British Embassy had been aware for some time that Sidqi's interpretation of the Sudan Protocol was at odds with that of the foreign secretary, particularly on the Sudan's right to secede from the Egyptian Crown. James Bowker, the British chargé, had kept Whitehall fully informed of the struggle to get the Protocol accepted, including Sidqi's denial that the agreement allowed for any right of Sudanese secession. Bowker's reports alarmed the British prime minister. After reviewing the minutes of Bevin's talks with Sidqi, Attlee became even more disturbed. "Our records here," he cabled Bevin, "do not show that Sidky ever agreed in so many words that the Sudanese would have the right to eventual secession. You put the point to him very clearly at your private meeting at Claridge's on the evening of October 24th and at other meetings and Sidky always rode off." In the face of Sidqi's repeated statements in Egypt, Attlee suggested, they should inform him immediately of the need for an agreed interpretation in writing. Anxious to avoid yet another démarche that might lead to charges of British insincerity and "breach of faith"

15. Anglo-Egyptian Treaty Negotiations, 1945-47, Secret, 12 March 1947, FO 371/62962, PRO; and C.S. letter no. 104, 3 December 1946, MP 571/2.

16. C.S. letter no. 104, Secret, 3 December 1946, MP 571/2; Foreign Office to New York, no. 2410, 22 November 1946, and draft, FO 371/53260, PRO. The original letter is missing from the files. Sargent gave this description of its contents to Bevin.

from the Sudanese, Attlee also sent a message to intercept Huddleston in Cairo, asking the governor-general not to use his letter without further instructions.[17]

Bevin agreed with the prime minister. "In addition to referring Sidky to the oral understandings reached in London," he ordered Bowker, "you should . . . say . . . it will be necessary to have an exchange of letters . . . at the time of signature of the treaty." Bevin could not give way now on the rights of the Sudanese: "The policy of His Majesty's Government is to deal with Sidky, his government and people on a fair and equal basis. But we cannot ride rough-shod over the Sudanese and arrest their aspirations. The British people would never stand for that. The Sudanese must be free to decide their future status. The United Nations would support us in that." Despite this apparently categorical defense of Sudanese self-determination, however, the Foreign Office soon began to back away from any demands that might endanger the treaty.[18]

It is clear from the documentary evidence that the Foreign Office officials, like the Egyptians, understood that they were attempting to square a circle in the Sudan Protocol. "Had Sidky kept his mouth shut," Sargent telegraphed Bevin, "we could have taken our stand on the *ipsissima verba* of the Sudan Protocol and argued convincingly in Parliament and elsewhere that the phrase about the right to choose the future status did include the choice of secession." The Foreign Office indignantly insisted that the Egyptian prime minister was to blame for the mess in which the treaty negotiations now found themselves. "It was Sidky's indiscreet disclosures in Cairo . . . which have debarred us now from taking our stand on the text of the Protocol and have forced us to demand from Sidky a clear definition of what we both understand the text to mean." Yet as Bowker reported from Cairo, Sidqi would be unlikely to agree to any written clarification. Consequently, Sargent and the Foreign Office suggested instead "simultaneous statements" to be read in the British and the Egyptian parliaments at the time of ratification.[19]

Meanwhile, in Cairo, Huddleston was outraged. As soon as he had set down in the Egyptian capital, he had been presented with the Foreign Office telegram instructing him not to use Attlee's letter. When it was suggested that the letter might be amended, removing the categorical assurance of the Sudanese right to secede from Egypt, the governor-general indignantly responded that without that assurance, the letter would be "useless." Refusing to return to Khartoum,

---

17. Cairo to Foreign Office, nos. 1711 and 1712, 18 November 1946, and Foreign Office to New York, no. 2303, 19 November 1946, FO 371/53260, PRO. Sargent summed up the situation for Bevin on the twenty-second, "It seems clear now . . . that the issue which will decide the fate of the Treaty is the question whether the Sudanese are, when the time comes, to have the right to secede from Egypt notwithstanding the unity of the two countries under the Egyptian Crown."

18. New York to Cairo, no. 17, 19 November 1946, Secret, FO 371/53260, PRO.

19. Cairo to Foreign Office, no. 1724, 20 November 1946, and Foreign Office to New York, no. 2411, 22 November 1946, Top Secret, FO 371/53260, PRO.

Huddleston demanded an unequivocal reply from the British prime minister to the hypothetical question, "Have the Sudanese the right to secede from the Egyptian Crown or not when the time for them to make their choice arrives?" Unless the answer was in the affirmative, he warned, he could not return to the Sudan. Awaiting an answer to this ultimatum, on 23 November Huddleston met with Sidqi Pasha.[20]

Huddleston's meeting with Sidqi made clear the vast difference of outlook between the Egyptians and the Sudan Government. Attlee had encouraged the governor-general to meet both Sidqi and King Farouk in the hope that he might induce them to support a policy of rapid Sudanization and self-government in the condominium. In fact, it seems clear that Sidqi Pasha never believed that such a course was either feasible or likely. Taking the same line with Huddleston that he had previously with Bevin, Sidqi insisted that the Sudanese were still in a "backward state." They would take a long time even to reach self-government, "so what was the good of talking about independence now?" The new treaty was only to run for twenty years, Sidqi went on; did the governor-general really think that the Sudanese would be ready for self-government before then? "A great many of the Sudanese certainly do think so," Huddleston replied. Regardless how long it took, "100% of the Sudanese want . . . the clearest possible statement that the right eventually to decide their own status shall include the right to secede."[21]

The Egyptian premier refused to understand the extent of opposition that truly existed among the independence factions in the Sudan. Like most Egyptians, he insisted on viewing the Sudan as an Egyptian province and the Sudanese as Egyptian subjects. Sidqi apparently believed that the Umma Party was little more than a British creation and Sayyid 'Abd al-Rahman, its leader, nothing but a British stooge. At the very outset of the meeting, Sidqi complained to Huddleston of an interview 'Abd al-Rahman had given to the *New York Times*, threatening violent resistance to the imposition of Egyptian sovereignty over the Sudan. These, Sidqi indignantly declared, "were the words of a rebel . . . an incitement to rebellion." When Huddleston defended the sayyid, noting that he had been "severely provoked" by Egyptian press articles denouncing him as a rebel and threatening that the "wages of rebellion were death," Sidqi responded that in Egypt the papers were free to write what they liked but that 'Abd al-Rahman was a responsible leader of a Sudanese party. The governor-general should see 'Abd al-Rahman when he returned to Khartoum, Sidqi insisted, and "warn him about his attitude." Ironically, even as they were speaking, Sayyid

---

20. Foreign Office to New York, no. 2410, 22 November 1946, Secret, FO 371/53260, PRO; and C.S. letter no. 104, 3 December 1946, MP 571/2.
21. Record of Meeting between Sidky Pasha and Governor-General on 23 November 1946, FO 371/53261, PRO.

'Abd al-Rahman, on Huddleston's advice, was on his way to London to lay the independents' case before the British Government.[22]

Sayyid 'Abd al-Rahman had suggested as early as October that he should go personally to London to argue against Egyptian sovereignty. At the time, he had been dissuaded in order to avoid any potential rebuff at a particularly delicate stage in Anglo-Egyptian negotiations. When Huddleston realized his own mission was not going to succeed, he reopened the matter, encouraging Sargent and Attlee to receive the Mahdist leader, ostensibly as a means of reassuring him about the "symbolic" nature of Egyptian sovereignty in the Protocol. The governor-general reached back to the turbulent days of the Egyptian revolution to make his argument, pointing out the "close historical parallel" of 'Abd al-Rahman's desire to put his case to London and Zaghlul Pasha's demand in February 1919 to state Egypt's case before the Paris Peace Conference or the British Cabinet. Huddleston's remarks are of particular historical interest because of his personal role in the earlier events:

Wingate, the High Commissioner in Egypt, strongly recommended that Zaghlul should be allowed to come—but not to the point of saying "I know for certain that there will be . . . a general anti-British rising in Egypt if you refuse. Therefore if you will not take my advice I must resign." Zaghlul's appeal was turned down—there was a general rising—a number of unarmed British . . . were murdered—a much larger number, far larger than was known at home, of fanatically excited Egyptians were killed. I know because I helped to kill them; I was then in military command of all Upper Egypt.

Even if the protocol must stand, Huddleston argued, allowing 'Abd al-Rahman to make his case might be just the concession that would "win him over." At the least, it would give the Sudan Government a breathing space, since a general rising of the independents was unlikely with 'Abd al-Rahman out of the country. In fact, despite these arguments, Huddleston probably hoped that 'Abd al-Rahman would convince Attlee of the impossibility of imposing Egyptian sovereignty on the Sudan.[23]

Eventually, the Foreign Office agreed that 'Abd al-Rahman should be allowed to come to London. As the governor-general expected, Attlee found that "S.A.R. did not show any sign of understanding that the sovereignty of the King of Egypt could be anything else than absolute power." After his first meeting with the Sudanese leader on 28 November, it was clear to the prime minister that 'Abd al-Rahman would never be convinced of the British point of view

---

22. Ibid. The Egyptian premier particularly complained that the Mahdist leader had refused to apologize for the destruction of King Farouk's portrait during the attack on the Ashiqqa club in Omdurman.

23. In his notes for a discussion with the minister of state on 12 November 1946, the governor-general marked this particular topic "most important." See correspondence and notes on 12 and 13 November 1946, FO 371/53260, PRO.

concerning sovereignty. Frustrated by the encounter and with the governor-general bombarding him with messages from Cairo demanding even further measures to safeguard the Sudanese from Egypt, Attlee finally answered Huddleston's hypothetical question.[24]

In a revised letter replacing the one he had given Huddleston in London, Attlee stated categorically: "His Majesty's Government are for their part determined that nothing shall be permitted to deflect the Sudan Government . . . from . . . the preparation of the Sudanese for self-government and for the task of choosing freely what their future status is to be." He reiterated that the Sudanese would be "free to choose the future status of the Sudan," and he even quoted Sidqi Pasha's observation to Bevin in October: "His Majesty's Government consider that, in the words used by the Egyptian prime minister to the British foreign secretary, nothing in the proposed treaty can prejudice the right of the Sudanese to achieve their independence nor bind a people in search of liberty. The Egyptian prime minister pointed out . . . this was a universal principle . . . not a matter for incorporation in a treaty." The prime minister also reiterated his assurances to 'Abd al-Rahman that nothing in the Sudan protocol could prejudice the right of the Sudanese to "complete independence." Any form of "direct Egyptian administration," he had told the Sudanese leader and now repeated to Huddleston, would be "resisted" by the governor-general as contrary to the protocol. This was as far as Attlee would go. Although Huddleston pressed him to insist that the Egyptians too must publicly adhere to this definition of the agreement, the prime minister could do no more. "Sir H. Huddleston is unreasonable," Attlee minuted to Sargent. "We cannot give the Sudanese any more rights against Egypt than already exist." It was enough. Huddleston made plans to return to Khartoum in the first week of December.[25]

While 'Abd al-Rahman made his case in London, in Cairo Sidqi Pasha finally obtained the consent of the Egyptian Parliament for signing the treaty that he and Bevin had initialed in October. Officially notifying the British Government on 1 December that Egypt was now prepared to sign the treaty with its two annexes, Sidqi invoked the initialled agreement and expected Bevin to recommend ratification of the documents to the British Cabinet. The Egyptian ambassador informed the Foreign Office that his government was unable to consider any exchange of letters. If Britain insisted on this, 'Amr Pasha warned, then the treaty was "doomed." 'Amr begged the British to stand "only on the documents already agreed and disregard any other interpretations, whether in the Press or

24. Ibid. See also C.S. letter no. 104, 3 December 1946, MP 571/2. Record of an interview of Sayed Abdul Rahman el Mahdi with the prime minister at No. 10 Downing Street on November 28th, 1946, and Minute by Attlee, 30 November 1946, FO 371/53261. For Abd al-Rahman's visit, see FO 371/53261 and 53262, PRO.

25. Attlee to Huddleston, 30 November 1946; Foreign Office to Cairo, no. 2038, 30 November 1946, Secret; and Minute by Attlee, 30 November 1946, all in FO 371/53261, PRO.

Notes by Sidky to the Egyptian Delegation." In effect, to get the treaty signed, the Egyptians wanted Bevin to leave differences over interpretation for the future.[26]

The official Egyptian notification forced Bevin's hand. As the Foreign Office reported on 2 December, "The time has come when we must now make up our minds whether we are going to ... sign the Anglo-Egyptian Treaty as it stands ... or whether we are going to maintain our insistence on an exchange of interpretations." Expressing the general Foreign Office consensus, Sir Robert Howe warned that insistence on letters now would certainly lose the treaty. The results would be a period of unrest and difficulty for the British in Egypt. Moreover, Farouk and the parties that had supported the treaty would be antagonized. "While I am certain that we shall have a lot of trouble in Egypt if we do not sign the Treaty," Howe wrote, "I am not quite so certain that the situation in the Sudan, if the Treaty is signed, would be as bad as the governor-general makes out." Accepting 'Amr Pasha's argument, Howe advised Bevin to take his stand on the words of the Sudan Protocol "as they are written." Whatever Sidqi may have found it necessary to say "for internal consumption" was not binding on the British Government. Unable to decide whether to insist on some form of agreed interpretation, Bevin hesitated—and in Khartoum the governor-general once again stole the initiative.[27]

THE END OF ANGLO-EGYPTIAN NEGOTIATIONS

Huddleston returned to the Sudan on 5 December. Within two days he made known to both the Sudanese and the British officials the terms of Attlee's letter. On 7 December, the governor-general publicly reiterated Britain's pledge that the Sudan, after attaining self-government, would be free to choose its own status, including complete independence from both co-domini if it so desired. As the repercussions exploded in the Egyptian press, on 8 December Sidqi Pasha—aged, ailing, beset by his enemies and having finally lost the confidence of his king— resigned as prime minister of Egypt. His successor, al-Nuqrashi Pasha, who had also been his predecessor at the head of the minority government, proved even more strident in his denunciation of both the governor-general and the British interpretation of the Sudan Protocol. The unity of Egypt and the Sudan, he told a cheering Egyptian Parliament, was permanent—there could be no question of

26. See especially a note by Sir Orme Sargent on a conversation with Amr Pasha, the Egyptian ambassador in London, 27 November 1946, FO 371/53261, PRO and draft telegram from the Foreign Office to Bevin, undated but sometime in the first week of December 1946, FO 371/53262, PRO.

27. Note by Howe, 2 December 1946, FO 371/53262, PRO. This note also refers to Bevin's hesitation as expressed in telegram no. 2004 of 27 November 1946, and subsequent telegrams.

separating the two. Two weeks later, Huddleston repeated Attlee's pledge, and publicly flourished his letter, in a speech at El Obeid. As the Sudan Government refused to be silent, or even moderately discreet in its emphasis on the British interpretation of the Protocol, Anglo-Egyptian relations reached a new low.[28]

Huddleston and the Sudan Political Service had done their best to overthrow the British foreign secretary's "appeasement" policy toward Egypt. Although they had been unable to get the Bevin-Sidqi Protocol shelved, along with its admission of Egyptian sovereignty, they had forced Whitehall to adhere to a strict interpretation of the Protocol, an interpretation that would preserve the Sudanese right to self-determination. At the same time, Huddleston had reinforced the position of the Sudan Government by extracting a written promise from Attlee that Egypt would not be allowed to "interfere" in the administration of the condominium. Neither the governor-general nor the Political Service chiefs believed that the Egyptians would honor their pledge to leave the Sudan alone. After Huddleston's return from London, they deliberately pursued a policy geared toward challenging Egypt's interpretation of the Protocol and exposing its true intentions to infiltrate the condominium. As they expected, the Egyptians proved extremely obliging.

On 13 December 1946, the Sudan Government informed the Foreign Office that pursuant to its policy of Sudanization and the terms of the 1936 treaty, it would not renew the contract (due to expire in January) of the present Egyptian grand kadi, Shaykh Hassan. Instead, it proposed to appoint a Sudanese to the post. A week later, on 21 December, Khartoum informed the Egyptian Government of the decision. As the Egyptians predictably protested at the elimination of their highest official in the Sudan, so too this action precipitated a crisis between the governor-general and the British Government. Once again, in the midst of Bevin's efforts to reach agreement with Cairo, the governor-general had done "something salient" and aroused the Egyptian nationalists.[29]

On 23 December, al-Nuqrashi Pasha summoned Ambassador Campbell to discuss the situation. Tactfully, the Egyptian premier broached the possibility of "modifying" the governor-general's decision. Its effect on Egyptian opinion at the present moment, he told Campbell, would be "disastrous"—the post of grand kadi was the only high-level position occupied by an Egyptian. Moreover, it was

28. Anglo-Egyptian Treaty Negotiations, 1945-47, Secret, 12 March 1947, FO 371/62962, PRO. In fact, Sidqi had been ill for some time. Despite denials that his resignation had anything to do with the governor-general's statement, however, it seems more likely that this episode triggered Farouk's decision to replace him. The British Embassy was privately informed that the king had decided Sidqi's relations with the British were too "strained" to achieve an agreement. Minutes by Scrivener and Howe, 9 and 10 December 1946, and accompanying telegrams in FO 371/53262/J 5205, PRO.

29. Khartoum to Cairo, no. 140, 13 December 1946, and Cairo to Foreign Office, 23 December 1946, FO 371/53263, PRO.

a post with significant religious overtones. Campbell played canny, reminding al-Nuqrashi of both the governor-general's authority under the Condominium Agreement and the Anglo-Egyptian commitment to Sudanization. Agreeing that Huddleston had the authority to make such a decision, the Egyptian prime minister nevertheless reiterated that the timing was deplorable. Although Egyptians could only "rejoice" that a Sudanese was ready for such a responsible post, at this juncture in Anglo-Egyptian relations Huddleston's action would inevitably be interpreted in Egypt as proof of Britain's policy to separate the Sudan from Egypt. Al-Nuqrashi suggested instead that a post of "deputy Grand Kadi" be created for the Sudanese candidate, whose position as mufti could then be filled by yet another Sudanese.[30]

Bevin personally responded to the crisis over the grand kadi. Dictating a reply to Campbell on Christmas Eve, the foreign secretary agreed that termination of the present kadi's contract seemed "most inappropriate in view of the delicate situation." Bevin also had orders for Huddleston:

I would be glad if the governor-general would refrain from making any announcement until I have had time to consider the subject carefully. In the meantime I would be grateful if he would observe the greatest circumspection. I will of course consider any views he may wish to express before coming to a final decision. . . . the most appropriate course would seem to be to let the Kadi carry on for another year until the present delicate Sudanese-Egyptian relations are in a less explosive state.

Still trying to obtain an acceptable treaty, the foreign secretary saw the appointment of the grand kadi as a bargaining chip. On 28 December, Bevin instructed Campbell to tell al-Nuqrashi "that if we can secure some settlement on the Treaty H.M.G. might find themselves able to meet him over the Kadi, extending the . . . term of appointment for a further period."[31]

Bevin assumed that the final decision concerning the appointment of the grand kadi was his to make. Trying to act toward the Sudan Government in the same way that the colonial secretary functioned with the colonies, the foreign secretary did not appreciate the nuances of Huddleston's "constitutional" relationship with the co-domini. Bevin's effort to use the appointment of an internal Sudan Government official as a political "carrot" for the Egyptians, however, violated

---

30. Khartoum to Cairo, no. 154, 25 December 1946, FO 371/53263, PRO. Cairo to Foreign Office, no. 1940, 23 December 1946, FO 371/53263, PRO. Campbell too was irritated with Huddleston: "It is unfortunate that this incident should coincide with present moment in Treaty negotiations when we are trying to get Egyptian Prime Minister to help in breaking deadlock and when one of the difficulties is Egypt's fear that His Majesty's Government are aiming at permanent separation of Sudan from Egypt." The obvious solution, of course, was to extend the kadi's term for yet another year.

31. Foreign Office to Cairo, no. 2157, 24 December 1946, and no. 2169, 28 December 1946, FO 371/53263.

every principle of trusteeship with which the Sudan Political Service had come to identify itself over the years. Huddleston was furious. Far from living up to the promises Attlee had made to prevent any interference in the administration, Bevin now seemed blithely willing to distribute Sudan Government offices as political bribes for Egyptian cooperation. This was an old pattern of "colonialism" that the Sudan Government believed it had long ago outgrown in its role as "Guardian" of the Sudanese. The governor-general reacted swiftly to what he now interpreted as a violation of his own prerogatives and the pledges made to him in London.

On 29 December, Huddleston telegraphed an uncompromising reply to Bevin's "instructions."

My action in replacing Egyptian Grand Kadi was taken under Article 11(2) of 1936 Treaty, which gives me full and unqualified authority. I am aware of no precedent for interference of His Majesty's Government with governor-general's power to appoint Sudan Government official.

Moreover, before my departure from England I was given most categorical assurance by Mr. Attlee that my constitutional powers in administration of the Sudan would not be infringed, and I was especially urged to push forward Sudanisation as quickly as possible.

There was a qualified Sudanese to fill the grand kadi's post, Huddleston continued, and under the treaty he should be appointed as soon as the present kadi's term expired. Furthermore, any attempt to use the post as a bargaining chip would quickly become known to the Sudanese and might well undermine his authority. Consequently, Huddleston refused point-blank to allow Bevin to politicize the appointment of a Sudan official. "I am unable," he ended his despatch, "to acquiesce in Secretary of State's proposal."[32]

Bevin was taken aback by Huddleston's response. In a more diplomatic telegram, Patrick Scrivener, the head of the Egyptian Department, rephrased the foreign secretary's position:

I think there is some misunderstanding. I do not question governor-general's authority under Article 11 of 1936 Treaty. But in present case one partner in the condominium has made pressing diplomatic representations to the other in regard to an appointment in which he is interested. The other partner, while in principle agreeing with the governor-general, is disposed, in return for a general settlement of the whole Sudan question, to indicate at the right moment that he may be able to meet

---

32. Khartoum to Cairo, no. 157 (repeated to Foreign Office no. 62), 29 December 1946, FO 371/53263. Huddleston also had recourse to that nightmare of secret diplomacy, the leak: "If Foreign Office message is delivered to Nokrashi its terms will in all probability leak to the Sudanese within a few hours of delivery as did my despatch of December 13th 1946 to Nokrashi." Whether this was a warning or a delicately veiled threat, the implication was clear.

the Egyptian request. Procedure, as I see it, would in that event be for both Governments to recommend to governor-general that present Kadi's appointment should be extended for an agreed period.

Meanwhile, with discussions under way between the co-domini, the governor-general should allow the present Kadi to continue on a day-to-day basis until the co-domini had together reached some decision. "We cannot brush aside Egyptian representations on this matter without discourtesy and . . . political unwisdom," Scrivener wrote. In his own less-compromising hand Bevin added, "Prime Minister and I both agree that the new appointment should not be made pending further instructions."[33]

Bevin was not used to having subordinates refuse his orders. Huddleston's reply had drawn him up sharply. The permanent officials in the Foreign Office hastened to explain the difficulty of the situation to him. The relationship between the governor-general and the foreign secretary was not like that between the colonial secretary and the governor of a colony. The governor-general's position was bolstered by international treaty and the original Condominium Agreement. The foreign secretary's instructions concerning the grand kadi had raised a constitutional issue with potentially disastrous implications. "This is clearly a delicate matter," warned Sir Eric Beckett, head of the Foreign Office Treaty Department, on 31 December, "When the G.G. lunched with me when he was last over here he raised purely casually the question as to whether anybody could give orders to the governor-general or not, and mentioned that Maffey seemed to hold the doctrine that nobody could give him orders and, what is more, nobody could sack him if he did not choose to resign." Although Huddleston admitted Maffey had perhaps gone a bit far, the implications of the conversation disturbed Bevin; as the governor-general continued publicly to champion Sudanese self-determination, thereby undermining Anglo-Egyptian negotiations, Bevin's concern deepened.[34]

Late in December, al-Nuqrashi again complained about Huddleston's activities and attitude. The Egyptian premier warned Ambassador Campbell that Huddleston's statements were undermining all the work done by the British and Egyptian governments to smooth over their differences and sign the treaty.

---

33. See Foreign Office to Cairo, no. 2174 (repeated to Khartoum no. 73 Immediate), 30 December 1946, and draft in Scrivener's hand with Bevin's addition, FO 371/53263, PRO.

34. See Minute by Beckett, 31 December 1946, FO 371/53263, PRO. Warily, the head of the Treaty Department agreed that, "legally speaking," neither co-dominus could alone give instructions to the governor-general—but if they gave a joint recommendation it should be regarded as binding. As for the governor-general not being sacked, Beckett found Maffey's position "absurd." If the co-domini joined together and announced that the governor-general had been replaced, then clearly his position would be impossible. Huddleston neither dissented nor agreed with this view.

Indeed, the governor-general's continual declarations of policy constituted "a challenge which, in its directness and violence, had no example since Cherif had refused to evacuate the Sudan in 1884 and His Majesty's Government had got Nubar, the Armenian, to accept their demand." Considering the repeated assurances of the British Government, al-Nuqrashi observed, Egyptians could only conclude that Huddleston was "deliberately pursuing a policy of his own, namely, the encouragement of the Sudan to separate from Egypt." Although Campbell denied the charge, in fact al-Nuqrashi had eviscerated the problem. With an air of resignation, Campbell himself privately lamented that the almost daily statements emanating from Huddleston, the Political Service, and Sayyid 'Abd al-Rahman were ruining chances for a settlement: "One feels rather helpless . . . they partake of the inevitability of the actions of Fate . . . and I have a horrid feeling that we must expect more of them. Indeed a vicious circle."[35]

Bevin did his best to bring the governor-general to heel. After receiving al-Nuqrashi Pasha's complaints, on 2 January 1947, the Foreign Office sent a cable to Cairo, repeated to Khartoum, urging that the moment had now come to "soft-pedal in the Sudan." If there was any further public controversy, it should be handled by Whitehall. Again intervening personally, Bevin added, "I must ask the Governor General should make no more extemporous statements on this issue but should consult us." Huddleston would have none of it. Although he reported that he had now made all the statements necessary to persuade the Sudanese to accept symbolic sovereignty, he refused to have his hands tied in the future; "In the absence of any immediate and explicit public statement by His Majesty's Government on their interpretation of the Sudan Protocol, I feel I must reserve the right to counter any statement made public in Egypt which conflicts with assurances which Mr. Attlee authorised me to give to the Sudanese. . . . maintenance of public order demands that I should have discretion to reassure Sudanese immediately if the need arises." Again warned off a direct confrontation by his permanent officials, Bevin accepted Huddleston's reservation "conditional on his rejoinders being kept strictly within the four corners of the Prime Minister's assurances" and with the understanding that no statement would be made in Khartoum except in the case of a "grave local emergency." Once more, the governor-general had successfully withstood the foreign secretary.[36]

The incident of the grand kadi had involved the internal administration of the Sudan. The other major controversy that "envenomed" Anglo-Egyptian relations

---

35. Cairo to Foreign Office, no. 1970, and Campbell to Howe, personal, 31 December 1946, FO 371/62939, PRO. Scrivener displayed less patience: "The whole of Nokrashi's attack can be paraphrased 'cet animal est mechant, lorsqu'on l'attaque il se defend.' If we had wanted the Sudan we should have taken it in 1924."

36. See draft telegram with Bevin's addition, Foreign Office to Cairo, no. 15, 2 January 1947; Khartoum to Cairo, no. 3, 5 January 1947, and Foreign Office to Cairo, no. 79, 10 January 1947; with accompanying minutes, all in FO 371/62939, PRO.

after Sidqi Pasha's resignation, however, epitomized what Bevin came to believe was the real stumbling block in the Sudan—an outdated imperial arrogance in the Sudan Political Service itself. Shortly after Huddleston's return to Khartoum in December 1946, the annual Palace reception was held to celebrate King George's birthday. In a clearly provocative gesture, the chief Egyptian staff officer in the condominium presented himself at the main Palace entrance, which was traditionally reserved for those on the official Entrée List. Since neither he nor any of his predecessors had ever been on the list, he was refused admittance and was directed instead to the same door that he habitually used to attend official functions. Publicly protesting, he declined to attend the party altogether, thereby committing, in Huddleston's eyes, a gross discourtesy to the British monarch. The governor-general demanded an apology, which the Egyptian refused to give. For nearly two months, Huddleston would have nothing to do with his own senior Egyptian military official.[37]

When King Farouk's birthday approached in February 1947, Khartoum raised the issue again. Huddleston refused to invite the chief staff officer to the garden party honoring the Egyptian monarch until a formal apology had been made for the insult to King George. Eventually, with both Bevin and al-Nuqrashi Pasha intervening, Huddleston got his apology. In the meantime, however, the foreign secretary was struck by the absurdity of such personal episodes being blown out of proportion until they required the intervention of senior government ministers to resolve them. Bevin found the custom of the entrée grotesquely out of date—a perfect example of the imperial legacy he was trying to eliminate in Anglo-Arab relations. As his negotiations with Egypt deteriorated, his irritation with Huddleston only increased.[38]

In January 1947, Bevin offered al-Nuqrashi numerous variations on two basic alternatives: the signed treaty, with an Anglo-Egyptian Conference on the Sudan instead of the Bevin-Sidqi Protocol; or the treaty with the Protocol and agreed understandings about an "unrestricted" Sudanese right to self-determination, as well as means for securing Egypt's "permanent interests" in the Sudan. In either case, the foreign secretary also offered to make a unilateral statement guaranteeing that His Majesty's Government would "place no obstacle in the way if the Sudan eventually chose to remain united to Egypt." Bevin even invited al-Nuqrashi to London for face-to-face discussions. Al-Nuqrashi responded with a new draft Sudan protocol embodying terms of reference for Bevin's proposed conference—terms of reference, however, that excluded any mention of Sudanese rights of self-determination and that insisted on the framework of the

---

37. The story of the chief Egyptian staff officer is in FO 371/62941 and 62942, PRO. Huddleston later told Robertson that he thought it had been this affair that "did for me." He knew Bevin had seen the correspondence and had dealt with the matter personally.

38. Ibid. See especially Howe to Campbell, Personal and Confidential, 17 February 1947.

common Crown between the Sudan and Egypt. When Bevin remained firm that his compromise proposals must not prejudice the issue of Sudanese self-determination, al-Nuqrashi rejected them altogether.[39]

Still Bevin refused to give up. On 23 January he cabled yet another Sudan protocol, this time referring only to the freedom of the Sudanese to exercise their choice "in accordance with their political aspirations and . . . the principles of the Charter of the United Nations concerning non-self-governing territories." This further effort evoked yet another challenge from Khartoum. Persistent as ever, Huddleston had followed the telegram traffic between London and Cairo. With an irony now familiar in Anglo-Sudanese relations, Bevin's new proposal brought a stern warning from the Palace: "Any alteration to the protocol, in particular where future status is concerned, will immediately appear to the Sudanese . . . in the light of a concession to Egypt and therefore if this alteration is accepted by Nokrashi I shall almost certainly be forced to repeat in full all the assurances and promises of future choice contained in Mr. Attlee's letter of November 30th 1946 and telegram 2038 of November 30th to Cairo."[40]

In fact, Huddleston need not have bothered. As Campbell made it clear that Bevin had gone as far as possible, al-Nuqrashi diplomatically responded that he must consult the Egyptian Council of Ministers, though he had little hope they would agree. As expected, they rejected Bevin's proposal. Instead, in early February the Egyptian premier officially informed the British ambassador that Egypt would refer the entire matter of the Anglo-Egyptian treaty to the United Nations. Anglo-Egyptian negotiations were dead.[41]

After nearly a year, Bevin's strenuous efforts to find a compromise had come to naught. The foreign secretary had done his best to maintain an evenhanded and fair approach to the treaty negotiations. He acknowledged that the Egyptians could never accept the possibility of an unfriendly regime in the Sudan. The only question was whether the British administration should be carried on "in antagonism to Egypt or in friendly collaboration." "I prefer the latter," Bevin had declared in a draft Cabinet Paper on 1 January 1947, "and we should make a declaration in this sense." The problem was that because of the governor-general's conduct, Egypt might repudiate the Sudan Protocol: "Her mind has been poisoned against us." Bevin blamed Huddleston personally for the failure of

---

39. Foreign Office to Cairo, Secret, 9 January 1947, FO 371/62940, PRO, summarizes Bevin's efforts.

40. Ibid. Also Minute by Howe, 22 January 1947; Foreign Office to Cairo, no. 173, Top Secret, 23 January 1947; Cairo to Foreign Office, no. 226, 25 January 1947; Foreign Office to Cairo, no. 191, 25 January 1947; and Khartoum to Cairo, no. 19, 25 January 1947, all in FO 371/62941, PRO.

41. Minute by Howe, 22 January 1947; Foreign Office to Cairo, no. 173, Top Secret, 23 January 1947; Cairo to Foreign Office, no. 226, 25 January 1947; Foreign Office to Cairo, no. 191, 25 January 1947; and Khartoum to Cairo, no. 19, 25 January 1947, all in FO 371/62941, PRO.

the Anglo-Egyptian treaty negotiations. "The Governor-General's attitude . . . has been very difficult. He assumes that he is a dictator and that no one has any control over him." With his Egyptian policy in disarray over the Sudan question, Bevin decided the time had come to begin again—this time by constructing a Sudan policy directed from London instead of Khartoum. Predictably, the first casualty of Bevin's new policy was Huddleston himself.[42]

---

42. Draft Cabinet Paper, never distributed, 1 January 1947, FO 371/62939, PRO.

5

The United Nations Debacle
and After

If there were risings here . . . on account of a U.N.O. decision to give Egypt a share in the Sudan, I could not expect the loyalty of my British staff to put down such risings—because they sympathise with the anti-Egyptian feelings of the Sudanese.

—James Robertson, July 1947

The Egyptian decision to refer both the Anglo-Egyptian Treaty and the Sudan question to the United Nations in the winter of 1947 marked a change in the pace of condominium politics. Although announcing its intentions, Egypt made no immediate move to carry through on the threat. Meanwhile, the British foreign secretary, Ernest Bevin, tried to reassert his authority over the "rogue" administration in Khartoum. While the foreign secretary did his best to reorient the Sudan Government, and to bring it into line with his plans for an eventual Anglo-Egyptian alliance, the Sudan civil secretary pursued his own plans for constitutional, administrative, and economic development, to consolidate the victory against Egyptian claims in the condominium. Despite Bevin's new initiative, the Political Service under Robertson stood firm against all efforts to suborn its self-conceived mission in the Sudan.

BEVIN'S REVENGE

Sir Hubert Huddleston officially retired from his post as governor-general of the Sudan in March 1947. Defended in the British Parliament by both Bevin and Attlee against Egyptian charges that he had repeatedly overstepped his authority, he was awarded a G.C.M.G. (Knight Grand Commander of St. Michael and St. George) in recognition of his services to the condominium. The British Government denied all rumors that Huddleston had been driven from office. The governor-general had remained in the Sudan a year beyond his original appointment, in spite of bad health, the Foreign Office insisted, and had now expressed a desire to seek a less debilitating climate. The Egyptian paper *Akhbar al-Yawm* more accurately suggested that the decoration signified "concealing the body under flowers as is the British custom." Huddleston's successor was Sir Robert Howe, previously one of Bevin's under secretaries and the first "diplomat" to be appointed to the Palace in Khartoum. Although the Foreign Office publicly denied that Huddleston's replacement marked a British effort to placate Egyptian opinion, Bevin himself privately commented that it might lead "to turning over of a new page in treaty negotiations." Despite the official story, Huddleston had in fact been sacked.[1]

With Huddleston out of the way, and despite his pledges not to intervene in internal administration or to change the status of the Sudan without consulting the Sudanese, in March 1947 Bevin moved unilaterally to transform the Sudan administration into a true condominium. On the twenty-fifth, he telegraphed Sir Orme Sargent from the Moscow meeting of the Council of Foreign Ministers, outlining a completely new Sudan policy: "The first step is to attempt to create a better atmosphere over the Sudan question, which may afford an opportunity for the treaty negotiations to be reopened. . . . I desire to emphasize . . . that the Sudan is a condominium and that we are partners with Egypt, and that my view has been that the policy adopted in 1924 . . . and again in 1942, has to be gradually modified. . . . a new atmosphere should be created by administrative measures." The most practical move to show that a "new spirit" had entered Britain's dealings with Egypt, Bevin believed, was to associate Egyptians with the administration of the condominium.[2]

On 29 March the foreign secretary telegraphed Sargent again suggesting the immediate establishment of a joint Anglo-Egyptian-Sudanese Council, which would supervise the preparation of the Sudanese for self-government, act as an arbitration board for Anglo-Egyptian disagreements over the Sudan, and advise the governor-general concerning appointments in the administration. "We shall also be glad," Bevin wrote, "To see Egyptians serving in the Sudan Colonial Service and other branches of the administration on the same footing as the

1. *Akhbar al-Yawm*, 15 March 1947, extract from Arabic Press Summary no. 401, and Bevin to Sargent, no. 71, 14 March 1947, Personal, FO 371/63043, PRO. Huddleston and the Political Service had hoped that he would stay on through the Egyptian appeal to the United Nations, but both Bevin and the Embassy pressed for his departure. Huddleston was also unpopular at no. 10 Downing Street. Bevin personally pressed Attlee to give the governor-general "at least a barony" or a privy councillorship instead of the lesser GCMG, but the prime minister coldly refused— one of the few times he actually stood up to Bevin in such a matter (see correspondence in FO 371/63043, PRO). Huddleston himself believed that the incident of the Chief Egyptian staff officer had been the last straw as far as Bevin was concerned. His own pungent account may be found in a file in the Robertson Papers, SAD, but it is extremely frustrating for the historian. Even after thirty-five years, Robertson determined to preserve his chief's reputation intact for posterity, stipulating that no copies or direct quotations could be made from the file.

2. Bevin to Sargent, Top Secret, no. 353, 25 March 1947, FO 3´ ₃2943, PRO.

British and Sudanese officials. . . . We trust that a greater number of suitable Egyptian candidates than hitherto will be forthcoming." Discrimination against Egyptians in matters of precedence or etiquette would cease "forthwith," and the right of entrée "and other antique survivals" should immediately be abolished. As for the future status of the Sudan, Bevin concluded:

I do not deny and would not deny the unity of Egypt and the Sudan under the Egyptian Crown, and this would surely mean that whatever decision the Sudanese might come to, the Sudan would always continue to have some special relationship with Egypt. His Majesty's Government . . . and the Egyptian Government have a common objective . . . the establishment of a friendly and strong Sudan capable of administering its own internal affairs. . . . His Majesty's Government hope that Egypt will play a larger part in this than . . . hitherto. His Majesty's Government are certainly not opposed to the Sudanese choosing in the end to be bound to Egypt by some special ties and would certainly do all in their power to promote harmonious relations between Egypt and the Sudan.

The new governor-general should "make every effort to ensure that the spirit as well as the letter of the . . . 1936 Treaty in respect of the Sudan [is] henceforth properly observed."[3]

It is difficult in retrospect to escape the conclusion that Bevin's policy toward the Sudan as a means of placating the Egyptians was internally self-contradictory. The foreign secretary continued to insist that he wanted to do nothing that would prejudice the right of the Sudanese to self-determination or that would compromise the process of Sudanization of the condominium administration. Indeed, he insisted that his policy was to increase the pace of Sudanization as far as possible. At the same time he proposed greater Egyptian participation in the administration and an acknowledgment that with Farouk as the joint sovereign, the two countries must always be bound in a special relationship. The contradictions escaped neither the Sudan Political Service nor Bevin's permanent officials.[4]

On 28 March, Sargent expressed the general Foreign Office feeling in his reply to Bevin's instructions. It amounted to an indictment of the foreign secretary's previous policy: "A year ago we had a large fund of goodwill in Egypt, and if this has been now more or less dissipated and replaced by growing hostility . . . this is largely due to the long series of concessions which we have made to Egypt over the last twelve months without exacting any immediate return." The permanent under secretary recited the litany of British compromises:

First of all we agreed to revise the Treaty. We then agreed to complete evacuation. . . . Later on we waived our right to maintain the military facilities we enjoyed under the 1936 Treaty; then we waived our rights to intervene in the event of menace of war, substituting for these rights a mere consultative body. Lastly we admitted the unity of

3. Bevin to Sargent, Secret, no. 448, 29 March 1947, FO 371/62943, PRO.
4. Ibid.

the Nile Valley under a common Crown, and now even the departure of Sir H. Huddleston is being represented as an attempt to placate Egyptian public opinion.

"My conviction," Sargent concluded, "is that this series of concessions, however justifiable at the time, has been interpreted as a sign of the growing weakness of Great Britain, the proof of which is seen daily in Arab eyes in our inability to put down terrorism in Palestine and the humiliations imposed by Jewish gunmen on our soldiers there. . . . We must avoid . . . anything at this stage that will give the impression that His Majesty's Government are still making concessions because they are frightened of Egyptian displeasure or because they are doubtful of . . . their case before United Nations Organisation."[5]

In Khartoum, the Sudan Political Service also worried about the foreign secretary's direction. They rightly interpreted Huddleston's replacement by a career diplomat, known to be one of Bevin's favorites, as a prelude to Bevin's intervention in the internal administration of the condominium in order to "appease" the Egyptians. Robertson himself blamed Bevin's new initiative on the advice of James Bowker, the chargé in the British Embassy in Cairo. Bowker had visited the Sudan in February 1947 to discuss Huddleston's position as well as to get a firsthand view of the situation for Bevin. Although in Khartoum Bowker seemed to accept arguments against increased Egyptian participation, in March Bowker wrote to the Foreign Office, and even to Howe, urging that several "high technical posts" be given immediately to Egyptians. Other Embassy suggestions included creating an Egyptian "Deputy Governor-General."[6] From Khartoum, Robertson complained that these suggestions were "absolutely contrary to the constitution of the Sudan Government." How could it be to the welfare of the Sudanese, he demanded, if Egyptians were to be appointed even, as Bowker himself admitted, "at the expense of good Government"? Robertson noted: "To do this is to surrender the moral justification for us being in the Sudan at all, and to lose the confidence of the Sudanese of whom the great majority believe we are honestly trying to give them a square deal. One of our main assets is the justice and honesty of our administration." Warning of the probable consequences of a policy along the Embassy lines, Robertson concluded, "We might ultimately come up against a new Mahdia." Although Huddleston was leaving, the Political Service had no intention of allowing the Embassy to dictate administrative policy in the Sudan.[7]

---

5. Sargent to Bevin, Top Secret, no. 425, 28 March 1947, FO 371/62943, PRO. Bevin was stung by Sargent's evaluation. "I agree . . . that concessions are useless," he cabled back, "but I do not agree that our policy . . . has been a policy of concessions, and I feel that this suggestion was uncalled for. . . . I do not think we can be accused of a policy of weakness."

6. For Bowker's tour and his personal report to Bevin, see the report and minutes of his interview with the foreign secretary on 17 February 1947, FO 371/62942, PRO. Also Bowker to Howe, 14 March 1947, FO 371/62942, PRO.

7. Robertson to Bowker, Top Secret, 26 March 1947, FO 371/62943, PRO.

With growing uneasiness, throughout March and into April the Sudan Government kept abreast of the new direction in which Bevin's policy appeared to be moving. Writing to Mayall, the Sudan agent in London, Robertson complained that the "snake in the grass" was Bowker, whose continual suggestions for more "appeasement" were increasingly dangerous. Moreover, from Khartoum's perspective it seemed as if the Sudan was losing all its friends in high places. Not only had Huddleston been replaced, but Patrick Scrivener, head of the Egyptian Department and normally sympathetic to the Political Service, retired, leaving in the Foreign Office a temporary vacuum that had little chance of being filled by anyone knowledgeable about the Sudan. As Whitehall seemed to be closing its doors on them, members of the Political Service turned elsewhere for support against the Egyptians. Bypassing the Foreign Office entirely, at the end of March Mayall and Sir Thomas Creed, the Sudan legal secretary who was home on leave, privately approached other members of the British Cabinet to sound out the apparent shift in Bevin's policy.[8]

On 30 March, Creed reported to Robertson the results of a confidential meeting with the colonial secretary, Arthur Creech Jones: "Creech Jones was insistent that the Cabinet decision regarding the future administration of the Sudan stands and that he regards the assurances given by Attlee to H.E. and S.A.R. as binding on H.M.G." If attempts were being made to whittle away these assurances, Creech Jones insisted, they had no Cabinet authority behind them and must be "purely departmental."[9] The moral, Creed wrote, was plain:

Any proposals put forward by the Ambassador, Bowker and the rest of the Cairo people should be regarded with the greatest suspicion, as should those of the Foreign Office. I personally trust none of them to fulfill H.M.G.'s undertakings unless their attention is repeatedly drawn to them. If you sup at the Embassy, I trust that you will sup with a very long spoon indeed. The object of the Ambassador, Bowker and the rest . . . is even now to secure a treaty at all costs.

Beware and again I repeat beware, and particularly of the Ambassador and Bowker. The more charming and conciliatory they appear, the more they are to be distrusted. These are hard words but their ways are not our ways. We are accustomed to put our cards on the table; they are not. . . . if you open the door an inch to the F.O. and the diplomats they will force it wide open unless they are watched continually.

Even Creech Jones seemed to share this view; during their meeting the colonial secretary had insisted on the need to maintain public interest as well as "the utmost wariness."[10]

---

8. Robertson to Mayall, 18 February, 13 March and 23 March 1947, Robertson Papers, SAD, (hereafter cited as RP) 521/6.

9. Creed to Robertson, 30 March 1947, RP 521/7.

10. Ibid. Creed appreciated the implications of this approach to the colonial secretary and begged Robertson to keep it "strictly confidential and personal," in view of "the utmost frankness with which the conversation was conducted on both sides."

In addition to this extraordinary approach to another Cabinet minister, Robertson also took the unprecedented step of conducting a propaganda campaign to challenge Egypt's interpretation of the condominium and Sudanese history in general. On 4 March he created a small committee composed of R. J. Hillard, the director of economics and trade, K.D.D. Henderson, assistant civil secretary, and J. W. Cummins, deputy financial secretary, to prepare "a Sudan Government case, should the Sudan question go to U.N.O." The principal task of the Hillard committee was to answer Egyptian charges that they had been unjustifiably excluded from their share in the condominium administration and that both Sudan Government and British policy aimed at eliminating all Egyptian influence from the Sudan, separating the Southern from the Northern Sudan, and encouraging the Sudanese to be anti-Egyptian in order eventually to create a "nominal independent Sudanese state under British influence." The result was a publication entitled *The Sudan: A Record of Progress*, an apologia for the condominium administration and a classic statement of much of the Political Service myth.[11]

Nor did Robertson confine himself to such blatant propaganda efforts. Again going beyond the normal bounds of his authority as a "civil servant" he worked behind the scenes to prevent a Foreign Office "sellout" of the Sudanese. After Newbold's death he had renewed his own acquaintance with Margery Perham, continuing to send her huge amounts of material on the Sudan, both statistical and classified. The two soon became friends, and Robertson asked for her help in conveying the "truth" of the Sudan situation to the British public, as well as to more "enlightened" elements of the government. Indeed, it was partly through Perham that the Political Service approached Creech Jones, for the two were fast friends and of like mind in questions of African colonial policy. Besides Perham, who wrote numerous articles and letters in *The Economist* and *The Times*, Robertson also canvassed Elizabeth Monroe, Rita Hinden of the Fabian Colonial Bureau, and old Sudan hands now in Parliament, such as Colonel Dodds-Parker and Major M. J. Wheatley. Meanwhile, Mayall inspired Parliamentary questions that frequently put the Foreign Office on the spot.[12]

While Creed, Mayall, and Robertson did their best to maintain support for the Sudan Administration, all three realized that the key to resisting effectively an appeasement policy would be the new governor-general. Although they had all met Howe in his capacity as an assistant under secretary, they knew little or

---

11. Robertson to Hillard, Most Secret, and Robertson to Governors and Department Heads, Most Secret, 4 March 1947, CS/SCR/97.H.1, FO 371/62943, PRO.

12. See especially letter from Robertson asking for help and detailing the reasons for his anxiety about "unfortunate trends of policy which seem to show that the Foreign Office and Cairo Embassy are looking for ways of appeasing the Egyptians at the expense of good government in the Sudan, and of the welfare of the Sudanese"; with copies to Hinden, Perham, Dodds-Parker, Wheatley, Munroe, and Mayall, Secret and Personal, 7 April 1947, RP 521/7.

nothing about his views on the Sudan—if indeed he had any. Still coping with the emotional shock of losing Huddleston, to whom all were personally as well as professionally devoted, the senior officials of the condominium found it difficult to be objective about his successor. Huddleston himself was more far-sighted. Despite the fact that Howe was Bevin's protégé and handpicked nominee for the Palace, Huddleston consistently told his staff that no one could sit in Gordon's chair without becoming completely pro-Sudanese; "Even if anyone comes to curse," he wrote to Robertson, "it is about 100 chances to one that he will, like Balaam, remain to bless."[13]

Although Huddleston proved right in the longrun, Howe's first visit to the Sudan Agency on 3 April 1947, shortly before his departure for the Sudan, sent warning tremors running from Wellington House to Khartoum. In conversation with Mayall, he asked "what . . . would be the local effect in the Sudan if, during his first few weeks as Governor-General, he were to have to make a public statement to the effect that more Egyptians would be joining the Sudan Administration?" Shocked, the Sudan Agent at first prevaricated and then gave his private opinion that such a course would be "tragic" for everyone and "possibly fatal" for Howe himself. The Umma would certainly oppose such a policy, perhaps even violently, and even the Ashiqqa would probably not like it. As for the British, all would dissent from the announcement. Robertson too was "very shocked" at Howe's gambit and hoped fervently that it would not come to pass.[14]

Despite his initial "try-on" of Bevin's policies, Howe in fact became as staunch a defender of the Political Service viewpoint as Huddleston had been. Indeed, Huddleston himself, after his "handing-over" interview with Howe in April, seemed not only satisfied with his successor but genuinely hopeful about the future of the Sudan. Noting that Creed and Mayall displayed a lack of warmth toward Howe, however, Huddleston warned Robertson and the rest of the Service against cold-shouldering their new master. The important thing, Huddleston reminded them, was to "reeducate" Howe along the right lines. If this could be done, Bevin would find it hard to resist the advice of his own man in Khartoum. Howe justified Huddleston's faith in early April when he supported Foreign

---

13. Quoted in Robertson to Mayall, 2 April 1947, RP 521/7. For views of senior members of the Political Service on Huddleston's replacement by Howe, see correspondence between Robertson and Mayall from mid-March to May 1947. Also letters to Robertson in April from Creed, Luce and Huddleston himself, in RP 519/4.

14. Mayall to Robertson, 3 April 1947 and Robertson to Mayall, 15 April 1947, RP 521/7. Howe suffered in the eyes of the Political Service from more than his affiliation with the Foreign Office. The son of a train engineer and the product of a grammar-school education rather than the more exalted public school, he was not a member of that elite level of British society from which the Political Service was wont to draw its membership. Even Lascelles in the Foreign Office thought it a mistake to admit men with Howe's background into the diplomatic service—they simply were not "up to it."

Office opposition to the foreign secretary's proposed administrative concessions to the Egyptians.[15]

With Howe adopting the Political Service position and with the foreign secretary confronted by staunch opposition from his own permanent officials, Bevin's new policy of creating a true condominium in the Sudan soon faltered. When anti-British agitation increased in Egypt in March, by April even the Embassy had become cautious about allowing further Egyptian participation in the condominium. The Cabinet too, as Creech Jones had told Creed and Mayall, proved firm in its resolve to avoid further concessions. As it became clear that Egypt would indeed refer to the United Nations, the attention of the foreign secretary and his office shifted away from a resumption of treaty negotiations and onto the probable line of Egyptian attack, and the formulation of an appropriate defense. By the summer of 1947, Bevin's initiatives had finally played themselves out, and the Sudan question went into abeyance, pending a United Nations decision. Publicly, the Foreign Office decided to stand on its own treaty rights and the Sudanese right to self-determination. On 16 May 1947, in a statement to Parliament drafted by his permanent officials, Bevin declared there would be "no attempt to appease the Egyptian Government at the expense of the Sudanese people."[16]

THE SUDAN QUESTION BEFORE THE UNITED NATIONS

The prospect of Egypt's appeal to the United Nations only heightened differences between Khartoum and the British Foreign Office. While London continued to be primarily interested in Britain's position on the Suez Canal, Robertson and the Sudan Government carried on their efforts to oppose Egyptian claims in the Sudan by creating a viable "independent" Sudanese state that would yet retain its need for the expatriate Political Service. As for the Sudanese themselves, they were, as ever, divided along sectarian lines. Unable to prevent the pro-Egyptian nationalists from going to New York in support of al-Nuqrashi Pasha, the civil secretary encouraged the Independence Front of Sayyid Sir 'Abd al-Rahman al-Mahdi to send a competing delegation. The Sudan Administration too fielded a contingent headed by Mayall and Creed, to represent, as Robertson put it, the "vast majority" of the Sudanese who were still content with the rule of the Sudan Government. What Robertson really wanted, however, was an end

---

15. For Huddleston's mood, see Mayall to Robertson, 10 April 1947, RP 521/7. "He thinks that Bevin has a mania to go down in history as the great treaty-maker. He has accomplished the French treaty, he is some way forward in extending the Russian treaty to fifty years, and he feels a minute matter such as the Egyptian treaty can be taken in his stride. . . . the interests of the Sudanese may, in Bevin's view, appear insignificant and almost incidental." For Howe's resistance to the new direction, see his minute, no date but probably 2 April 1947, in FO 371/62943/J 1533, PRO.

16. Great Britain, *Parliamentary Debates (Commons)*, 16 May 1947.

to the condominium regime and some sort of British or even international trusteeship under which the Political Service might continue to prepare the Sudanese for self-government and eventual self-determination. Such views were anathema to the Foreign Office.[17]

In late April 1947 Robertson sent Mayall a news release outlining Khartoum's position, for dissemination through the Foreign Office publicity organizations. His central thesis was that, in the interests of the Sudanese, the condominium should be abolished and the present Sudan Administration placed under the direct supervision of the United Nations. "The present condominium has never, in fact, functioned as such," the memorandum asserted, and had been practical only so long as Britain controlled Egypt as well as the Sudan. The Egyptians were generally disliked by the Sudanese, nor could they be trusted with the Southern Sudan, which must be safeguarded until it had been brought up to the same level of development as the North. When Mayall passed this on to the Foreign Office, D. W. Lascelles, who had replaced Scrivener as head of the Egyptian Department, reacted strongly.[18]

In a vein of studied bewilderment, Lascelles told Mayall the Foreign Office could not sponsor Khartoum's paper in its present form: "The ethics of the whole Sudanese set-up are a bit puzzling to a newcomer like myself, so I may be entirely wrong in supposing that a government A, the head of which owes his position to appointments by governments B and C, has an obligation of loyalty not to announce to the world its desire to sever all connexion with both at the earliest possible moment." Apart from the question of loyalty, it was hardly incumbent on Britain to publicize with its own funds a policy such as that advocated by Khartoum, and it was "rather eccentric of the latter to expect it to do so!"[19]

Lascelles belittled the Political Service insistence that Sudanese welfare should be the sole future criterion for policy, without regard to the question of treaty rights. Such ideals sounded "very wide and handsome" but could hardly be endorsed by His Majesty's Government, which was itself preparing to stand on its treaty rights in both Egypt and the condominium. Nor was it wise of the Sudan Government, "consisting of British officials who owe their position exclusively to these same treaty rights," to express such ideals without considerable qualifications:

What Khartoum are in effect proposing to say publicly is: "never mind how we got here; we're here now, and doing a good job of work, so let's be internationalized and be confirmed in office by the new international management." This, apart from being

17. For Robertson's attitude toward the Sudanese delegations, see Khartoum to Foreign Office, no. 130, 7 August 1947, and Robertson to Creed, no. 104, 9 August 1947, FO 371/62947.

18. The "Dudley" memorandum was drafted by one of Robertson's assistants. See correspondence in RP 521/8, especially Lascelles to Mayall, 9 May 1947.

19. Ibid.

entirely contrary to His Majesty's Government's attitude, is a very dangerous line intrinsically. If the whole past history, the question of sovereignty and the treaties are to be swept aside so cavalierly, is it really likely that . . . the United Nations, with its numerous anti-British and still more numerous anti-Imperialist elements, would accept the whole proposition *telle quelle*? Think of all the little governments with jobs to find for their friends!

Lascelles found it incomprehensible that British administrators in the Sudan should make such a marked distinction between the best interests of the Sudanese and those of Britain. Surely the two must be virtually coincident?[20]

The Foreign Office especially worried about the question of tactics at the United Nations. Robertson's observation that the condominium had never been more than a fiction might be true, but it was also a damaging admission of one of Egypt's major complaints. "If there never was a genuine condominium, then the 1899 Agreement and the Sudan Protocol of 1936 are meaningless and worthless scraps of paper. In that case what right have the Secretariat to be in Khartoum at all? The British right of conquest—though the conquest was effected with Egyptian money and mainly Egyptian troops, and was expressly to restore the authority of the Khedive of Egypt?" Nor did the head of the Egyptian Department favor Khartoum's contention that the South must be afforded special protection for some time to come. Such arguments now would only give rise to yet further suspicions that Britain intended to separate the North and the South, keeping the latter for herself. ("That might indeed be a very good solution, but it is not at all likely to appeal to the world in general at the present stage.") Variations in the "propaganda lines" of the two governments should be "quite marked," Lascelles insisted, but they should not actually clash; "The aim should be counterpoint, not discord."[21]

Under considerable pressure, Robertson eventually backed away from his publicity memorandum. The Foreign Office had telegraphed directly to Howe, complaining about the divergence of official policy. Even Mayall had been "frankly disturbed by the violence" of Lascelle's reaction. Although Robertson later wrote disingenuously to the flummoxed Sudan agent that it had been simply a "trial balloon," the memorandum had reflected faithfully the prevailing attitude of the Political Service. "What has in fact happened," Robertson commented, "is that we (Sudanese and British) acquired last autumn an attitude of suspicion of H.M.G. which will be very hard to get rid of. All we want really is to be convinced that H.M.G. will put the Sudan's interests first and for H.M.G. to agree that we, as a S.G., have a duty first and foremost to the Sudanese."[22]

---

20. Ibid.

21. Ibid.

22. Mayall to Robertson, Personal, tel. no. 989, 9 May 1947; Robertson to Mayall, 24 May 1947, and enclosure titled "Notes on Lascelles Letter," RP 521/8. Also Sargent to Howe, Secret, no. 122. 8 May 1947, FO 371/62944, PRO.

In a classic statement of the Political Service self-image, late in July Robertson wrote personally to Lascelles, explaining the fundamental difference of outlook between the Sudan Government and the British Foreign Office.

Our position is different from yours, because your loyalties and duties are to H.M.G. while ours are to the Sudanese who pay us and whose servants we are. We think that . . . we should speak for them, and try to interpret what they think to you, and the world, U.N.O. included. The Governor-General, who still has his F.O. outlook (though I think he is growing Sudan minded!) tells me that we are appointed by H.M.G. and Egypt to administer the Sudan, but have no mandate to speak for the Sudanese. Most of us don't quite accept this, as after all H.M.G. and Egypt don't pay us, and don't come into day by day contact with the Sudanese, who are beginning to develop a national sense, and of whom many expect us to be their mouthpiece.

Administrators, like anyone else, Robertson pointed out, had a "pride of trade," and the Political Service could hardly be expected to greet with joy the prospect of all their work "going to hell, and a decently run country being allowed to fall into the chaos which one sees in Egypt."[23]

In his role as spokesman for the Sudanese, Robertson had not given up his views on trusteeship. At the same time, he believed that the Political Service held the delicate balance of power in the Sudan: "The Sudanese who are sensible and think about things know that they can't yet run their country; that if we went and left them alone there would be civil war, and that if the Egyptians came in our place, there would also be civil war." But the Sudanese also distrusted the British Government, which after all had worldwide commitments to look after, particularly since it had already demonstrated its willingness to impose Egyptian sovereignty over the Sudan in exchange for its military base in Egypt. The Sudanese solution, Robertson told Lascelles, was to get rid of the condominium, place the Sudan under a trusteeship with Britain as the administering power, and rely on the Trusteeship Council to guarantee rapid implementation of self-government. This might be idealistic, placing too much faith in the United Nations, Robertson admitted, "but it is not an unreasonable faith (is it?) when all the powers pay lip service to U.N.O. and base their policy upon it, and when since the Atlantic Charter the world has rung with these ideas."[24]

While Robertson and Lascelles argued, on 11 July 1947 the Egyptians finally submitted their case to the United Nations Security Council. The essence of al-Nuqrashi's argument was that the Anglo-Egyptian Treaty of 1936 was now out of date and should therefore be considered void. During the hearings in August, he outlined the entire history of Anglo-Egyptian relations from an Egyptian point of view. The 1936 treaty, he declared, was merely the capstone of Britain's traditional policy of imperial domination on the Nile. "An alliance of this sort is but another form of subordination. It masks a relationship which is both unbalanced and undignified. It ties Egypt to the British economy; it subjects

23. Robertson to Lascelles, 23 July 1947, RP 521/8.
24. Ibid.

Egypt to the vagaries of British diplomacy; and it imprisons Egypt within the orbit of British imperial power." As for the Sudan, the Egyptian premier accused the British of having adopted a policy "designed to sever the Sudan from Egypt; discrediting Egypt and the Egyptians; creating discord between them and the Sudanese, and dissension among the Sudanese themselves; instigating and encouraging artificial separatist movements." Despite a "malevolent propaganda" that had of late "pictured the unity of the Nile Valley as a concept of Egyptian imperialism," al-Nuqrashi reiterated throughout the hearings that the Sudan was a part of Egypt itself. "We shall not forsake the Sudanese," he thundered. "We shall do everything in our power to protect them from a foreign, alien imperialism, from losing their identity in a vast conglomeration of subject peoples."[25]

In spite of al-Nuqrashi's rhetoric, the members of the Security Council were unmoved, perhaps troubled by his appeal to the doctrine that treaties were binding only so long as the circumstances in which they were made continued to prevail, or by his categorical rejection of any consultation with the Sudanese themselves "while they are hampered by the British occupation." Certainly, the British delegation was pressuring members behind the scenes. Arguing before the Security Council, the British representative, Sir Alexander Cadogan, disposed of the first half of the Egyptian brief by pointing out that al-Nuqrashi's argument was generally unacceptable in international law. As for the second half, Cadogan related the course of the Bevin-Sidqi talks, asserting that the agreement initialed by the two statesmen had not been implemented for only one reason: "Egypt was not prepared to accord in the future to the Sudanese people the right of self-determination which it had claimed for Arabs elsewhere." He later reiterated," The Sudan's full right of self-determination is not, apparently, admitted by the Egyptian Government."[26]

While al-Nuqrashi and Cadogan argued their cases before the Security Council, the various Sudan delegations found little opportunity to make their own presence felt. Lascelles and Robertson never did see eye to eye on the question of Political Service loyalties, but the Foreign Office had made its point: Mayall and Creed were under instructions to coordinate with their British counterparts as closely as possible, while maintaining an official air of neutrality and cooperation with both co-domini. At the same time, they also kept in close contact with the Independence Front representatives. As for Isma'il al-Azhari, he and his small National Front contingent were effectively a part of the larger Egyptian entourage. Much to their chagrin, al-Nuqrashi kept them in the background. Consequently, although the Security Council delegates were wary of both Sudanese contingents, the freer presence of the Independence Front must

---

25. United Nations, *Proceedings of the General Assembly*, 11 July 1947.

26. Ibid. Al-Nuqrashi's doctrine, observed the French delegate, was the same one that Hitler had used to tear up every peace treaty he had ever made.

have contrasted sharply with Egypt's claims of having to overwhelming Sudanese support, claims bolstered only by a seemingly tame al-Azhari.[27]

In the end, a Brazilian resolution that Britain and Egypt should return to the negotiating table or should "seek a solution of the dispute by other peaceful means of their choice" generally expressed the outlook of the Security Council as a whole, although it unexpectedly failed to pass by one vote. All subsequent resolutions also failed to obtain a majority, and on 10 September the Security Council adjourned *sine die* without having resolved the issue. The principal Egyptian contentions, however—that the treaty should be declared null and void for "historical" reasons, and that the Sudanese should be considered part of Egypt without consultation as to their wishes—had been clearly rejected by the international community.[28]

From Robertson's viewpoint, the result of the United Nations hearings was reasonably satisfactory. Although the condominium remained intact, so too did the present Sudan Government with its policy of preparing the Sudanese for self-government and self-determination. Moreover, the Political Service's insistence that many Sudanese did not in fact favor union with Egypt seemed to have been accepted by the international body. Nevertheless, the attitude of both the British delegation and the Sudan Government representatives had planted the seeds of serious doubt about the Sudan Government's intentions in the minds of the Umma delegation. The Independence Front had not expected the Political Service, as well as the British Government, to take exception to their demands for a termination of the condominium and the immediate development of self-government. Even more disconcerting, the section dealing with the Southern Sudan in *A Record of Progress* had not only suggested that the region must be considered a special case, requiring "safeguards" against Northern domination, but even left open the question whether it ought not to be detached from the Sudan altogether and included in some "Central African" territory. A chastened and sobered Independence Front delegation returned to Khartoum in September.[29]

---

27. Ibid. Robertson himself drafted the Sudan Government delegation's instructions in Howe's absence: Robertson to Creed, Most Secret and Personal, 7 July 1947, FO 371/62946, PRO. See also Robertson to Speaight [in the Cairo Embassy], CS/SCR/97.h.1/3, 1 April 1947, FO 371/62943, PRO; Khartoum to Cairo, Top Secret, no. 131, 27 May 1947, FO 371/62944, PRO; and Note of conversation between Robertson and Abdullah Bey Khalil, CS/SCR/36.M.8, 28 June 1947, FO 371/62946, PRO.

28. United Nations, *Proceedings*, September 1947. Sir Orme Sargent characterized the conduct of the Anglo-Egyptian dispute at the United Nations as "farcical and inept" (2 September 1947, FO 371/62948, PRO).

29. Sudan Government, *The Sudan: A Record of Progress* (Khartoum, 1947); Record of Meeting with Umma Delegation and Members of British Delegation to the United Nations, 16 August 1947, FO 371/62947, PRO. "The members of the party . . . appeared to be rather shaken," Lascelles wrote, "explaining that they had not realised before that we should regard the making of their claim [for an end to the condominium and immediate independence under the present Sudan Government] as a spoke in our

The inability of the United Nations to make a judgment threw the entire Anglo-Egyptian question back to the co-domini themselves, and condominium politics soon interfered once more with the Sudan Government's internal policies. Despite the breakdown in Anglo-Egyptian treaty negotiations, Robertson had continued with his plans to implement the Sudan Administration Conference recommendations for a Legislative Assembly and an Executive Council. In the aftermath of the Security Council hearings, however, he became increasingly worried about the question of condominium approval before the plans could be implemented. The Foreign Office had made clear Britain's unconditional endorsement of the principle of Sudanese constitutional advance. Privately, they had encouraged the civil secretary to finalize the proposals as quickly as possible for their full propaganda effect at the United Nations. Al-Nuqrashi Pasha and the Egyptian Government too publicly approved the idea of Sudanese self-government but argued that true self-government would be impossible so long as British administrators and British troops remained in the condominium to intimidate the Sudanese.[30]

By the time the Security Council hearings began, the Egyptian position had hardened, and al-Nuqrashi insisted that so long as the British remained in the Sudan the true feelings of the Sudanese could never be properly expressed. Moreover, since the Administration Conference did not include representatives of either the Ashiqqa or Egypt, its deliberations were of little consequence. Such sentiments, coupled with the British attitude at the United Nations, alarmed Robertson's internal "allies," Sayyid 'Abd al-Rahman al-Mahdi and the Independence Front, who now threatened to withdraw their cooperation from the government.

As the debate over constitutional advances seemed to be caught up with the whole question of Anglo-Egyptian relations, the Independence Front became increasingly worried that Britain might yet sell out the Sudanese in exchange for a treaty. During the summer, 'Abd al-Rahman began to complain at the delays in setting up the Legislative Assembly and the Executive Council. In late July he obtained an audience with the new governor-general. 'Abd al-Rahman badgered Howe about the lack of support he was receiving from the Sudan Administration. The government, he insisted, should immediately withdraw support from Sayyid 'Ali al-Mirghani and the Khatmiyya (the real power behind the pro-Egyptian party in the Sudan) and should silence Egyptian attacks on himself, the administration's "only loyal supporter." In addition, the government

---

wheel." For Azhari's disappointment with al-Nuqrashi, see also Fouracres to Robertson, Secret, 26 September 1947, FO 371/62948, PRO.

30. Worried that Egypt might insist that the proposals required prior consent of the co-domini, Robertson suggested the transparent device of promulgating them as an amendment to the existing governor-general's Council Ordinance. Foreign Office legal experts thought it would be hard to defend such unilateral action before any international tribunal (FO 371/62947, PRO).

should provide both political and financial support for the Umma Party. The Mahdist leader even suggested that Howe should consult him privately before making major policy decisions. The independence parties had not worked with the Government to prolong condominium rule, 'Abd al-Rahman warned, but to achieve self-government and self-determination: they would continue to cooperate only if condominium rule was terminated and self-government implemented quickly.[31]

Although neither Khartoum nor the British Foreign Office was much impressed by 'Abd al-Rahman's demands or threats of noncooperation, Robertson too was tired of waiting on the Egyptians. He also worried about Embassy talk of an Egyptian deputy governor-general or Egyptian appointees to the Executive Council. The September adjournment of the Security Council without a settlement gave him an opportunity to reaffirm the Sudan Government's commitment to Sudanese self-government and self-determination. While Howe was away on leave, on 13 September 1947, only three days after presenting the new constitutional proposals to the co-domini, Robertson issued a proclamation on his own authority as acting governor-general:

The deliberations of the Security Council on the Anglo-Egyptian disputes have reached a deadlock. Whether or no . . . negotiations are resumed at an early date, the duty of the Sudan Government and of the Sudanese people is clear.

The Government is determined to press swiftly on with its plans for the new Legislative Assembly and Executive Council following closely the recommendations of the Sudan Administration Conference, to allow no interference with its general policy of Sudanisation and economic development and to ensure the maintenance of public security, law and order by firm action against any who may wish to disturb the peace or to further their aims by unlawful means.

Once again, in an effort to forestall Egyptian demands, Robertson had asserted the independence of the Sudan Government from the co-domini in its obligations to the Sudanese.[32]

---

31. The delay, 'Abd al-Rahman asserted, was "implanting doubt" about the Government's intentions. Record of conversation at the Palace in Khartoum between the Governor-General and Sayyid 'Abd al-Rahman, 26 July 1947, with attached correspondence and Foreign Office minutes, FO 371/62947, PRO. The next day 'Abd al-Rahman suggested to J. S. Owen that the Government should "rig the elections and ensure that a pro-Government majority will be returned," by broadening voter qualifications in the towns and instructing British provincial officials to use their paternalistic authority to let voters know which candidates should be returned. Owen "expressed surprise at this undemocratic suggestion"—and asked for details (Note by Owen, 30 July 1947, FO 371/62947, PRO).

32. Cairo to Foreign Office, no. 869, 13 September 1947, FO 371/63054. See also telegrams and minutes from 30 August to 30 September 1947, FO 371/62948, PRO.

RENEWED ANGLO-EGYPTIAN NEGOTIATIONS:
THE KASHABA-CAMPBELL TALKS

Robertson's unilateral proclamation precipitated another protest from the Egyptian Government against the Sudan Administration's "separatist" policy in the condominium, but it also contributed to a shift in Egyptian strategy. The outcome of the United Nations hearings had shocked the Egyptian Government. They had fully expected to be upheld in their case, both for the abrogation of the 1936 treaty and for their claim of Egyptian and Sudanese unity. It had become clear, however, that the Security Council was especially disturbed by Egypt's refusal to consider the Sudan's right to eventual self-determination. With Robertson's statement seeming to take the moral high ground of defending Sudanese rights, al-Nuqrashi decided to respond to the Sudan Administration Conference recommendations in a more positive vein. In mid-October he wrote to Howe that the proposals had been submitted while he was still in New York, and it would take some time to study them. He did not reject them outright, however, but suggested that Egypt too might make its own amendments and counterproposals. In December, the Egyptian premier followed up with a lengthy memorandum, analyzing the Administration Conference proposals and insisting that they did not go far enough toward true Sudanese self-government.[33]

At the heart of al-Nuqrashi's complaints was the continuing overriding power of the governor-general. In addition, he observed that the Khartoum plans did not envisage either the creation of full Sudanese ministers or even Sudanese parity with British members on the Executive Council. Even worse, there had been no Egyptian participation in the development of the proposals, nor apparently were Egyptians to be included on the Executive Council. Al-Nuqrashi even called into question the representative nature of the scheme, since major Sudanese elements, those favoring unity with Egypt, had not participated in the Administration Conference. And there were other difficulties. The plans did not provide for immediate universal manhood suffrage and direct elections throughout the Sudan. Nor did they specifically guarantee "constitutional freedoms," such as free speech and rights of assembly. The most controversial Egyptian demand, however, was that all legislation approved or rejected by the governor-general should be subject to ratification by the co-domini themselves: it was nothing less than an attack on the condominium structure that had been set out in the 1899 Agreement.[34]

Neither Khartoum nor the Foreign Office believed that al-Nuqrashi's memorandum reflected a genuine Egyptian desire to see self-government in the

---

33. Cairo to Foreign Office, Top Secret, no. 2060, 24 October 1947, FO 371/62948, PRO; al-Nuqrashi to Howe, 11 December 1947, Howe to Sargent, Top Secret, 14 December 1947, and minutes and memoranda on Egypt and the Sudan in FO 371/62949 and 69155, PRO.

34. al-Nuqrashi to Howe, 11 December 1947, Howe to Sargent, Top Secret, 14 December 1947, and minutes and memoranda on Egypt and the Sudan in FO 371/62949 and 69155, PRO.

Sudan; it was simply an effort to "overbid" the British for Sudanese support. But the Egyptian proposals were embarrassing. Transforming the Administration Conference recommendations into draft legislation, in December Robertson made adjustments to meet some of the Egyptian criticisms. Nevertheless, neither Robertson nor Howe would accept Egypt's principal political demands—the wholesale appointment of Egyptians to the Executive Council and the right of the co-domini to approve all Sudan legislation or to act as arbiters of any disagreement between the Legislative Assembly and the Executive Council.[35]

Apart from its effect in the Sudan, the Egyptian memorandum also had ramifications for Anglo-Egyptian treaty negotiations. Much to Khartoum's alarm the Embassy in Cairo suggested that a treaty was still possible if Britain met some of the political demands in the memorandum. Once more it pressed for Egyptian participation in the condominium, particularly in the new constitutional bodies. The Foreign Office too was tired of Khartoum's attitude and Robertson's constant harping about a "new Mahdia." Lascelles minuted in January 1948: "The temper of Sudanese opinion is a real problem for the Sudan Government, but it is sometimes difficult to avoid the impression that the Sudan Govt.—or at any rate certain members of it—have been largely responsible for creating it and are rather proud of it. It is not only the indigenous Sudanese who take the line that their country 'should be left to manage its own affairs' regardless of its status as a condominium and . . . a part of the Middle East as a whole." As Khartoum stubbornly opposed a compromise with Egypt, on 10 January, Bevin and his senior advisors met in London with the governor-general and the ambassador in an effort to resolve their differences and develop a coordinated Sudan policy.[36]

Bevin's principal concern remained Britain's strategic and defense interests. At the same time, he did not want to seem insensitive to "legitimate" Sudanese demands for self-determination. Trying to reconcile these divergent priorities, he now proposed a comprehensive plan that would bring the Sudan into the framework of his schemes for the Middle East as a whole and at the same time defuse the Sudan crisis in Anglo-Egyptian relations. Agreeing that the Legislative Assembly and Executive Council could not be held up indefinitely, he approved Howe's proposal to send the draft legislation to al-Nuqrashi as soon as it was ready, informing the Egyptians that it was being submitted to the Advisory Council for the Northern Sudan for approval before promulgation. Should Egypt refuse to go along, the new constitutional bodies would be set up by the governor-general unilaterally, with full support from Britain. In the

35. Ibid. Al-Nuqrashi's response surprised both the Sudan and the British governments. Robertson admitted it had been "a shrewd piece of work" (C.S. letter no. 1/48, MP 571/4).

36. Minute by Lascelles, 8 January 1948, FO 371/69155. Robertson blamed the enthusiasm of A. E. Chapman-Andrews, Bowker's successor as minister of state in the Cairo Embassy, for the renewed campaign to get a treaty settlement at the Sudan's expense (C.S. letter, no. 1/48, 10 January 1948, MP 571/4).

meantime, however, Campbell would propose to Egypt the creation of a tripartite body, with the Sudan as an equal member, to supervise development of the condominium toward complete self-government. Rapid economic development schemes in the Sudan should also be undertaken on this tripartite basis. Finally, Bevin wanted to include the Sudan as an equal member of the Joint Defence Board, which formed the basis of his plans for a settlement with Egypt.[37]

In February, Campbell opened talks with the Egyptian foreign minister, Kashaba Pasha, on the basis of Bevin's new policy. As a preliminary measure, he suggested to the Egyptians a joint Anglo-Egyptian technical commission, which would examine the constitutional proposals together with the experts of the Sudan Government. Although Robertson agreed to this idea, he was adamant that the commission should be truly "technical" and not "political." When Kashaba Pasha provided a list of probable Egyptian members, the civil secretary complained that they were "fanatical" supporters of unity of the Nile Valley— just the sort of Egyptian politicians he did not want interfering in the Sudan. He need not have worried: on 1 March the Egyptian Cabinet rejected the proposal.

The principal Egyptian demand remained the same—more participation in the condominium administration. Convinced that no agreement would be possible without a concession along these lines, Campbell pressed Khartoum again to accept the appointment of an Egyptian deputy governor-general. Tired of such tactics, and anxious lest action be postponed too long on the constitutional proposals, at the end of February Robertson telegraphed the Foreign Office warning that if there was much further delay, the governor-general would feel obliged to go ahead with the proposals as agreed during the January meeting at the Foreign Office. Once again, however, an alarmed ambassador insisted that nothing be done prematurely to alienate the Egyptians; in early March, Howe returned to London for yet another round with Bevin.[38]

On 12 March and again on the eighteenth, Howe once more fought out the whole question of Egyptian participation in the condominium. Following Robertson's brief, he stood firm against all arguments for appointing Egyptians to the proposed Executive Council simply for being Egyptian: like everyone else in the Sudan Government, they must work their way up through the administrative services. No British members sat on the Council simply by virtue of their nationality, Howe and Robertson insisted, but only in their capacities as

---

37. Record of Meeting in the Foreign Office on 10 January 1948, by Lascelles, with accompanying minutes, FO 371/69155, PRO.

38. For Khartoum's opposition to an Egyptian deputy governor-general, see telegrams and minutes in FO 371/69156, PRO. On Robertson's advice, Howe resisted the deputy governor-general scheme as "unnecessary and dangerous" on the grounds that "native officials would be in supreme authority in the Sudan whenever I left Khartoum and would have direct access to all papers on His Majesty's Government's policy towards Egypt and the Sudan." (Minute by McDermott, 1 March 1948, FO 371/69156, PRO).

senior civil servants. So it must be for the Egyptians. In the end, Howe agreed to name senior Egyptian condominium officials to two of the three Executive Council seats reserved for his discretionary appointments and to include the senior Egyptian Irrigation Department official in all Executive Council meetings dealing with Nile waters—but only in exchange for full Egyptian support of the new constitution. On Robertson's advice, Howe reiterated the dangers of holding up the legislation indefinitely, with or without Cairo's approval.[39]

Despite Khartoum's warnings against undue delay, Campbell's negotiations with Kashaba Pasha continually dangled the prospect of a settlement before Bevin's eyes. Eventually, in early May the Egyptians agreed that a "committee," made up of Kashaba and Campbell himself, should consider the draft Sudan constitution. Three weeks later, the two men agreed on a five-point program along Bevin's lines: establishment of an Anglo-Egyptian-Sudanese committee to supervise Sudanese progress toward self-government; an Anglo-Egyptian committee to supervise elections to the Legislative Assembly; appointment of two Egyptian condominium officials to the Executive Council; inclusion of the senior Egyptian staff officer at all Executive Council Meetings involving defense discussions; and continuance of the present administrative system for three years, subject to renewal.[40]

On 4 June 1948 the Foreign Affairs Committee of the Egyptian Senate rejected the Kashaba-Campbell agreement on the grounds that Egyptian members of the Executive Council should be given full ministerial status and that two places were inadequate considering the preponderance of British members. Privately, Robertson believed the real sticking point had been the inclusion of Sudanese on an equal basis on the committee to supervise self-government. Whatever the reason, as he had predicted all along, nothing short of equal participation in the administration would satisfy the nationalists in Cairo. By the end of May even the Embassy agreed that Khartoum must proceed without Egyptian acquiescence if necessary. On 14 June, the British Government publicly announced that it would no longer "stand in the way of the governor-general doing as he thinks fit" concerning the constitutional reforms. On 19 June 1948, Sir Robert Howe promulgated an ordinance creating the first constitutional government of the modern Sudan and called for elections the following November. For the next several years, Anglo-Egyptian negotiations were effectively dead.[41]

---

39. See Mayall to Robertson, Personal and Secret, 22 March 1947, RP 521/11; Chapman-Andrews to Campbell, Top Secret, no. 381, 15 March 1948, FO 371/69157, PRO; and the Minutes of a Meeting in the Foreign Office, Top Secret, 12 March 1948, FO 371/69193, PRO.

40. For the course of the Kashaba-Campbell talks, see especially Kirk, *The Middle East*, 140-41.

41. Ibid.

6

Cutting the Gordian Knot: From Treaty Abrogation to Revolution in Egypt

> The Sudan administration is coming to run Sudan external affairs, and to feel that it may do so uncontrolled in the promotion, at an enhanced tempo, of the Political Service's programme that has been developing since 1924. . . . If the Sudan administration is allowed to do this, it may very easily run Anglo-Egyptian relations into a crash.
>
> —Sir Ronald Campbell, May 1949

In January 1950, the popular nationalist Wafd Party won a landslide victory in the Egyptian elections. In March, the new Egyptian ministry of Mustafa al-Nahhas Pasha reopened negotiations with the British Foreign Office for revision of the 1936 Anglo-Egyptian treaty. As ever, there were two elements to the negotiations: the question of a military alliance that would satisfy British strategic needs for a general Middle East defense policy while at the same time assuaging Egyptian nationalist demands for "evacuation" of the Suez base; and the Sudan question. Between March and August, the military aspects of the negotiations held center stage. In August, however, as an Umma campaign for self-government reached a crescendo in the Sudanese Legislative Assembly, the Egyptians finally made it known that they would conclude no military alliance that was not also linked to a resolution of the Sudan problem. Not until December 1950, however, were negotiations on the Sudan formally opened.[1]

NEGOTIATING WITH THE WAFD

As had happened four years earlier, the new round of negotiations over the Sudan ended in a complete deadlock. Neither side could now retreat from the positions they had taken in 1946: al-Nahhas Pasha, like Sidqi Pasha before him,

---

1. For the Anglo-Egyptian talks, and especially the significance and outcome of the December negotiations, see Louis, *The British Empire*, part 5, chapter 4.

was bound by the twin slogans "evacuation" and "Unity of the Nile Valley." And thanks to the work of the ever-watchful Sudan Political Service, with its friends in Parliament and press alike in Britain, the British Government too was inescapably tied by its various pledges to Sudanese self-government and eventual self-determination. Al-Nahhas himself set the tone when, in November he declared at the opening of the Egyptian Parliament that the 1936 treaty was "null and void," called for "total and immediate evacuation," and pledged himself to "building the edifice of civilization in the entire Nile Valley" and the "unity of Egypt and the Sudan under the Egyptian Crown." With such rhetoric, there was little chance of agreement. The subsequent decision of the Sudan Government to accept the Umma demand for a debate on self-government in the Sudanese Assembly only further incensed the Egyptian premier—so much so that he threatened to "deny communications" to British troops in the Canal Zone. Although a crisis was momentarily averted, Anglo-Egyptian relations remained as stormy as ever.[2]

There were strong external pressures for Anglo-Egyptian agreement, however. In the spring of 1950 the Korean War had broken out. Confronted by what they believed to be a growing bid for world hegemony on the part of the Soviet Union, not only the British Government but also the Americans were anxious for a settlement that would secure the Middle East militarily. As Whitehall came under increasing pressure from Washington to resolve its differences with Cairo, the Sudan Political Service found itself once more under attack from the British Embassy in Cairo. Even after Bevin's abortive December talks with the Egyptian foreign minister, Salah al-Din, in February 1951 the new ambassador to Egypt, Sir Ralph Stevenson, still believed agreement might be possible, with concessions from Khartoum. At any rate, he insisted, the Egyptians would no longer separate the Sudan problem from the military negotiations.[3]

Over the next several months Robertson revived his successful 1946 tactics, stonewalling all the Embassy proposals that seemed to "appease" the Egyptians at the expense of the Sudan. When Stevenson submitted a draft of points on which the co-domini might agree and included references to "the people inhabiting the Sudan," the civil secretary complained that it seemed "a suspicious periphrasis for 'Sudanese.'" Instead of the ambassador's formula that the Sudanese should choose "the system of relationship with the people of Egypt which will best answer the needs of the inter-dependence of Egypt and the

2. Ibid. See also telegrams, correspondence, memoranda, and minutes in FO 371/80359, especially Khartoum to Foreign Office, no. 195, 17 November 1950, reporting effects of the Egyptian "Speech from the Throne." For al-Nahhas Pasha's threat, see also minute by Bowker, 11 December 1950, FO 371/80360, PRO and especially Cairo to Foreign Office, no. 867, 12 December 1950, FO 371/80359, PRO.

3. Cairo to Foreign Office, no. 867, 12 December 1950, FO 371/80359, PRO. For the American position, see Louis, *The British Empire*, and especially Peter L. Hahn, *The United States, Great Britain, and Egypt, 1945-1956* (Chapel Hill, N.C., 1991).

Sudan," Robertson suggested the Sudanese should "choose freely for themselves their form of Government and their relationship with Egypt." He added: "To involve the use of 'interdependence' would be misleading for both are 'dependent' on the Nile but neither on the other . . . this phrase will immediately recall the [formula] of 'the common crown' which had to be abandoned in 1946 as a result of Sudanese protests." When Stevenson deliberately excluded references to the potential Sudanese choice for independence, the civil secretary reminded both the Embassy and the Foreign Office of Bevin's numerous pledges concerning Sudanese independence. In short, a tedious time was had by all. Eventually, the most Robertson would agree to was the appointment of a joint tripartite commission, "somewhat on the lines of the United Nations Commissions in Libya and Eritrea," which would help the Sudanese toward achieving self-government and self-determination as well as formulating their future constitution.[4]

As Anglo-Egyptian negotiations faltered, in the summer of 1951 the Egyptian Government once again took offense at the civil secretary's internal policies. This time al-Nahhas Pasha complained about the proceedings of the Constitutional Amendment Commission, which the civil secretary had convened in 1949, pursuant to the wishes of the Legislative Assembly and the leading Sudanese parties, to consider further steps toward full Sudanese self-government. When both Robertson and the British ambassador defended the Commission, the Egyptian premier reiterated that Egypt had never recognized the legality or the representative character of the Legislative Assembly. Al-Nahhas had obviously had reports about the nature of the commission's constitutional proposals and was convinced that it was yet a further British effort to make the Sudan's separation from Egypt irrevocable.[5]

Relations with Khartoum deteriorated even further, and the military negotiations with Britain finally reached an impasse in August; by the fall al-Nahhas had decided to follow through on his previous threat. On 8 October 1951, the Egyptian prime minister introduced legislation into the Chamber of Deputies abrogating both the 1936 Anglo-Egyptian treaty and the 1899 Condominium Agreement. The next day further bills were presented outlining a self-governing constitution for the Sudan and proclaiming Farouk "King of Egypt and the Sudan." On the tenth, after passage of the legislation by unanimous vote, al-Nahhas Pasha proclaimed to a cheering Parliament the eternal unity of the Nile Valley under the Egyptian Crown. Although neither the Wafdist prime minister nor the Sudan Political Service officials in Khartoum

---

4. See spate of telegrams with accompanying minutes between Cairo, Khartoum, and the Foreign Office in late January and February 1951, FO 371/90152, PRO.

5. See, for example, Alexandria to Foreign Office, no. 88, 27 July 1951, FO 371/90153, PRO.

realized it, al-Nahhas had taken the first irrevocable step toward both the end of the condominium and the downfall of the Egyptian monarchy.[6]

ABROGATION AND RENEWED ANGLO-EGYPTIAN NEGOTIATIONS

Egypt's abrogation of the Condominium Agreement of 1899 in October 1951 came as something of a surprise to the Sudanese political parties. Although they had anticipated a repudiation of the 1936 treaty, none believed Egypt would also abandon the condominium. The surprise was matched momentarily by "delight," as Governor-General Sir Robert Howe reported to the Foreign Office on 17 October. All the Sudanese except the Ashiqqa categorically denied al-Nahhas Pasha's assertion of Egyptian sovereignty over the Sudan and repudiated in turn the new constitution he had laid down for the country along with his abrogation of the treaties. Instead, both the Independence Front of Sayyid 'Abd al-Rahman al-Mahdi and the Nationalist Front of Sayyid 'Ali al-Mirghani drew closer than they had ever been in denouncing Egyptian pretensions and agreed that the hated condominium had now come to an end. At the same time, both were displeased by the reaction of the British Government, which denied the validity of al-Nahhas's action and declared that the treaties remained in force. For the Umma in particular, Britain's stance seemed almost a betrayal of all its pledges. Moreover, it cast the entire situation further into doubt. Was the Sudan now independent? Or, as Britain insisted, was the condominium still in force?[7]

For anti-Mahdist members of the Constitutional Amendment Commission, led by Ahmad Mahgoub, the prevailing question was an entirely theoretical one: where did sovereignty over the Sudan now reside? Meeting continuously in emergency session in the week following al-Nahhas Pasha's proclamations, the Sudanese members of the commission debated what should be done. Eventually, the six Nationalist Front members resolved to telegraph the secretary general of the United Nations requesting that a United Nations Commission take over the Sudan Administration pending some decision by the Sudanese themselves. On 26 October, Howe reported on the situation to the Foreign Office. Like the Sudanese, the Political Service too believed that Egypt's actions had now finished the condominium.[8]

Howe virtually endorsed the Sudanese plan to approach the United Nations. He disliked the idea of an international commission from the United Nations itself, however, and suggested instead the creation of a trusteeship in the Sudan like that in Tanganyika, with the specific goal of instituting self-government quickly. This would have "many advantages," he believed. "It would leave the

---

6. For al-Nahhas's declaration and the British response, see telegrams and minutes in FO 371/90153, PRO.

7. Khartoum to Foreign Office, no. 131, 17 October 1951, FO 371/90154, PRO.

8. Khartoum to Foreign Office, no. 144, 26 October 1951, FO 371/90154, PRO.

present British-led administration in day-to-day control under His Majesty's Government, the sole state responsible for administering Sudan (now that Egypt has repudiated the condominium). . . . It would be generally acceptable to the Sudanese with the exception of Ashigga and would offer the best guarantee for the South." Above all, he asked London to consider the proposals urgently, before the situation deteriorated in the Sudan. As the Foreign Office prevaricated, rather appalled by the suggestion of United Nations interference, on 29 October the National Front members resigned from the commission and sent their telegram to New York. While they waited in vain for a reply that never came, Howe decided the commission itself was no longer viable and dissolved it. The condominium's status remained unresolved.[9]

In part, the Foreign Office hesitation was unavoidable: on 25 October elections in Britain had resulted in a Conservative victory. Both Winston Churchill, now prime minister, and Anthony Eden, now Foreign Secretary, as well as the whole of their party, had committed themselves during the election campaign in the strongest terms to the principle of Sudanese self-determination. At the same time, however, they were also committed to protecting Britain's position in the Canal Zone. Clearly, acceptance of Egypt's unilateral abrogation by the Conservative Government in London was unthinkable. Although Robertson and the Political Service counted on the Conservatives for better support than they had had from the Labour Government, the practicalities of Britain's strategic position in Egypt remained as dangerous to Khartoum's purposes as ever. Consequently, while both the Sudanese and the Political Service hoped the condominium was dead, London still refused to agree.

Eden agreed with his Foreign Office officials that unilateral abrogation was "contrary to international law"—whatever Egypt might think, the agreements stood. Nor did the Foreign Office favor associating the Sudan with the United Nations. Not only would an approach to the United Nations be inconsistent with its position that the treaties were still in force, but this approach might also have serious repercussions in Britain's other non-self-governing territories like Nigeria, Malta, and Malaya. Not least, as one Foreign Office official noted, a United Nations commission or trusteeship would "tie our hands irrevocably, and make it impossible ever to induce the Sudanese to accept even a 'symbolical' union with Egypt." This in turn would make an eventual Anglo-Egyptian agreement "much more difficult and probably impossible." Having decided once again to retain the condominium structure, on 15 November 1951, the new foreign secretary rose in the House of Commons to repudiate the Egyptian abrogation and to reassure the Sudanese: "His Majesty's Government find it

---

9. Ibid.; see also Khartoum to Foreign Office, 30 October 1951, FO 371/90154, PRO. Abrogation also caused the Political Service considerable anxiety about threats to its security, particularly from Egyptian army units in the condominium. As rumors flew in mid-October that the Egyptian troops were about to attack British units, Howe informed London that he had decided to disarm the Egyptians and ship them back to Cairo. It might have been 1924 all over again.

necessary to reaffirm that they regard the governor-general and the present Sudan Government as fully responsible for continuing the administration of the Sudan. . . . His Majesty's Government are glad to know that a constitution providing for self-government may be completed and in operation by the end of 1952." Once they had attained self-government, Eden concluded, "it will be for the Sudanese people to choose their own future status and relationship with the United Kingdom and with Egypt." From the Sudanese viewpoint, it was too little too late—nor was Egypt deterred from confrontation.[10]

With no satisfaction from the United Nations, with British troops still occupying the Canal Zone, and with the British governor-general still ensconced in the Palace in Khartoum, the Egyptian Government of al-Nahhas Pasha had essentially run into a brick wall. On 26 January, smoke rose above the *suqs* and the garden villas of Cairo as the Egyptian people vented their sense of humiliation and frustration at the hands of the Ingeleez. Shepherd's Hotel, the Turf Club, and all symbols of Britain's imperial dominance over Egypt went up in flames. Frightened by the mob violence, and secretly delighted with the chance to get rid of the Wafdist prime minister whom he hated, King Farouk dismissed al-Nahhas Pasha and returned to a government by Palace appointees— first in the person of 'Ali Mahir Pasha and, six weeks later, Hilali Pasha.

Confronted by widespread destruction of British property, loss of British lives, and a deteriorating situation in Egypt, Sir Winston Churchill called for a show of strength, proposing reinforcement of the Suez Canal Base by a joint Anglo-American force. Instead, the Americans pressed the British to reopen talks as quickly as possible to take advantage of the weakness of the new Egyptian Government and at last obtain a collective Middle East defense agreement. Even more than the chaotic situation in Egypt, the entry of the Americans into the problem of Anglo-Egyptian negotiations presented a direct challenge to the Sudan Political Service.[11]

For Robertson, the Sudan question was a moral one—for the Americans it was purely strategic. With virtually no feel for political implications in the condominium, the American ambassador in Cairo, Jefferson Caffery, convinced the State Department that only one thing stood in the way of Anglo-Egyptian agreement—recognition of Farouk's personal sovereignty over the Sudan. And the only thing standing in the way of British recognition of Farouk's

---

10. Minute by Roger Allen, 2 November 1951, with notation "I agree," by Anthony Eden, FO 371/90154, PRO. For Eden's statement see Great Britain, *Parliamentary Debates (Commons)*, 15 November 1951. The Umma Party subsequently joined the other Sudanese parties in calling for a plebiscite in the Sudan, as proposed by the Egyptians, but the suggestion was never pursued seriously.

11. The most important foreign policy principle in Churchill's government was to maintain Anglo-American unity. In Egypt, as earlier in Palestine, this was not always easy. The British particularly disliked the attitude of Jefferson Caffery, the American ambassador in Cairo, and frequently asked the State Department to instruct him to coordinate with his British colleagues in Egypt.

sovereignty, Caffery believed, was "the obstinacy of Sir James Robertson." For his part, Robertson later wrote in his memoirs that the southern-born American ambassador could never understand why the future of "ten million bloody niggers" was more important to the Political Service than the defense of the Middle East. Whether this disparaging remark was justified or not, one thing was perfectly clear: with the cold war in full swing, for the State Department, strategic questions always took precedence.[12]

The course of negotiations between Britain and Egypt through the winter and spring of 1952 provides a study of international diplomacy at its most tedious. Their effect may be summed up in a single word—futile. Despite American pressure, the British Government never seriously considered acknowledging Farouk's sovereignty over the Sudan before the creation of a Sudanese Parliament that might be consulted on the question. For the purposes of the present argument, however, it is important to point out the continuing role played by the Political Service, and especially Robertson, in stiffening Foreign Office resolve and commitment to the preservation of Sudanese self-determination. Moreover, the U.S. pressure for a settlement was, more than anything else, responsible for the postponement of Robertson's plan to implement a draft constitution based on the proposals of the Constitutional Amendment Commission and to hold elections before the end of 1952. If either intention had been carried out, the history of the modern Sudan would undoubtedly have been very different.

Even before the new year Anthony Eden had signified his willingness to resume negotiations in November 1951 in spite of Egypt's abrogation of the treaties. In December, the British ambassador in Cairo telegraphed the Foreign Office, suggesting that an agreement might yet be reached if they could settle the question of Farouk's "nominal sovereignty" over the Sudan. In January, Robertson picked up the implications from the telegram traffic between the Embassy and the Foreign Office. His subsequent letter to Roger Allen, head of the African Department, opposing any recognition of sovereignty, "nominal" or otherwise, elicited exasperated comment in the Foreign Office. "If the Sudan Government spent as much time and energy in trying to find a way of reconciling Anglo-Egyptian differences as they do finding objections to any suggestion . . . by Cairo," wrote one official, "we might have settled the problem long since." The official added: "Whether out of suspicion or prejudice, or both, the Sudan Government are clearly determined to have no part of King Farouk, and though I say it with hesitation, I do not think that we can count on their loyalty to canvass in the Sudan any proposal involving limited recognition of King Farouk's title which might in the future become part of H.M.G.'s

---

12. FO 371/96896, PRO; Robertson, *Transition*, 150. As Martin Daly has pointed out, Robertson's quote seems to have a suspiciously mixed Anglo-American provenance.

policy." It was an accurate assessment; mutual suspicion, even animosity, continued to mark relations between Whitehall and Khartoum.[13]

Despite Khartoum's objections, goaded by the United States, Eden accepted both the British and the American ambassadors' advice that negotiations could go forward only if Britain resolved the issue of Farouk's sovereignty. In mid-January, after discussions with Dean Acheson, the British foreign secretary telegraphed new proposals to Ambassador Stevenson in Cairo. In exchange for a joint statement looking forward to Sudanese self-government in 1952, pending which the Sudan Administration should continue unhindered, Britain would agree that the Egyptian legislation concerning Farouk's title and even the constitution for the Sudan need not be repealed. After self-government had been attained, the Sudanese would choose their future status by plebiscite, to be overseen by an international commission. In the meantime, Britain would refrain from discouraging other countries' acknowledgment of Farouk's title as king of the Sudan. The underlying principle, Eden wrote, was an agreement to differ on the sovereignty question before Sudanese self-determination: thereafter, the Sudanese would be free "to unite themselves with Egypt . . . or to choose independence, or to apply for membership of the British Commonwealth."[14]

Like Ernest Bevin before him, Anthony Eden now ran into the stone wall of the Sudan Political Service. On 21 January Howe responded to the new suggestions with all the outraged conviction of his Political Service officials. "Whatever may be said," he telegraphed the Foreign Office, "the proposal . . . reduced to simple terms, is that, as the price of settlement of defence problems, His Majesty's Government would agree: (a) to recognise the King of Egypt as King of the Sudan; and (b) to recognise the recently enacted Egyptian constitution for the Sudan." These two undertakings by the British Government, Howe insisted, "cannot be reconciled with solemn pledges given . . . in the House of Commons and elsewhere" that the Sudanese would be consulted about changes in their status and that they would be free to choose their future status. "Sudanese would regard any agreement on lines . . . above as a flagrant breach of His Majesty's Government's word." It might have been Sir Hubert Huddleston berating Ernest Bevin at the time of the Bevin-Sidqi Protocol in 1946.[15]

Over the next several months, all suggestions for an Egyptian approach that included formulas for recognizing or ignoring the title of the Egyptian monarch were stymied by Khartoum. Raising again the specter of violence, like that of 1946, both Robertson and Howe refused to allow any retreat from the British Government's "pledges" to sustain Sudanese independence from Egypt. Eden himself became increasingly exasperated over Khartoum's constant references to

---

13. Robertson to Allen, 6 January 1952, Secret, and accompanying minute by D.V. Bendall, 16 January 1952, FO 371/96902, PRO.

14. Foreign Office to Cairo, no. 130, 19 January 1952, Secret, FO 371/96902, PRO.

15. Khartoum to Foreign Office, no. 18, 21 January 1952, Secret, FO 371/96902, PRO.

his "promise" of Sudanese self-government in the speech to Parliament the previous November. In the margin of one telegram he minuted "a wish I think." Nor did Robertson confine himself to ordinary channels of protest. As before, he reopened his network of Sudan supporters in Britain. The result was a flood of correspondence and Parliamentary questions that both annoyed and impressed the Foreign Office with the strength of opposition to any admission of Egyptian sovereignty—and the determination of the Political Service to organize it. So unnerving did it become that the Foreign Office threatened to "reconsider" its relations with the Sudan Agency in London if Mayall, now a publicity agent for Khartoum, did not stop using his access to "classified information" in the agency to fuel the campaign.[16]

Both British and American efforts to find a solution to the dilemma continued throughout the spring. Formula after formula was tried. The governor-general's title should be changed to that of "viceroy." This would appeal to the Egyptians, Stevenson said, so long as he was the viceroy of the Egyptian king alone—but no, insisted the Sudan officials; to hold the Sudanese, he would have to be viceroy for Queen Elizabeth as well. The Americans even suggested reviving an ancient title that might have less political impact, calling Farouk "Lord of Darfur, Kordofan etc." It was all to no avail. In mid-March, on the verge of yet another approach to Hilali Pasha, in Khartoum Robertson laid a draft constitution for the Sudan before the Legislative Assembly. With full publicity, he announced the new document as the fulfillment of Sudanese aspirations for complete self-government and the prelude to self-determination. As in 1946, the civil secretary had done "something salient" to bring Anglo-Egyptian negotiations back to earth.[17]

As a storm of protest broke from the Cairo Embassy, on 7 April Robertson and Howe telegraphed the Foreign Office, suggesting a new approach to Egypt:

We should start by asking the Egyptians to accept the new draft constitution and urge them to encourage the unity of parties taking part in elections. At the same time we might invite Egyptians to join an Anglo-Sudanese commission to supervise elections and we would undertake to complete elections and set up new government by latter part of July. This government . . . as a result of unity parties participating in the elections, would be fully representative and with the elections supervised by a tripartite commission presumably fairly elected would appoint delegates to attend the Anglo-Egyptian joint negotiations not later than August, in the meantime talks on defence could go ahead.

---

16. See, for example, letters and accompanying minutes in FO 371/96903, PRO, especially note by Bowker concerning his interview with Mayall on 25 February 1952. Eden's disputation of his "pledge" is on several telegrams: see Khartoum to Foreign Office, no. 82, 15 April 1952, FO 371/96854, PRO for an example.

17. The American proposals with British commentary and revisions are in FO 371/96903. For Robertson's tabling of the draft constitution, see also Khartoum to Foreign Office, no. 82, 15 April 1952, FO 371/96854, PRO.

The Embassy response, as Robertson had foreseen, was not sanguine. Stevenson and his advisors agreed that elections should be supervised by a tripartite commission but insisted that the Egyptians would never agree to the draft constitution, particularly chapter 11. At any rate, they insisted, further efforts must be made to obtain Egyptian agreement before the constitution should be promulgated and elections held.[18]

Like the Embassy, the permanent officials of the Foreign Office were also concerned about Khartoum's attitude. In the aftermath of presenting the draft constitution to the Assembly, the Sudan Government had begun to make preparations for introducing a new currency and even a set of postage stamps with the phrase "Self-Government 1952," in commemoration of the presentation of the constitution on 7 April. In short, Robertson seemed to be acting as if self-government and the inauguration of the modern Sudanese state were already an accomplished fact. On the eleventh, Sir William Strang sent a personal letter to Howe tactfully explaining that nothing had yet been decided, that they must take "some account of Egyptian pride," and that presentation of the constitution at such a delicate stage "might have wrecked everything." With a request that Khartoum should keep London better informed about actions likely to affect Anglo-Egyptian relations, Strang invited Howe and his advisors to a roundtable conference with Stevenson at the end of April.[19]

In fact, there was considerable miscommunication between the British officials and those of the Sudan Government. London and the Embassy functioned under the assumption that the condominium was still in effect. The Political Service, apparently, did not. On 12 April Robertson responded to Embassy complaints about the draft constitution in a telegram that well-illustrated Khartoum's different outlook.

Its form and timing are the logical and inevitable consequence of
(a) the destruction of Condominium by Egypt in October last and
(b) the declaration by Her Majesty's Government in November that the Sudan should have full self-government by December 1952.
(a) made a constitution of some kind necessary to fill the political vacuum and (b) imposed speed in its preparation.

---

18. Khartoum to Foreign Office, no. 74, 6 April 1952, FO 371/96854, PRO. Tired of Khartoum's persistent opposition, even as they fought the Sudan Government in Whitehall, Embassy officials apparently decided to take a page out of Robertson's book. The result was a series of articles in various British papers criticizing the Sudan Government for its obstructionist attitude in Anglo-Egyptian relations. On the eighth, a lead article in *The Times*—"officially inspired," according to Mayall—attacked the Political Service and questioned the introduction of the draft constitution at such a critical moment. Indignantly, Robertson mobilized his own correspondents to reply.

19. Minute by Roger Allen, 10 April 1952, and Strang to Howe, 11 April 1952, FO 371/96854, PRO.

A further limiting factor was that the present Legislative Assembly's life was due to end this summer.

Robertson also denied the Embassy's contention that the new constitution would "sever the link between the Sudan and Co-domini." "Egypt herself did that," the civil secretary maintained, "and it was not within the competence of the Sudan Government to put back the link."[20]

The April meeting accomplished little rapprochement between the Political Service and the Embassy staff. The ambassador again raised the issue of the king's title. Robertson and Howe insisted that any recognition of sovereignty for Egypt would be unacceptable to the Sudanese. Eventually, they agreed that the Egyptians should be approached about the question of a joint commission to oversee the elections—which might still be held in the summer between the end of Ramadan and the beginning of the rains. On one point the foreign secretary, Anthony Eden, supported the Sudan officials—he would not break his pledge to the Sudanese by recognizing Farouk's title. Stevenson was sent back to Cairo with instructions to give nothing away. Relations between the Embassy and the Palace remained cool.[21]

Robertson was heartened by the foreign secretary's apparent determination to "stand firm" on the pledges he had made to the Sudanese in November. Returning to Khartoum, the civil secretary pressed forward with a final draft of the constitution, taking into account the recommendations of the Legislative Assembly. Anxious to avoid further delay, he proposed to implement the new constitution by amending the existing ordinance. Under the Legislative Assembly Ordinance, so long as they received no joint instruction from the co-domini to the contrary, after six months the Sudan Government would be free to proceed on its own. By 9 May 1952, the final draft had been sent to the co-domini for comment; now, as Robertson wrote to Perham, all they could do was wait.[22]

Convinced that Britain would give an "all clear" even if the Egyptians refused to cooperate, as they had done in 1947 when the Legislative Assembly was instituted, Robertson decided to allow the natural dissolution of the assembly that summer without extending its life. He expected that fresh elections would certainly take place before the end of the year. "I think that failure to seek the extension of the Assembly's life," he later wrote in his memoirs, "was probably one of the greatest mistakes I made as civil secretary, for it resulted in there being no representative body for about fifteen months." It was not entirely

20. Khartoum to Foreign Office, no. 78, 11 April 1952, FO 371/96854, PRO.

21. There was a series of meetings at the Foreign Office and in Eden's room in the House of Commons from 21 to 26 April 1952. The minutes are in FO 371/96904, PRO. See also Robertson to Perham, 7 May 1952, MP 536/7.

22. Robertson to Perham, 13 May 1952, MP 536/7.

Robertson's fault: he could hardly have anticipated the coup d'état in Egypt toward the end of July.[23]

THE EGYPTIAN REVOLUTION AND AFTER

In July 1952, Judge Muhammad Salih Shingiti, of the Sudan High Court of Appeals, visited the Sudan Agency in Cairo. In the course of discussions with the Sudan agent, C. E. Fouracres, Shingiti observed that the reason King Farouk was so adamant on the question of his title to the Sudan was his fear of revolution in Egypt. If he could just obtain recognition as king of the Sudan, Shingiti pointed out, the monarch himself would be the primary tie binding the two countries together; consequently, no Egyptian Government would threaten its claim to the Sudan by abolishing the monarchy. It was a clever argument and may actually have gone to the heart of Farouk's insistence on the title. Certainly, in the summer of 1952, when revolution did finally come to Egypt in the military coup of the Free Officers' Movement, the deposition of Farouk proved to be the first step in a transformation of Egyptian attitudes toward the condominium. In the meantime, however, the matter of the king's title stymied all efforts at a solution of the Sudan question.[24]

After considerable floundering, eventually the Foreign Office suggested direct consultation between the Egyptian Government and the independent parties in the Sudan. It was an idea not unwelcome to the Sudan Political Service. During the Bevin-Sidqi negotiations it had encouraged both the British and the Egyptian governments to see Sayyid 'Abd al-Rahman and judge his determination for independence for themselves. Although prime minister Attlee had agreed and been duly impressed by the Mahdist leader's intransigence, the Egyptians had refused. Now, with Anglo-Egyptian talks in abeyance, Hilali Pasha decided he had nothing to lose. Where his predecessors had bullied, the Egyptian premier now tried to buy 'Abd al-Rahman, both with money and, if rumor was correct, with the title of "Viceroy of the Sudan." In May, the Egyptian premier invited the Mahdist leader to send emissaries to Cairo to discuss the situation.[25]

'Abd al-Rahman was nervous about the Egyptian approach. He worried that dealings with Cairo at Egypt's request might compromise him in the eyes of the Sudan Government. Consulting Howe and Robertson, the Mahdist leader asked their advice. When Howe reassured him, explaining that both he and the British Foreign Office thought it a good idea to convince the Egyptians that Sudanese nationalist feeling was not just a fiction of the British, 'Abd al-Rahman promised that under no circumstances would he "betray" his benefactors; he would not accept Farouk's title over the Sudan, nor address the Egyptian

23. Robertson, *Transition*, 148.

24. In Alexandria to Foreign Office, no. 1021, 12 July 1952, FO 371/96907, PRO.

25. The telegrams detailing Abd al-Rahman's invitation are in FO 371/96905, PRO.

monarch as his sovereign. Coordinating his activities with Robertson, in mid-May he sent representatives to Hilali Pasha.[26]

While Sayyid 'Abd al-Rahman's visit to Egypt precipitated flurries in the political salons of Omdurman and Khartoum, in Egypt itself the situation was growing ever more precarious. Since the outburst of violence on Black Saturday the previous January, public sentiment had been hardening against both the British and those Egyptian classes who were seen as collaborators. The king in particular was rapidly losing his popularity—what little he had left. Al-Nahhas Pasha's dismissal had alienated the Wafd, and although 'Ali Maher had stabilized the situation temporarily, his replacement by Hilali after so short a time, combined with continuing British occupation of the Canal Zone and the Sudan, resulted in the habitual deadlock in Egyptian politics. Convinced that the Americans would, as one British observer put it, "play the *deus ex-machina*" to get them out of their predicament, the Egyptians refused to budge over the question of Farouk's title. By June the situation had begun to deteriorate quickly.[27]

Robertson watched the situation in Egypt with a certain satisfaction. He had warned the Foreign Office all spring that "appeasement" over the title would only alienate the Sudanese without gaining any long-term advantage in Egypt. "My own belief," he wrote to Perham in April, "is that Egypt will break up into chaos . . . any appeasement will have no effect. They are so corrupt, rotten and impracticable that they are valueless as allies." Anxious as ever to hold the Sudan together and prevent it from being dragged down in the wake of a capsizing Egyptian monarchy, Robertson continued to press for permission to hold elections. "I have great hopes," he told Perham, "that if we could have the elections soon, we might achieve more unity than we have had for years; but time is always pressing on and delays are against us." Despite his efforts, as Egypt did indeed descend into chaos and under increasing pressure from the Americans, the Foreign Office and the Embassy continued to look for some formula that would acknowledge Farouk as king of the Sudan without betraying Eden's "pledges" to the Sudanese—all to no avail.[28]

While 'Abd al-Rahman negotiated with Hilali, in late June Palace intrigues brought about the Egyptian premier's downfall. A Palace lackey, Sirry Pasha, formed a new Cabinet, which soon failed for lack of talent. In the first week of July, Farouk dismissed Sirry, summoning Bahi al-Din Barakat Pasha, only to change his mind within hours and reinstate Sirry. The American Ambassador anticipated a return to power of the Wafd party, but at the end of July another crisis developed—this time between the king and his prime minister. When

26. Khartoum to Foreign Office, nos. 125 and 127, 16 and 17 May 1952, FO 371/96905, PRO; also Khartoum to Foreign Office, no. 136, 23 May 1952, and Record of a Meeting Held at Her Majesty's Embassy, Paris, 26 May 1952, between Eden and Dean Acheson, FO 371/96906, PRO.

27. Minute by R. Parsons, 6 June 1952, FO 371/96896, PRO.

28. Robertson to Perham, 3 April 1952, MP 536/7.

Farouk refused to appoint General Muhammad Neguib as minister of war, Sirry resigned. Hilali Pasha was summoned once more, but it was too late: on the night of 22 July, the Free Officers' Movement took control of Cairo, with General Neguib at their head. Frantically, Farouk telephoned the American Embassy, begging Caffery to intervene and obtain British support for the dynasty. Eden refused to save the monarchy. On the twenty-fifth, Farouk abdicated and sailed into exile.[29]

Egypt was not officially proclaimed a republic until the following summer, but Farouk's fall essentially marked the end of the monarchy. It also threw both Anglo-Egyptian relations and the state of the condominium into uncertainty. 'Abd al-Rahman himself had been on the verge of visiting Cairo personally to meet Sirry Pasha when the military coup took place. Although the Egyptian army did not immediately take direct control of the government, instead reinstating 'Ali Maher Pasha as the new prime minister, on Robertson's advice the Mahdist leader cancelled his trip until it became clear what the change of regime might mean for the Sudan. In the short run, 'Ali Maher himself informed the British ambassador that he preferred not to discuss the Sudan for at least several months. His immediate task was to restore stability and confidence in Egypt and to carry out the reforms demanded by the army. Mindful of Eden's pledge not to hold up the new constitution, despite the revolution Robertson expected to proceed with elections at the latest after 9 November, the expiration date of the statutory six-month waiting period. It soon became apparent, however, that the new Egyptian premier was simply gaining time for Neguib and the army to develop their own approach to the Sudan problem.[30]

The underlying causes of the Egyptian Revolution of 1952 are beyond the scope of this study. The intervention of the army reflected not only a sense of frustration at the inconclusive Anglo-Egyptian negotiations but also a deep-seated disgust with the sterility and corruption of Egyptian domestic politics. One of the first items on the army's agenda, for example, was land reform. For the Sudan, however, the effects of Farouk's abdication and the rise of the army to power in the person of General Neguib were incalculable. Neguib himself was half-Sudanese and was both well known and liked in his mother's country. He had lived in the Sudan while his father served there in the Egyptian army and had attended Gordon College Secondary School with many of the now-prominent Sudanese politicians. On friendly terms with most of them, the general understood the Sudanese leaders and their feelings toward Egyptian domination. Moreover, the removal of Farouk gave Neguib a trump card to play: he could now drop Egypt's claim to sovereignty, thereby breaking the deadlock in Anglo-Egyptian negotiations and in Cairo's relations with the pro-independence Sudanese factions.[31]

---

29. The general course of events in July 1952, including 'Abd al-Rahman's negotiations with the Egyptians, can be found in FO 371/96907 and 96908, PRO.

30. Ibid.

31. Ibid.

For Robertson, Neguib's cutting of the Gordian knot spelled disaster. Fully alive to the dangers of the situation, the civil secretary began pressing London for immediate British approval of the draft constitution so that elections might be held and a Sudanese Government installed as quickly as possible. At the very least, he believed, Whitehall should make a statement reassuring the Sudanese that elections would be held soon and self-government implemented before the end of the year. As ever, the prospect of Anglo-Egyptian agreement negated all his efforts.[32]

Even before the fall of the Egyptian monarch, the Foreign Office had been preparing yet another approach to resolve the Sudan question. The heart of their proposals was the establishment of a tripartite commission, composed of British, Egyptian, and Sudanese representatives, under a "neutral" chairman, to oversee elections for the new Sudanese parliament and afterward to "advise" the governor-general on the exercise of his powers regarding constitutional development and preparation for Sudanese self-determination. In addition, a list of amendments would be suggested for the draft constitution to meet both Egyptian and Sudanese criticisms. Robertson's vehement objections had watered these proposals down to the amendments plus an international commission that would only supervise the elections, without constraining the governor-general's constitutional powers. After considerable debate in August, and despite the fall of 'Ali Maher's government and the assumption of power by Neguib himself, in mid-September Ambassador Stevenson presented the British plans to the Egyptian premier. As Robertson feared, Neguib used the British initiative to stall for time.[33]

Although Stevenson warned Neguib that the foreign secretary must soon give his approval to the Sudan Government to proceed with the new constitution before the 9 November deadline passed, the Egyptian begged that he be given time to study the proposals and respond to them. By the last week of September his real intentions became clear. On the twenty-second, he personally telephoned the leaders of the major Sudanese political parties, including the Socialist Republican Party and Sayyid 'Abd al-Rahman, inviting them to Cairo for consultations. On the twenty-ninth, the chairman of a new "Sudan Sub-Committee" of the Egyptian High Military Committee, Major Salah Salam, met with British Embassy staff members and outlined a revolutionary change in Egyptian policy toward the Sudan: Egypt would no longer insist on unity with the Sudan but would accept the principle of complete self-determination for the Sudanese. So, far from blocking the implementation of self-government, Egypt would now encourage the unity parties in the Sudan to participate in the upcoming elections. At the same time, however, Salam asked Stevenson for a postponement of "one to two months" to enable all the parties to prepare for the elections. On 3 October, Neguib himself informed the ambassador that he would

32. Ibid.

33. Memorandum, "The Sudan: Proposed Approach to the Egyptian Government," with accompanying minutes, 14 August and 9 September 1952, FO 371/96908, PRO.

prefer to wait until after his talks with the Sudanese to make a definitive response to the British proposals. The stage was being carefully set for a complete British *démarche*.[34]

Neguib had cut Egypt free from the demands of the monarchy; now he also displayed more perspicacity toward settling the Sudan problem in Egypt's favor than all previous Egyptian governments combined. In his talks with the Sudanese representatives he agreed in principle that the Sudanese must be able to decide for themselves their future status. Tailoring his discussions to the audience at hand, however, the general also focused on the Sudan Political Service itself as the ultimate stumbling block to an immediate settlement of the Sudan question. Finally in a position to outbid both Britain and the Political Service, the new Egyptian leader made the most of his opportunity. All that he asked from the Sudanese in exchange for his assent to a new constitution was the removal of British influence from key positions in the Sudan before the Sudanese decided their status and their relationship with Egypt. In short, full Sudanization must take place before the Sudanese exercised self-determination; only thus, Neguib argued, could they express their views freely and without the possibility of coercion or "outside" influence.[35]

Neguib did his best to convince the Sudanese that he had broken with the mistakes and ill-faith of his predecessors. Not only did he now offer recognition of the Sudanese right to full self-determination, he also began to undermine the Political Service by pressing for changes in the draft constitution to curtail the powers of the governor-general. According to the Sudan agent in Cairo, the Egyptian strategy was simply to offer each Sudanese delegation whatever it most wanted. As party after party made the pilgrimage to Cairo, the Egyptians racked up more and more agreements. The most important agreement, that of 'Abd al-Rahman and the Umma, Neguib saved for last. In October, after first meeting in London with Anthony Eden, the Mahdist leader finally went to Cairo to hear Neguib's offer personally.[36]

The Egyptian volte-face on the question of Egyptian-Sudanese unity essentially paved the way for a rapprochement between Cairo and the Sudanese Independence Front. Despite all his protestations of friendship and loyalty to the Sudan Government and the British, 'Abd al-Rahman had become increasingly worried that the Political Service, or at least influential members in the provinces, were actively working against him in favor of the Socialist Republican Party, a "centrist" party of tribal shaikhs and nazirs who feared the establishment of a Mahdist monarchy. Moreover, he had never been entirely happy with some specific provisions of the new constitution, particularly the

---

34. Khartoum to Foreign Office, nos. 241, 243, and 252, 22 and 30 September 1952, and Cairo to Foreign Office, nos. 1457 and 1468, 30 September and 3 October 1952, all in FO 371/96909, PRO.

35. Neguib's agreements with Sudanese are in FO 371/96911, PRO.

36. Ibid. A comparative analysis of the various agreements and Egypt's eventual submission to the British Government is in FO 371/96912, PRO.

status of the South and references to the governor-general's "special responsibilities." He also consistently pressed for direct elections in all Northern constituencies, a move he believed would favor his own adherents. On 11 October, 'Abd al-Rahman raised these issues during his meeting with Eden in London. It is clear from the transcripts that although the foreign secretary denied any connection between the British and the Socialist Republican Party, he could not fully convince the Mahdist leader that district commissioners at the local level were not working against him. Nor was 'Abd al-Rahman satisfied with Eden's defense of the need for indirect elections as recommended by the governor-general. Although he promised Eden that he would remain true to the British, by the time he left London the Mahdist leader was ripe for an offer from the Egyptians.[37]

General Neguib was only too happy to accommodate 'Abd al-Rahman. In exchange for the sayyid's signature, Neguib solemnly promised to put an end to Egyptian support for the "unity" parties and to halt all pro-Egyptian propaganda in the Sudan. In addition, he agreed that elections would be held before the end of the year. Furthermore, he suggested that all Northern constituencies should be directly elected and the governor-general's powers restricted through the appointment of a supervisory commission. The new commission would supersede the governor-general in case of emergency, in external affairs, and with regard to Sudanization. Self-determination would be postponed for three to five years to allow complete Sudanization before the Sudanese decided their future status. Worried about continuing delays in setting up the new government, and still half-convinced that the Sudan Government was backing the Socialist Republican Party against him, the Mahdist leader accepted the Egyptian offer.[38]

Sayyid 'Abd al-Rahman's acquiescence provided the capstone to the Egyptian premier's achievement. On 30 October, the Egyptian Government publicly announced that it had at last accomplished what Robertson himself had tried—but failed—to achieve for years, Sudanese unity on a plan for self-government and self-determination. With all Northern Sudanese political parties in agreement, Robertson's "united front" had finally come into being—but against the Political Service rather than in support of it. In effect, 'Abd al-Rahman had signed the death warrant of the Sudan Political Service and brought all Robertson's efforts to perpetuate its influence in an independent Sudanese state to naught. Despite Robertson and Howe's valiant rearguard action, which centered on the lack of representation of or consideration for the views of Southerners and the rural Sudanese, nothing now stood in the way of final Anglo-Egyptian agreement on the future of the Sudan.[39]

---

37. Meeting of the Secretary of State with El Sayed Sir Abdel Rahman El Mahdi on 11 October 1952, FO 371/96910, PRO.

38. Cairo to Foreign Office, nos. 1614 and 1617, 30 and 31 October 1952, FO 371/96911, PRO.

39. Ibid.

7

Resolution

We have always had in our minds here the possibility of a landslide of Sudanese political parties . . . to Egypt, once the Egyptians were permitted to return to the Sudan. The unqualified crowning stupidity of the Egyptian politicians in the past was not to have realised this. It is Neguib's achievement that he has had the wit to realise the cards which Egypt has always held.

Sir Robert Howe, January 1953

On 2 November 1952, the Egyptian Government formally presented the British Ambassador and the Foreign Office with a memorandum outlining its proposals for a resolution of the Sudan question, based on its agreements with the Sudanese parties. The heart of the Egyptian plan was the creation of three commissions to prepare the Sudanese for self-government and self-determination: the Governor-General's Commission, composed of five members—two Sudanese, one British, one Egyptian, and one Pakistani or Indian—which would oversee his exercise of certain key powers; an electoral commission of seven members—three Sudanese, one British, one Egyptian, one Indian or Pakistani, and one American (the Indian or Pakistani to act as chairman)—to oversee the upcoming parliamentary elections; and a Sudanization committee—composed of an Egyptian, a British, and three Sudanese members (assisted by one or more nonvoting members of the Civil Service Commission acting purely as advisors)—to speed up Sudanization of the administration, the police, the Sudan Defence Force, and "any other Government posts that may affect the freedom of the Sudanese at self-determination." Although at the time Howe referred to these Egyptian suggestions as "half baked proposals," in fact they provided the basis for eventual Anglo-Egyptian agreement.[1]

---

1. Note from Egyptian Government to British Government Concerning . . . the Sudan, 2 November 1952, and Khartoum to Foreign Office, no. 290, 4 November 1952, FO 371/96911, PRO.

For the first time in the history of the condominium, Neguib's proposals gave Egypt the initiative in the Sudan. His agreements with the Northern Sudanese placed Robertson and the Political Service in an awkward position. On the one hand, the new Egyptian-Sudanese rapprochement seemed to have answered both Khartoum's and London's avowed desires for a consensual solution to the Sudan question based on Sudanese self-government and eventual self-determination. Yet Neguib's proposals, combined with the demands of the Northern Sudanese politicians, threatened to destroy the very basis on which the Political Service itself had envisioned the development of the independent Sudanese state. Neguib maintained that Northern Sudanese would not countenance any special status for the Southern Sudan in the constitution. Turning the Political Service's own arguments against itself, he insisted that he could not possibly agree to conditions opposed by the Sudanese political parties. He himself refused to budge from the principle that the Political Service must be either Sudanized or replaced by "neutrals" to ensure free and impartial elections. Both problems soon centered on the powers of the governor-general under the new constitution and the extent to which he would be bound to consult and accept the advice of the new Governor-General's Commission.[2]

Robertson was appalled by the new Egyptian proposals. On 7 November, in a tone of desperation, he wrote to Margery Perham enlisting her aid once more to expose Egypt's continuing efforts to dominate the Sudanese and draw them into Cairo's orbit. Transmitting a rough copy of the Egyptian memorandum and his own comments, he asked Perham to use the information "among your acquaintances in high quarters." Although as a civil servant, he could not appear to be concerned, opinion at home should know "what the Egyptian note really means." He wrote, "Neguib has succeeded in holding up our elections and self-government and all our work for two years past is now in the melting pot. It is very disheartening." Dilution of the governor-general's powers, particularly where the Civil Service and the South were concerned, as well as in the case of "an emergency," spelled potential disaster. Neguib's mandatory terms of reference for the new oversight Commission would mean rule by committee, thereby destroying the most fundamental element of any transitional government, a strong executive. Above all, Robertson believed, it meant an opening for the Egyptians to return to their old tricks in the condominium.[3]

Perham responded to Robertson's plea for help by writing a lengthy article along his lines for *The Times* on 17 November. In the meantime, Robertson also mobilized other members of his British "Sudan network." On the

2. See negotiations in FO 371/96912, PRO and especially note of an interview between Robertson and Neguib, 19 November 1952, FO 371/96916, PRO.

3. Robertson to Perham, 7 November 1952, MP 536/7. Robertson blamed Sayyid 'Abd al-Rahman for the *démarche*. "I don't think S.A.R. and his chaps know what they have done as S.A.R. has already told his tribal people that the five man commission is purely advisory. He was carried away by adulation in Cairo, and I hear that he is extremely gratified by his royal reception."

fourteenth, two ex-Political Service members now in Parliament, Mott-Radclyffe and Dodds-Parker, wrote to the Foreign Office warning that the "fundamental basis" of the Egyptian note seemed to be the elimination of British influence in the Sudan. Limitations on the governor-general's powers meant the British were "virtually being requested to abdicate all our rights and trusteeship in advance without any reference to the Sudanese Assembly or Parliament." Demands for Sudanization threatened a "serious weakening of law and order, of the authority of the tribal leaders, and particularly of the administration of the Southern Sudanese." Indeed, the proposals seemed to imply removing Southern safeguards altogether, in which case, "anxious about their position as a backward non-Moslem minority in a Moslem State," Southerners might refuse to enter the new Parliament. Not least, Egypt's electoral plans would inevitably entail a year's delay of elections. Despite a postscript denying any collusion with Perham, whose article appeared before their letter was delivered, it was clear that all had been inspired by the same source: the Sudan civil secretary.[4]

Even as the "Sudan lobby" in London thus carried his views by proxy to the Foreign Office and the British public, Robertson himself was in Cairo, trying once more to hold the Egyptians at bay. On 2 December, he wrote again to Perham, reporting on the state of negotiations with Neguib. During his two weeks in Cairo in mid-November, he had held the line on the major issues. Indeed, he had managed to persuade the Egyptians to agree that the Civil Service at least should remain the sole responsibility of the governor-general. The main points of difference now, he wrote, were the South, the powers of the Governor-General's Commission, and whether the powers of the commission, as well as its appointment, should be referred to the Sudanese Parliament for its decision. Insofar as the commission was concerned, Robertson laconically admitted that the British had conceded most of the powers demanded for it by the Egyptians: "but we are sticking out for real authority in the case of an emergency affecting law and order." Of the three issues, he believed, the South would probably be the most difficult.[5]

THE PROBLEM OF THE SOUTH

The problem of the Southern Sudan, as it was raised by the Political Service in its fight against the Egyptian proposals, was a controversial one. Both at the time and since, Sudanese and other critics of the British have insisted that it was a cynical effort to prevent ultimate Anglo-Egyptian agreement and to retain British influence in the newly emerging Sudanese state. In fact, the documents

4. *The Times*, 17 November 1952, and letter by Mott-Radclyffe and Dodds-Parker, 14 November 1952, FO 371/96913, PRO. Robertson also wrote to Mayall, who apparently spread the word.

5. Letter by Mott-Radclyffe and Dodds-Parker, 14 November 1952, FO 371/96913, PRO. Robertson to Perham, 2 December 1952, MP 536/7.

suggest that the Political Service concern for the South was both sincere and legitimate. In the official mind of the Sudan Political Service, the special status of the Southern Sudan was as old as the condominium itself and largely a function of the African slave trade. Under both the Turco-Egyptian regime and the Mahdiyya, the South had been a primary source of merchandise for Egyptian and Northern Sudanese slave markets. Since one of the pillars of the Political Service justification for being in the Sudan was the suppression of slavery, the South easily fit into the role of benighted orphan, saved by the forces of civilization from the clutches of Arab slavers. Compounding the image were the inescapable, fundamental differences between North and South—geographic, ethnic, and cultural.

Although the Sudan Government over the years had certainly pursued policies that reinforced these differences, the reasons for such policies were considerably less nefarious than either Sudanese or Egyptian nationalists believed. In fact, though bound by the exigencies of imperial strategy to administer the region, the "Orientalist" members of the Political Service in Khartoum, steeped as they were in the cultural milieu of the Middle East, neither understood the African South nor wanted to. Just as the Northern Sudan had been left in the hands of the Political Service by a neglectful British Foreign Office, so for most of the condominium period the South was left by an uninterested Khartoum to the care of the "bog barons," eccentric members of the service who spent the bulk of their careers administering the Nuer, Dinka, Shilluk, Bari, Zande, Toposa, and all the other peoples in the "Zoo," as they habitually called it.[6] Indeed, for many members of the Political Service it was an open question whether the South should not be separated from the North and administered along "African" lines with East Africa or Uganda. Such views stemmed not from any long-term plan to maintain British imperial control, however, but rather from a thoroughly rational and pragmatic recognition of the intrinsic differences between the two regions and their inhabitants, as perceived from Khartoum. Indeed, the sentiment

---

6. The South traditionally began just north of Fashoda, or Kodok as it was renamed after the Marchand incident, and was marked on its northern borders by the Bahr al-Arab, flowing east from French Equatorial Africa into the Bahr al-Ghazal and the White Nile, and the Baro River, which rises in the Ethiopian highlands, running west past Gambeila to join the White Nile at Malakal. The sudd begins just south of Malakal. For administrative purposes the South was divided into three provinces: Mongalla to the southeast, bordering Ethiopia, Kenya, and Uganda; Bahr al-Ghazal to the southwest, bordering Uganda and French Equatorial Africa; and Upper Nile in the northeast, bordering Ethiopia. The bog barons were generally holdovers from the days of military rule. Ex-army officers, they were usually recruited on a nonpensionable contract basis and remained their entire careers in the South. Crusty and eccentric to a degree, they formed a unique branch of the Political Service. In later sections I have deliberately misapplied the term to regular members of the Political Service whose length of tenure and outlook on the South seem to qualify them for the group. For examples, see especially K.D.D. Henderson, *Set under Authority* (Somerset, 1987), chapter 6, and Collins, *Shadows*, chapters 1, 4, and 9.

for division was almost entirely to be found within the Political Service, especially among the Southern administrators—not in the British Government at all.[7]

Whatever the historical reasons for administrative differences between North and South, however, by 1945 the realities of Anglo-Egyptian politics made any further moves toward separation moot. Despite speculation in the Political Service, in fact the Sudan Government never had the authority to accomplish a separation between North and South. In the spring of 1946, the question was finally settled by the Administration Conference on Closer Association of Sudanese with the Government. When the Sudanese members of the Administration Conference asked whether they were to consider the whole Sudan in their deliberations, including the South, the chief justice of the Sudan, C.C.G. Cumings, pointed out that legally there was no difference between North and South: the conference's terms of reference must therefore cover the whole Sudan.[8]

Robertson himself soon became firmly committed to the concept of a unified state encompassing both North and South. "The South is certainly at present economically connected with the Northern Sudan more closely than with Uganda or the Belgian Congo," he wrote to the governors in July 1946, "and from the natural configuration of the country presumably this will always be the case." The next December he went further, warning the governors, "We should . . .

---

7. Scholarly speculation on the administrative separation of North and South has varied considerably: from arguments that the South was a "sop" to Christian missionary societies, whom Wingate and Cromer wanted to keep out of the Northern Sudan where their presence would inflame "fanatical" Muslim sentiments, to more carefully documented, but still nebulous, allegations of a British conspiracy to separate the regions in the time-honored tradition of *"divide et impera."* In fact, so contradictory is the evidence of underlying motivation that even the Political Service itself seems to have had no firmly held convictions in the matter. For the arguments concerning Christian missionaries see Norman Daniel, *Islam, Europe, and Empire* (Edinburgh, 1966), part 3. For alternate views of Northern and Southern Sudanese historians, see also Mohammed Omer Beshir, *The Southern Sudan: Background to Conflict* (New York 1968), and Dunstan M. Wai, *The African-Arab Conflict in the Sudan* (New York and London, 1981). For the most recent scholarly account of the South, see especially Collins, *Shadows.*

8. Two weeks later, Robertson wrote categorically: "I have been asked by many people recently whether the Governor-General's statement at the opening of the Advisory Council refers to the Southern provinces of the Sudan as well as to the North. The answer is yes: the Sudan Government is not empowered to divide the South from the North, and economically and in other ways the South is very closely tied to the North." Despite the seemingly inevitable logic of including the Southern Sudan in any constitutional proposals, debate over the future of the area continued within the Political Service over the next year (CS/SCR/97.H.1., Civil Secretary to All Governors and Heads of Departments, 23 April 1946, Secret and Personal. Urgent, FO 371/53252, PRO; Proceedings of the Sudan Administration Conference, 24-25 April 1946, FO 371/63052; C.S. letter, 11 May 1946, MP571/2).

work on the assumption that the Sudan as at present constituted with possibly minor boundary adjustments, will remain one."

The policy of the Sudan Government regarding the Southern Sudan is to act upon the facts that the people of the Southern Sudan are distinctively African and negroid but that geography and economics combine (so far as can be seen at the present time) to render them inextricably bound for further development to the Middle-Eastern and Arabicised Northern Sudan; and therefore to insure that they shall by educational and economic development be equipped to stand up for themselves in the future as socially and economically the equals of their partners of the Northern Sudan in the Sudan of the future.

Although he sought the governors' advice, Robertson ominously included a warning: "*Urgency is the essence of the problem. We no longer have time to aim at the ideal; we must aim at doing what is the best for the Southern peoples in the present circumstances.*"[9]

Robertson worried about the reaction of the Southern administrators to his new policy, and not without reason. Just as he and the northern Political Service opposed Egyptian domination of the North, so the southern branch of the Service worried about Northern Sudanese domination of the South. Although the Southern governors eventually accepted that the two regions must remain united, they became concerned about the kind of relationship that would develop between the "unsophisticated" and "simple" Southerners and the more highly "developed" Northerners.

B. V. Marwood, governor of Equatoria, perhaps best expressed the attitude of the barons in a letter sent to his district commissioners announcing Robertson's new plans. "I believe he is right," Marwood wrote. "I do not regard the excision of the Southern Sudan and its attachment to neighbours on the South as practical politics nor in the best interests of the people themselves, for they would be 'Cinderellas' even more than they are now." On the other hand, Marwood also did not expect an immediate reunion of North and South: "The line I propose to take is to accept in the main the Civil Secretary's contentions but to press for safeguards and a period of 'trusteeship' till the South is vocal and knows its own mind." Still functioning in the full flush of paternalism, the bog barons wanted assurances that their charges would get a fair deal in the new Sudan: "safeguards" and "federation" between North and South became the twin themes of their reaction to Robertson's policy shift.[10]

---

9. Proceedings of the Sudan Administration Conference, 24-25 April 1946, FO 371/63052; C.S. letter, 11 May 1946, MP571/2.

10. Marwood to District Commissioners, 23 December 1946, Secret, reproduced in Beshir, *The Southern Sudan*, Appendix 3, 122-23. For the reactions of J.H.T. Wilson (District Commissioner, Jur River), T.R.H. Owen (deputy governor Equatoria, Bahr al-Ghazal sub-province), and E. H. Nightingale (District Commissioner, Rumbek), see Appendices 4 through 7 respectively.

As the Northern Sudan moved ever closer to self-government and self-determination, however, the Southern governors and district commissioners grew increasingly unhappy with the rapid pace of political developments in the condominium. Educated Southerners too began to worry that they might be forgotten or left behind in the North's rush for self-government. Moreover, as Robertson himself once observed, the behavior of the Northern Sudanese politicians toward Southerners increasingly bordered on folly. As the Northern political parties reached agreement with General Neguib, and as the prospect of self-government and even self-determination became more and more a foregone conclusion in the summer of 1952, both Southern administrators and educated Sudanese began to experience almost a sense of panic. Although at the time and later, Northern Sudanese nationalists accused the Sudan Political Service of using the Southern problem as a justification for continued "imperialism," the documentary record suggests that both Robertson and the governor-general were sincere in their fears for the stability of the Sudanese state if safeguards for the South were not included in the new constitution and, moreover, that their fears were far from groundless.

With the publication of the Egyptian proposals and the reports on Egypt's agreements with the Northern political parties, the civil secretary came under enormous pressure from the Southern Sudanese and their British administrators. There had been a "wave of alarmed protest from the Southerners," he wrote to Perham.

They have been sending petitions and telegrams to H.E. and me, and writing letters to the papers. We have suggested that the Northern political parties send down representatives to Juba, Wau and Malakal, and have asked that the Egyptian Government too might send one of their young officers. This should either result in their realising the strength of the Southern feelings, or the Southerners being persuaded that there is no harm intended. If it doesn't work, then I foresee an impasse, as the action of the politicians and the Egyptians has raised all these fears and suspicions in the hearts of the Southerners, which I had hoped we had partially allayed.

Despite all his warnings to both independents and Khatmiyya over the past several years, Robertson could only lament that Northern politicians seemed determined to alienate the South entirely.[11]

---

11. See for example, Robertson to Bishop A. M. Gelsthorpe, 22 March 1948, in Beshir, *The Southern Sudan*, in which he summarizes his policy: "We do not know how long the British will be able to administer the Sudan and keep out the Egyptians, and continue to influence the Northern Sudanese. The longer we can remain the better for the Sudan and the Southern Sudan. If we can therefore get the Northern Sudanese to co-operate with us, the better for the Southerner. . . . if therefore by administering the Sudan as one country and breaking down the barriers between North and South, we can maintain our influence, it is for the benefit of the South."

The civil secretary worried not only about the Southern Sudanese but also about the loyalty of his Southern district commissioners. He tried to use the pressure they were exerting as leverage in his struggle to retain the governor-general's powers for the South. In December he received a worried appraisal of the situation from T.R.H. Owen, governor of Bahr al-Ghazal Province. Southern reactions, Owen warned, "are only the beginning of a resentment toward any coercion into an un-safeguarded union with the North, a resentment which will grow in intensity and weight. It has been potential rather than actual hitherto simply because the masses are too hopelessly uncomprehending and have such a blind faith in us." Northerners had displayed "callousness and bad faith" toward their "junior partners" in the South. Now Southern district commissioners were being asked to encourage the South to continue cooperating with the Northerners. But how could Southerners willingly go into partnership with Northern politicians in the face of their agreements with Egypt? "How can we ourselves retain faith in the good sense and good conscience of the North?" Owen wanted to know: "Granted the full safeguards . . . we can continue to advise them so and I think we can prevail on them. If British care for them is not guaranteed, no district commissioner with any conscience can advise them to walk straight to the scaffold."[12]

Owen had raised the issues involved to the level of principle—even prophecy about the future civil war. In Khartoum, however, the civil secretary had to deal on a daily basis with the Northern Sudanese, who were considerably more organized and articulate than their Southern counterparts. In the struggle to retain the governor-general's position, Robertson had always been able to count on at least a few of the Northern Sudanese parties, notably the Socialist Republican Party of the tribal shaykhs and nazirs, the "countrymen" as he called them. In the face of continuing delays, however, which the Egyptians attributed to a Political Service desire to maintain Southern safeguards only to ensure its own continued control, the Northern Sudanese, including the Socialist Republicans, finally lost patience. Despite all his efforts to retain Southern safeguards, in January 1953 Robertson at last had his legs cut out from under him.

THE ANGLO-EGYPTIAN AGREEMENT OF 1953

Early in the New Year, tired of Robertson's continuing obstinacy, Neguib once again went over Khartoum's head, appealing directly to the Northern parties for agreement on the sticking points in Anglo-Egyptian negotiations. The most he would concede was that the governor-general should refer directly to the co-domini in case of his disapproval of legislation affecting the South; and only unanimous support from the co-domini would sustain his veto. In addition, Neguib reiterated that complete Sudanization must precede self-determination,

---

12. Owen to Robertson, 7 December 1952, with covering letter from Robertson to Allen, 14 December 1952, FO 371/96917, PRO.

which would occur three years after the institution of self-government. Elections should be direct wherever possible, but such determinations would be left up to the Electoral Commission. Finally, all British and Egyptian troops should be withdrawn before the election of a Constituent Assembly, which would finally establish the form of Sudanese self-determination. Crucially, he also agreed that nazirs and shaykhs would not have to stand down from their local positions in order to run for election to the new Parliament.[13]

On 11 January 1953, the Northern Sudanese political parties agreed in writing to Neguib's terms. This time, under enormous pressure from their colleagues, and with Neguib's agreement that they need not give up their local political roles in order to participate in the central government, even the Socialist Republican Party agreed to forego Southern safeguards and the governor-general's independent powers. Signing with the rest, they pledged themselves to "boycott any elections held under another constitution." For the Political Service, this second Egyptian-Sudanese agreement meant disaster. "What then do we do?" Robertson wrote despairingly, "There seems little point of struggling if all the political parties are with Egypt." Even Anthony Eden was displeased by the circumstances of Egyptian-Sudanese agreement—on Howe's telegram reporting the announcement he wrote in a hand less steady than usual, "could not be more humiliating."[14]

Robertson at least had some warning of the turn of events. For the rest of the Political Service, the new Egyptian-Sudanese agreement came as a shock. C. G. Davies, Sudan agent in London, perhaps best expressed the feeling of bewilderment in the Political Service. "I am quite at a loss to understand this move," he wrote on 22 January.

I think the only reasonable supposition is that our still rather immature Sudanese politicians have reached the limits of frustration and exasperation at the continuance of Anglo-Egyptian talks and the delay of the promised elections, and in the unhappy absence of any parliament or legislative assembly they are like ships without ballast, unable to hold a course against any strong wind. . . .

We look as though we have failed to hold the confidence of the Sudanese politicians or have been outbid by the Egyptians. The only hope that I can see still lies in getting a Sudanese parliament together somehow. It is just possible that this too is the wish of our Sudanese friends—but they go rather a tortuous way round to get it.

Bewildered or not, for the Political Service it was the end.[15]

On 8 February 1953, Robertson broke the news of impending Anglo-Egyptian agreement to the Sudan Political Service. Although the British Government had not yet responded to the new situation, he had little doubt now about the outcome: "Broadly speaking HMG find themselves in an unenviable position:

---

13. Khartoum to Foreign Office, no. 26, 11 January 1953, FO 371/102737, PRO.
14. Ibid. Also Robertson, *Transition*, 151.
15. Davies to Perham, 22 January 1953, MP 536/1.

failure to reach agreement with Egypt over the Sudan will almost inevitably lead to a revival of the attacks on British interests in Egypt, to guerilla warfare on the Canal, and perhaps to a British reoccupation of the Delta and the Egyptian cities. This could not be done without much bloodshed and loss of life." Acceptance of Egypt's plans would mean "a severe blow to British prestige throughout the Middle East, and a feeling of despair amongst British officials and loyal Sudanese here. The Southern Sudanese will feel they have been let down—and the tribal chiefs, loyal Sudanese officials, and the vast majority of Northern Sudanese will be resentful of a too early British withdrawal and at being left to the tender mercies of scheming politicians." He added: "American pressure on HMG is very heavy, however, and my own belief is that HMG will find it very difficult not to bow to the force of events. Possible civil war in the Sudan in the unknown future and administrative chaos in a few years' time are not likely to weigh so much as the apparent certainty of serious disorders and war conditions in the Canal Zone in a week or two's time." Howe agreed. Like Robertson, the governor-general saw little point in struggling. Neguib had "cut the ground from under our feet."[16]

If he went on with the draft constitution, Howe pointed out, he would have to elect a Parliament and form a government from among the tribal leaders and Southerners—and with the religious leaders supporting Egypt's proposals it was doubtful whether he could even count on the tribal leaders. In any case, neither group could produce enough trained men to handle the machinery of government. There was really only one alternative:

It is clear that until there is a Sudanese Parliament properly elected and established it may be impossible for the tribal leaders and the Southerners to make their opinion heard and I believe our best tactics now will be to accept the most reasonable terms which we can get from the Egyptians and bring the Parliament into being. Until then the situation offers limitless opportunities for trouble-making and misunderstandings, possibly leading to serious disturbances.

As a safeguard, the British Government should "stand fast" on the principle that the Sudanese Parliament itself would be able to discuss the projected Anglo-Egyptian agreement and make recommendations for either maintaining or amending it. Even then, there remained the problem of the South.[17]

The Southern problem proved to be the last major battle the Sudan Government fought in its efforts to salvage something from the aftermath of the Egyptian-Sudanese accord. On 9 January, Robertson wrote to Margery Perham that the South was one of the few issues on which both he and Howe were prepared to resign. Neither man had any illusions about the meaning, for the

---

16. C.S. letter no. 2/53, 8 February 1953, RP 525/15; Khartoum to Foreign Office, no. 28, 12 January 1953, FO 371/102737, PRO.

17. Ibid; also Khartoum to Foreign Office, no. 27, 12 January, FO 371/102737, PRO.

Southern Sudanese, of the rapprochement between Northern politicians and Egyptians. Nor did they underestimate the potential consequences. "The South have been contemptuously overridden," Howe complained to London, and there seemed little chance of preserving the governor-general's special powers over the region, as demanded by the Southerners themselves. Even worse, Northern politicians themselves seemed bent on alienating the South.[18]

For Robertson, the Southern problem now raised the specter of civil war and eventual dismemberment of the Sudan. As he noted with exasperation, the Southern issue was not one on which Northern Sudanese were entirely reasonable—even a "sensible man" like Mekki Abbas became "fanatical" when discussing it. Ironically, this Northern susceptibility was undermining the very unity of the Sudan that the civil secretary and governor-general were trying to maintain. "The attitude of the northern Sudanese at the moment," Robertson told Perham, "is intolerant, foolish, and calculated to antagonize the South more than ever." The Northern press too was neither tolerant, "nor . . . even truthful." Nevertheless, Robertson still hoped to effect a consensus. "My idea," he wrote Perham, "was that during the transitional period of self-government prior to self-determination the North and South should work out some formula to satisfy both sides . . . a federated South on the Ulster model might be the sort of thing. But this should be done by them themselves and not by us, as we would be accused of separating the two parts of the Sudan."[19]

Robertson soon decided that only by bringing North and South "face to face" could a real solution be found; the best way to do this was to get a Sudanese parliament elected as quickly as possible—that would include both sides. Howe agreed. "It may be that the real guarantee for the South rests in quite considerable strength allotted to them in the new parliament, if they can learn to utilize it. . . . Perhaps the best course is to agree with Neguib as quickly as possible and to rely on the Sudanese Parliament to show more common sense than the present political leaders have done." The difficulty was to prevent the South from boycotting the elections. British staff in the South could not be counted on to "use their influence" to get Southern cooperation, "for they will undoubtedly feel that the Southerners are being let down, and our promises to them being forgotten." On 13 January, Howe brought the three Southern governors to Khartoum for consultations.[20]

The governor-general's anticipation of the Southern staff's disapproval was wholly justified. At their meeting the Southern governors remained adamant: the great majority of Southerners would boycott any election held under a statute that deprived the governor-general of his special powers for the South and that removed British administrators from the South within three years. Failure to take

18. Robertson to Perham, 9 January 1953, MP 536/7; Khartoum to Foreign Office, no. 28, 12 January 1953, FO 371/102737, PRO.

19. Robertson to Perham, 9 January 1953, MP 536/7.

20. Robertson to Perham, 22 January 1953, MP 536/7; Khartoum to Foreign Office, no. 28, 12 January 1953, FO 371/102737, PRO.

these fears seriously would lead to a "deterioration in public security . . . as the southerners would consider that the British officials had let them down." Such a deterioration would probably manifest in a refusal to obey the government's orders, "and probable attack on the Northern Sudanese." Moreover, there would be "widespread resignation" of British officials if they were ordered to carry out such a policy. When Howe appealed to them directly, explaining that there must be some sort of compromise if they were to avoid "serious trouble" in the North, the governors "did not think that this contingency could weigh against their conscientious objection to any 'betrayal' of the South." At the very least, they insisted, the South should be allowed to express its views at a representative conference.[21]

While Robertson pursued the idea of a Southern conference, the Foreign Office decided to adopt Howe's proposed strategy to obtain agreement with Neguib as quickly as possible. "If we can secure Egyptian acceptance," Eden cabled Howe, "we should be well advised to clinch the matter." They would simply have to hope that a Southern boycott could be avoided. After further negotiations, in early February Britain finally accepted the Egyptian position that the governor-general could exercise his powers for the South only with the concurrence of his new oversight commission. This, Neguib insisted, in addition to the Southern share of a quarter of the seats in the new Parliament and two Cabinet posts, would suffice to protect Southern interests. Even the civil secretary admitted that no more could be done. As Britain and Egypt finally reached agreement, Southerners were simply not given time to react.[22]

On 14 February, Britain and Egypt formally signed the Anglo-Egyptian Agreement of 1953. The Sudan Government was to be completely Sudanized within three years. The draft constitution was to be revised to provide not only for Sudanese self-government along lines laid down by Robertson the previous spring, but also for a Governor-General's Commission, an Electoral Commission, and a new Sudanization commission, which would oversee elections and prepare the Sudanese for eventual self-determination in a "neutral" atmosphere. There was to be no mention of a special status for the South in the Constitution, but the governor-general would have a special responsibility to "ensure fair treatment to all the various provinces of the Sudan," subject to the agreement of his Commission. It was all Robertson could salvage. The Political Service sun had set, and a timetable for Sudanese independence had finally been given. No longer would the Sudan Political Service stand in the way of full Anglo-Egyptian agreement. If there was weeping and gnashing of teeth in

21. Khartoum to Foreign Office, no. 33, 14 January 1953, Emergency Secret, FO 371/102737, PRO.

22. Foreign Office to Khartoum, no. 52, 15 January 1953, Immediate Secret, FO 371/102737, PRO. Also Robertson to Perham, 22 January 1953, MP 536/7.

Khartoum, in London and Cairo permanent officials and Embassy staff must have rejoiced: the Sudan question had finally been resolved.[23]

ANGLO-EGYPTIAN RELATIONS AND DECOLONIZATION IN THE SUDAN

The signing of the Anglo-Egyptian Agreement on the Sudan in February 1953 marked a seachange in the course of Anglo-Egyptian relations, but it did not eliminate altogether the potentially disruptive role the Sudan might play in those relations. Indeed, if it presaged the end of the Political Service's influence, it also intensified the direct involvement of the British Government in the struggle to prevent a complete capitulation to the Egyptians in the condominium and to maintain British influence in the newly emerging Sudanese state. From 1953 until the declaration of Sudanese independence in January 1956, the history of the condominium provides an almost classic example of Britain's effort to maintain its prestige and influence even as it formally abandoned the trappings of empire. At the same time, however, a vestigial Political Service legacy remained to irritate both Egypt and, especially, the British Government.

In the wake of the agreement, Sir James Robertson decided to retire from his post because he believed that his office had now become redundant. With a Sudanese prime minister and a responsible Sudanese Government, Robertson would have been an embarrassment, particularly in the internal administration of the country. On the other hand, he had become indispensable to the governor-general, Sir Robert Howe, as an advisor on politics, both internally and vis-a-vis the co-domini. Although in March 1953 it was already clear that elections would be postponed and that self-government would therefore not be implemented before the end of the year, Robertson decided to divide the civil secretary's office into the functions of the anticipated Ministries of the Interior and of Foreign and Political Affairs, "so that the later transition will be as smooth as possible." The general functions of the internal administration were effectively put on "hold" for the time being. The "external and political side" of his work was taken over for Howe by W.H.T. Luce as "Advisor to the Governor-General."[24]

Luce was, as he described himself, by nature "an optimist." Like Robertson, he too saw the primary task of the administration, and especially the Political Service in its closing stages, to be the prevention of Egyptian hegemony and the rapid creation of an independent Sudanese state. "I think the only policy to follow now," Luce wrote to Margery Perham in January 1953, "is to try to get

23. The agreement is in Great Britain, *Parliamentary Papers*, Cmd. 8904 (1953). See also Cmd. 8766 (1953) and Cmd. 8767 (1953).

24. Robertson, Transition, 152; Robertson to Perham, 20 April 1953, MP 536/7; Letter from W.H.T. Luce (WHTL) to the Political Service (replacing Robertson's monthly C.S. letters), 17 April and 5 May 1953, Top Secret and Personal, MP 589/8. See also Robertson to Perham, 16 February 1953, MP 536/7.

the Sudanese to vote without too many parties boycotting the elections and without letting them be committed by H.M.G. or Egypt to anything before a Sudanese Parliament has had an opportunity to consider any new proposals." Even after the February agreement had "committed" the Sudanese, Luce maintained his hope that all would work out in the end.[25]

Luce had no illusions about the future. "I don't for a moment think that this country is going to have a smooth transition from the security and honest administration of the past 50 years to similar conditions under independence." Many of the policies and ideas the British had introduced, he expected, "will go by the board." "But I'm convinced that in spite of that there will remain with the Sudanese an abiding sense of the value of what we have done and been in this country." The important thing now, he believed, was to fulfill what he regarded as the ultimate British pledge to the Sudanese: "By hook or by crook we've got to get the Sudan its independence and that's the ball we've got to keep our eyes on for the present."[26]

The Sudan Government now had only one effective course of action. Although Howe insisted on a completely neutral attitude on the part of the Political Service, even the governor-general believed that the best hope for the future of the Sudan lay in independence. With this in mind, Luce and the senior administrators encouraged a rapprochement between the Umma and the Socialist Republican Party (SRP) as the leading elements of the movement for independence. At the same time, they also worked behind the scenes to detach the independent Khatmiyya members from the National Unity Party (NUP), which was still largely dominated by al-Azhari and the Ashiqqa. Although they had little hope of accomplishing a Khatmiyya/Umma alliance in favor of independence, they thought that the two groups might be brought to stop fighting each other at least until after the Egyptian threat had been dealt with and an independence-minded Parliament safely elected. The key to all these maneuverings lay in the attitude and public stance of Sayyid 'Ali al-Mirghani.

Sayyid 'Ali's position was never much in doubt. Above all else, he was determined to oppose any possibility of a Mahdist monarchy: even Egypt was preferable to Mahdism. At the same time, Mirghani did not really expect that there would ever be any real union with the Egyptians. He consistently repeated to Luce and other British officials that there was "no question" of going with Egypt. Yet, so long as there was a remote chance of the Mahdists gaining a majority in Parliament, Mirghani refused to divide the NUP or to throw his support to the independent Khatmiyya in any way that might improve the electoral prospects of the Umma. For this reason too he vacillated in giving his countenance to the SRP. In the end, Mirghani's refusal to support publicly either the independent Khatmiyya or the SRP brought about the demise of the latter as a viable party and forced the former to be submerged completely within the NUP. However, al-Mirghani extracted a price from the NUP—complete

25. Luce to Perham, 30 May 1953, MP 536/1.
26. Ibid.

control for the Khatmiyya of both the General Assembly and the Executive Council of the party.[27]

From the perspective of the Umma, 1953 was a year of disappointments. After the initial euphoria of the February agreement had worn off, Sayyid 'Abd al-Rahman and his chief lieutenants soon discovered that the warnings of Robertson and the other British administrators had been correct: not only did the Egyptians continue their propaganda efforts in the Sudan, they actually seemed to increase them. Moreover, the apparent willingness of the Sudan Political Service to accept and even encourage the SRP also seemed a betrayal to the Mahdists. Sayyid 'Abd al-Rahman increasingly felt himself isolated. He had foregone collaboration with the British in order to gain concessions from Egypt, only to discover that the concessions were worthless and that the British had perforce turned to other potential collaborators. In effect, Sayyid 'Abd al-Rahman's refusal to accept guidance and advice from the Political Service had thrown the potentially united front of the independence groups into disarray. Despite his efforts to salvage the situation, his withdrawal of support from the Political Service at a crucial moment in the Anglo-Egyptian negotiations had actually rendered them impotent. Sayyid 'Ali had gained the upper hand, and without some change in his position, there was now little that could be done. Sayyid 'Abd al-Rahman could only watch with bitter frustration as his hopes of a throne vanished.[28]

As the Mahdists and other independents watched with growing alarm a massive propaganda campaign designed to bring the Sudan into Egypt's fold, in Whitehall the British Government too finally woke up to the need for a British countermove. Ironically, resolution of the Sudan question had not brought Anglo-Egyptian agreement on the Egyptian question closer but in fact had made it harder to achieve. Not only were Britain and Egypt now finding it difficult to agree on the terms of the military side of their negotiations, but both the Conservative Government in London and the revolutionary government in Cairo found themselves bound more tightly than ever by domestic political considerations that were directly related to the Sudan Agreement. With cries of "scuttle in the Sudan" rising from its own imperialist backbenches, the British Government hardened its position in military negotiations. Having publicly abandoned claims to sovereignty over the Sudan, the government in Cairo too

---

27. Political Service efforts to effect a rapprochement between the Umma Party and the Socialist Republican Party are outlined in Luce's monthly letters between May and July 1953, in MP 589/8. For the rapprochement between the Khatmiyya and the NUP, see especially JWK/4, 2 August 1953, in the same file.

28. Luce's monthly letters between May and July 1953, in MP 589/8. During the summer 'Abd al-Rahman was finally persuaded by Abdullah Khalil, the general secretary of the Umma Party, to make a formal statement endorsing a republic in the Sudan rather than a monarchy. It was too late, however, to alleviate the suspicions of those who feared a Mahdist monarchy.

became more adamant in its demands for immediate and complete British evacuation, partly to prove its nationalist credentials.

As the new regime of Colonel Gamal Abdel Nasser became more recalcitrant, the Foreign Office at last accepted what the Political Service had argued all along (albeit for tactical reasons of their own): that an independent Sudan friendly with Britain would still give Her Majesty's Government a card to play in Anglo-Egyptian negotiations. Ironically, the end of the condominium and the demise of the Political Service itself finally brought Whitehall into full support of the Political Service goal. The moving force in this sudden British concern seems to have been the prime minister, Sir Winston Churchill.

There is an air of inevitability and fate in the presence of Churchill at the head of the British Government that finally granted Sudanese self-government and independence. It had been a long road since the day some fifty-five years earlier when, as a young subaltern, he had charged with the British cavalry at Omdurman, in the days of the old queen-empress, when the British Empire was at the height of its power and splendor. After the battle he had criticized Lord Kitchener's looting of the Mahdist capital and desecration of the Mahdi's tomb. Through the long years since, years of peace and war and imperial decline, he had risen to the top of the "greasy pole" to become the new queen's first minister— only to find himself at the end defending Kitchener's legacy. Throughout the years, Churchill had remained true to form, an unreconstructed imperialist to the last. Now nearly eighty, he found in the Sudan yet another call to arms to defend the empire which had always fascinated him with its siren song of power and glory. Churchill's presence casts an almost surrealistic glow over the final days of the condominium—a glow that conjures up images of blood and fire, and the last cavalry charge of the Empire.

Determined to preserve what was left of imperial prestige, Churchill persistently saw the Sudan problem in military terms. That he was perhaps reliving the past is suggested by his habit (whether from ignorance or old age is uncertain) of referring to Sayyid 'Abd al-Rahman as "the Mahdi." Like so many other British statesmen, Churchill never understood the neutral attitude of the Sudan Political Service in its role as guardian of the Sudanese. As the Egyptian campaign intensified, he became increasingly determined that something must be done to hold the country within the British sphere. Even while on vacation, cruising in the Caribbean, in mid-January 1953 the prime minister cabled Eden about events in the condominium. "We seem to have been ill served by our agents in the Sudan," he complained, "Money has evidently been freely used by the Egyptians. Surely we should now confront Neguib resolutely. . . . what happens here will set the pace for us all over Africa and the Middle East."[29]

As the British position continued to deteriorate, the Foreign Office agreed with Sir Robert Howe's suggestion that a senior British official should visit the condominium to counteract Egypt's influence. The result was a short trip in late

---

29. Churchill to Eden, Emergency Top Secret, Personal no. 12, 15 January 1953, FO 800/827, PRO.

March by the minister of state, Selwyn Lloyd. At the same time, pursuing an old Political Service recommendation, and on the advice of Ambassador Stevenson in Cairo, Eden now decided to appoint a United Kingdom trade commissioner, D.M.H. Riches, to act as Britain's direct representative in the Sudan. As might be expected, the legitimate "trade" side of Riches's office was relatively small compared with his real purpose, the gathering of political intelligence and the propagation of Britain's own views in the Sudan. The United Kingdom Trade Commission (UKTC) soon became the center of British efforts to woo the Sudanese away from Egypt.

Both Riches and Selwyn Lloyd found the remaining Political Service in a state of virtual disintegration, completely disheartened by what many regarded as the betrayal of the true Sudanese, the country man and the Southerner, to the politicians of the three towns. Although Robertson himself was helpful, offering the trade commissioner his house as a temporary office after he himself had left, Riches found the general attitude of the administration "insensitive" and "repellently off-hand" toward outsiders, "whether British or foreign." Moreover, as he reported with a certain exasperation, the ethical sensibilities of political service members made them less than ideal agents of British policy in the Sudan. There was the "major question of access to papers, consultation, and correspondence pending the completion of secure offices of our own," he wrote to the Foreign Office in early April.

On this I have been going very slowly as I think that the only hope of getting a proper working arrangement is with Luce when he arrives to take over in three or four days time. In the meanwhile . . . I have been reading material every day though there is much apprehension about this compromising "neutrality." Here again Robertson is being helpful. But the general belief of the administration in their neutrality— apparently above mundane things like national interests if not out of this world altogether—makes matters rather difficult.

Such reports soon roused the British prime minister to action.[30]

In April, Churchill telegraphed directly to Howe for the first time, encouraging the governor-general to tell his remaining people to drop their misplaced sense of neutrality. "Considering the methods Cairo have used and will certainly continue to use," Churchill pointed out, "there is surely no reason why all our faithful officials in the Sudan should not tell the people who trust them where their real interests lie. We must not take it all lying down. Pray do not hesitate to telegraph me." Like Huddleston before him, Howe was not to be bullied even by the prime minister of Great Britain—particularly a Conservative one of Churchill's ilk. His reply must have sounded like treason to the queen's first minister: "The problem of countering Egyptian action here is one of great

---

30. Riches to Roger Allen, 6 April 1953, FO 371/102792, PRO. For the formation of the UKTC, see earlier correspondence in this file, as well as correspondence in March 1953 in FO 371/102921, PRO. The UKTC Political Summaries for the Sudan are a valuable source for the last years of the condominium.

difficulty, on which the Foreign Secretary knows my mind. The governor-general is the agent of both the British and Egyptian Governments and in principle cannot therefore take that partisan attitude which any propaganda or counter-propaganda demands. . . . Our guiding principle here must primarily be to keep the ring . . . for the Sudanese themselves and to protect them as much as possible." Churchill, however, was neither an Attlee nor even a Bevin. On 16 April he responded sharply to what he obviously considered Howe's unsatisfactory attitude.

My colleagues and I hold that there is a great deal which the British members of the Sudan Administration can and should do to counteract Egyptian propaganda and pressure upon the Sudanese. . . .

The Administration should defend themselves strongly when attacked by the Egyptians. They should do everything they can to encourage the Sudanese to stand up for themselves in every way. I agree that, except when members of the Administration are attacked, they must preserve an appearance of impartiality. . . . but I cannot believe that a great deal cannot be done to unmask Egyptian intrigues.

Still, the governor-general did not take matters as seriously as did the prime minister.[31]

When Howe telegraphed his normal summer leave plans later in April, Churchill gave vent to his sense of outrage. His initial reaction was apparently so forceful that the draft telegram was subsequently removed from the files. The effect, however, is clear from the surrounding minutes and notes between Churchill and Eden. "Pray consider . . . this reply," the prime minister asked his foreign secretary, "and report to me upon the effect of his resignation, after its receipt, of the Governor. What is his pension and who pays it and will there be any power to withhold his pension after he is guilty of this desertion of his duty?" Eden prevented any precipitate dismissal of the governor-general, warning the prime minister of the difficulties inherent in getting the Egyptians to agree to a replacement. He also found Churchill's assessment unfair. In fact, Howe's wife was suffering from terminal cancer, and the summer heat of Khartoum was more than either she or the governor-general could bear. The summer leave was a traditional part of service, and Howe did not view the situation with as much alarm as did the prime minister. Nevertheless, Eden's redrafted version of Churchill's personal telegram to the governor-general still conveyed the Cabinet's sense of urgency and alarm at continuing Egyptian propaganda. Given the present crisis, and the Egyptian propaganda campaign, even Eden thought Howe must stay in the Sudan to show the Sudanese that they were not being

---

31. Churchill to Howe, no. 513, 10 April 1953, Personal Secret; Khartoum to Foreign Office, no. 275, 13 April 1953, Personal for Prime Minister from Governor General, Secret; and Foreign Office to Khartoum, no. 533, 16 April 1953, Secret Priority, all in FO 800/827, PRO.

abandoned to Cairo's machinations, as well as to bolster Political Service morale.[32]

Despite Howe's continuing rather low-key assessment of the situation, the Conservative Government remained worried about the Sudan and continuing Egyptian bellicosity over the Canal Zone. The documentary record suggests a kind of crisis mentality in Whitehall about both the Sudan and Egypt. At the end of April the Cabinet decided that if serious trouble broke out in the Canal Zone, amounting to a state of war, Khartoum would be reinforced immediately with two infantry battalions and sufficient air forces to disarm Egyptian troops in the condominium and "resume full control of the Sudan." Churchill saw the Sudan as a test case for Britain's continuing will to empire. "Firm action in the Sudan," he told the Cabinet, "might offset the damage to our prestige in the Middle East which would result from an unsatisfactory solution in Egypt." The chief of the Imperial General Staff suggested building up the Khartoum garrison to a full brigade: "Provided we held Khartoum and the Sudan Defence Force remains loyal, the Egyptians could do nothing to embarrass us unduly."[33]

In June, Churchill decided on a new approach to the Sudan problem—an outright alliance with "the Mahdi." When 'Abd al-Rahman visited London for the new queen's coronation, Churchill and Selwyn Lloyd saw him privately, offering full British support in exchange for a public break with Egypt and a repudiation of his earlier agreements with Neguib, on the grounds that Neguib himself had broken his pledges not to continue the propaganda campaign. Through the rest of the summer, negotiations between the British and the

---

32. For Churchill's anger at Howe's leave plans, see Prime Minister's Personal Minute, 21 April 1953, with the notational reference to a draft telegram "removed"; the response by Selwyn Lloyd, 21 April 1953; and Foreign Office to Khartoum, no. 553, 22 April 1953; all in PREM 11/544, PRO. Howe never did admit the urgency of the situation and insisted that he might easily leave Sudan affairs in the hands of an "acting" governor-general, as he had always done during the summers; anyway, he was scheduled to represent the Sudan in London at Queen Elizabeth's coronation. Not even Churchill suggested that Howe should not attend the coronation. "In the circumstances," however, Howe rather sulkily agreed to postpone his other plans "subject to discussion on arrival in London." Khartoum to Foreign Office, no. 312, 27 April 1953, Personal for Prime Minister, PREM 11/544, PRO. An incensed Churchill sent copies of Howe's reply to the Queen herself.

33. Cabinet Conclusions (53) extract, 29 April 1953, and Ministry of Defence to G.H.Q. Middle East Land Forces, 30 April 1953. Anticipating Howe's opposition to any military action in the Sudan, Churchill deliberately excluded the governor-general from the circuit of telegrams dealing with either Anglo-Egyptian military negotiations or British plans for defense of the Canal and reinforcement of Khartoum. Hearing of the plans through his own military advisors, however, in mid-May, Howe telegraphed the Foreign Office, insisting that he and he alone must be the "sole judge" of the need for measures to ensure the security of the Sudan. Churchill gave explicit instructions to ignore Howe's telegram; see telegrams and Prime Minister's Personal Minutes from 28 April to 29 May 1953 in PREM 11/544.

Mahdist leader continued on this basis, but in the end 'Abd al-Rahman held off as Neguib once more promised to stop Egyptian interference.[34]

Although 'Abd al-Rahman eventually did break with the Egyptians, by the end of the summer of 1953 it was too late—the tide in the Sudan had turned against him. In the November elections, despite all his efforts and those of the remaining British, the Sudanese electorate overwhelmingly voted for the Khatmiyya and the Ashiqqa. It was less a vote for unity with Egypt, however, than a vote against continuing suspicions of 'Abd al-Rahman's monarchical ambitions. The opening of the first Sudanese parliament on 1 March 1954 demonstrated the point better than any argument might have done. When General Neguib arrived to attend the opening ceremonies, pro-independence demonstrations precipitated a major clash with the police, resulting in thirty-four deaths and hundreds of injuries. Howe had to postpone the opening for ten days. Although it was clear that Mahdist supporters had organized the demonstrations and the violence, it was equally clear that the extent of the Ashiqqa victory did not reflect any widely held sentiment in the Sudan for unity with Egypt. As the new Sudanese Government of Isma'il al-Azhari took office, competition between Britain and Egypt for the affections of the future Sudanese state went on unabated.[35]

The last years of the condominium, under the self-governing regime of al-Azhari, were primarily marked by continuing British determination to prevent the Sudan from falling under Egypt's spell. The replacement of Neguib by Colonel Gamal Abdel Nasser made Britain's task easier. The Sudanese had been fond of Neguib, attributing his best qualities no doubt to his Sudanese mother. Even 'Abd al-Rahman liked Neguib and, with all the evidence to the contrary, apparently continued to believe in his sincerity. Nasser was a different story altogether. As his agent, Major Salah Salam, traveled throughout the Sudan trying to drum up support, the Sudanese trusted the Egyptians less and less. Eventually, Salam even tried to make trouble in the South, encouraging Southern leaders to visit Cairo and make their own agreements with Egypt, as the Northern Sudanese political parties had done in 1952. The effects of Salam's troublemaking became evident in 1955, when the Southern sections of the Sudan Defence Force revolted against al-Azhari's government and called for the British to return. Even for al-Azhari, the Southern mutiny was the last straw. At last, he

---

34. C.(53) 168, 11 June 1953, Secret, and C. (53) 197, 7 July 1953, Secret, both memoranda for the Cabinet by Selwyn Lloyd, in PREM 11/544. See also Howe to Churchill, 8 June 1953, and Selwyn Lloyd to Churchill, 9 June 1953, PREM 11/544.

35. The best summaries of events are in the Sudan Fortnightly Summaries of the UKTC from May through December 1953, in FO 371/102700-102702, PRO. For the election results, see also Khartoum to Foreign Office, nos. 603, 604 and 107, 30 November and 1 December 1953, and Riches to Eden, 4 December 1953, printed under title "Results in the General Elections for the Sudan House of Representatives," all in FO 371/102713, PRO.

turned to his traditional enemy, the governor-general of the Sudan, and listened to his advice.[36]

In 1955, Sir Robert Howe finally asked to be relieved as governor-general. He wanted to resign on 1 January 1955, effective 1 July, and to go on final leave in March. Despite Churchill's earlier irritation with him, by this time Howe's own prestige and the difficulties of replacing him with another British governor-general caused the Foreign Office virtually to beg him to stay on until Sudanese self-determination—which London now hoped to speed up to the fall of 1955. Howe's wife was dying, however, and he would agree to stay only if allowed considerable leave in England. Since British staff had already issued numerous complaints that he spent little time in the Sudan as it was, and that he was not even there to "shake them by the hand after all their years of service" as they were progressively Sudanized, eventually his original plan was accepted. His successor, Sir Knox Helm, took up his appointment as the last governor-general of the Anglo-Egyptian Sudan on 29 March 1955. Although initially Knox Helm actually tried to govern as well as rule, causing the Foreign Office considerable headaches, he was never more than a caretaker governor-general. (Indeed, after realizing he had authority but no power, Knox Helm became increasingly anxious to end his tenure in time to spend Christmas 1955 at home with his family.)

Convinced that continuing Egyptian propaganda and Salah Salam's visits might yet bring the Sudan under Egyptian domination—or even start a civil war that would give the Egyptians an excuse for military action—throughout 1955 Knox Helm did his best to persuade al-Azhari to short-circuit the three-year timetable which Britain itself had accepted in the 1953 Anglo-Egyptian Agreement. On 19 October 1955, Luce, still in place as the new governor-general's political advisor, went so far as to state publicly to a Sudanese newspaper, "If the Sudanese Parliament decided itself to proclaim independence, Britain would recognize its decision." In December the governor-general declared his intention to retire and urged al-Azhari to take the opportunity to proclaim independence—the alternative was appointment of a "neutral" replacement. The Sudanese prime minister finally took the hint.

Still wary of British intentions, and uncertain about his own position between the two great sects, the Mahdists and the Khatmiyya, throughout 1955 al-Azhari had procrastinated and hesitated. Finally, in the wake of the Southern rebellion, as the British proved their good faith by refusing to intervene, he took the bit between his teeth. With Knox Helm conveniently out of the country (almost certainly by prearrangement, or at least foreknowledge, despite denials to the contrary), Ismail al-Azhari laid a proclamation before the Sudanese Parliament declaring the end of the condominium and the independence of the Sudan. On 1

---

36. The Southern mutiny is covered in FO 371/113697-113699, PRO. For Salem's intrigues see also reports from the UKTC, especially no. 47, 12 November 1954, 19 November 1954, and memorandum "Anglo-Egyptian Relations in the Sudan," 23 December 1954, FO 371/108381, PRO.

January 1956, the independent Sudanese state, for which the Political Service had struggled so long, at last came into being.[37]

As for Anglo-Egyptian relations, continuing struggle in the Sudan certainly did not make them closer. Indeed, the ultimate victory of the British strategy, marked by al-Azhari's unilateral declaration of independence, may well have exacerbated anti-British feeling not only in the general Egyptian populace but especially within Nasser's revolutionary government. Anglo-Egyptian negotiations and Britain's withdrawal from Egypt in 1954 and 1955 went hand in hand with the continuing poker game in the Sudan. When the situation in Egypt threatened to reach crisis proportions, Churchill habitually ordered troops to stand by for a reoccupation of Khartoum. Indeed, on at least one occassion, only Anthony Eden's personal counterorder in the middle of the night prevented such a movement. Although it would be too much to attribute the Suez crisis to the legacy of bitterness created by the Sudan question, as opposed to all the other differences between London and Cairo, certainly the struggle over the condominium, which was in many ways a struggle over both Egypt's role as a regional imperial power and Britain's role as a global imperial power, contributed mightily to the general atmosphere of Anglo-Egyptian animosity. Moreover, by postponing any Anglo-Egyptian settlement for some eight years after the initial efforts to renegotiate the 1936 treaty, the Sudan issue made the eventual settlement not only more difficult, but considerably more fragile and unsatisfactory to both sides, especially to Britain. From London's perspective, as Anthony Eden once wrote about the 1953 Sudan Agreement, the outcome could not have been "more humiliating." Consequently, it is not too much to say that the Sudan Political Service helped generate the atmosphere of bitterness and frustration in which the Suez debacle would finally occur.

---

37. On Howe's retirement, see FO 371/108383, PRO. For Helm's efforts to persuade al-Azhari to declare independence early, see also correspondence in PREM 11/1649, PRO.

Conclusion: Imperialism or "Expatriate Nationalism"

The purpose of this study has been to examine the influence of the Sudan Government on Anglo-Egyptian relations between 1945 and 1953. Several conclusions may be drawn from this examination. First, it should be clear that, popular conceptions of imperialism notwithstanding, the Sudan Government in Khartoum, dominated as it was by the largely British Sudan Political Service, was by no means simply an agent of the British Government in London. Whatever the origins of the condominium government, by 1945 it had taken on a life of its own. The point is significant because, despite assertions to the contrary, it should now be clear that the Labour foreign secretary, Ernest Bevin, was indeed eventually quite willing to compromise the question of Sudanese aspirations for self-government and self-determination in exchange for a new treaty that would guarantee Britain's strategic requirements in Egypt. The "brick wall" that prevented him was the Sudan Government, which pursued an independent anti-Egyptian policy as a part of its own plans for the future of the Sudan. Even after the advent of the Conservative Government in London, which not only was more sympathetic to Sudanese aspirations (at least as represented by the Political Service) but also placed more emphasis on the strategic importance of retaining British influence in the Sudan as well as Egypt, Anthony Eden's efforts to reach some compromise were also stymied by an obstinate regime in Khartoum. Ultimately, the issue was resolved neither by compromise in the Sudan nor British intervention in Egypt but by the revolution of the Free Officers in Cairo itself. The ramifications of these conclusions are significant for a whole range of problems raised by the nature of the Anglo-Egyptian relationship.

Second, for those who have tried to resurrect his reputation, it should be clear that Bevin's noninterventionist policy was not equivalent to a moral concern for the rights of the Sudanese, as both the Sidqi-Bevin Protocol and his effort to reorient British policy toward the condominium in the spring of 1947 make clear. The dominant theme of Bevin's tenure as foreign secretary was power politics as usual—the only difference between the Labour Government and its Conservative counterpart lay in calculations of the most effective means to their ends in the Middle East, not a major shift in evaluating what those ends should be, nor even a shift in their sense of "morality" about choosing any particular means. At the same time, the choices made in London were often not a matter of positive long-term planning but rather of choosing the least bad of several unsavory alternatives. In formulating policy toward Egypt during this period, the British Government often functioned under outside influences that were beyond its control. Nowhere was this clearer than in the policies pursued toward the Sudan and the constraints placed on those policies by the government in Khartoum—which brings the inquiry back to the nature of British imperialism in the Sudan itself, at least as practiced by the Sudan Political Service.

Finally, the most intriguing question to emerge from this study, perhaps, is why did the Sudan Political Service, an elite British imperial administration, defy its masters not only in Cairo but also in London, to the clear detriment of British interests in both the Sudan and the Middle East as a whole? It is a question that is difficult to answer, and the answer itself may be impossible to prove. Some scholars have suggested that the underlying reason for the Political Service's extraordinary behavior is to be found simply in its members' "pride of trade," as Robertson himself once described it, and their desire not to see the Sudan Administration dissolve into the kind of corruption they perceived in Egypt. Such an interpretation, however, does not convincingly explain the strength of the Political Service's determination, nor the depth of its indignation whenever the British Government seemed to be "appeasing" the Egyptians at the expense of the Sudan. What, then, could have motivated these otherwise upright, seemingly honorable subjects of the British Crown?

Members of the Political Service responded throughout the period of Anglo-Egyptian negotiations as if they were themselves directly threatened by any Anglo-Egyptian rapprochement that might potentially place the Sudan under Egyptian rule. While it is true that such an outcome would have resulted in the demise of the Political Service, it is equally clear that such an event need not have threatened any particular individual within the service. Most were young enough to find other careers, and pensions could always be worked out one way or another. What was at stake, then, that its potential destruction should elicit such a passionate response from otherwise phlegmatic, not to say unimaginative, men like Robertson? Was it indeed only a pride of trade, or was it something larger than the self-interest of particular individuals; was it perhaps an idea to which these administrators had committed themselves in order to justify, not least to themselves, their rule in the Sudan? For it must surely be a commonplace that only some strong emotional appeal would cause men like Robertson, Huddleston, and the other members of the Sudan Government to so displace their allegiance from the home government under whose auspices they were recruited, and to whom they were at least nominally responsible, and give it instead to the Sudanese, who, as Robertson once put it, "paid our salaries." Clearly, some potent force, which on its face was inconsistent with the demands of either a British imperial identity or a British national identity, was at work within the British Sudan Political Service, overriding their sense of duty and loyalty toward their own country and allowing them, perhaps even requiring them, to oppose British policies in pursuit of their own goals for the Sudan.

Throughout Anglo-Egyptian efforts to renegotiate the 1936 treaty, Khartoum was clearly playing its own game, with its own goals in mind. Those goals, it seems, included the creation of a Sudanese state independent from Egypt and, if necessary, even from Great Britain. Although proof is beyond the scope of this study, the most logical conclusion, however remarkable, is that members of the Sudan Political Service were themselves functioning from a sense of Sudanese "nationalist" identity. Such a conclusion would certainly explain their opposition to any attempt to give the Sudan to Egypt. A concession of Egyptian sovereignty by Britain would immediately threaten such a nationalist identity, particularly among its expatriate adherents. This would also account for the depth of feeling against both co-domini, which the documents clearly show that the Political Service displayed. Moreover, it might also account for Robertson's efforts to forge a united Sudanese front against Egypt, without completely compromising the Political Service's own position, even when he realized that such a move would mean a more rapid timetable for Sudanese self-government and self-determination—indeed, for decolonization.

At the same time, a nationalism propounded by the Political Service, however much it might have attempted to woo the Sudanese themselves, would inevitably reflect not the true Sudanese experience but rather that of its creators—the expatriate British administrators. Consequently, it would appeal to the Sudanese only so long as it conformed to their own nationalist conceptions and goals. If the two visions of an independent Sudan ever collided, that of the indigenous Sudanese might well be expected to prevail over that of the expatriate imperial administrators. Such an interpretation is entirely consistent with the events of late 1952 and early 1953, when all Sudanese parties abandoned the Political Service to make their own deals with Egypt. Yet even if such an interpretation is accepted, this only raises further questions about the "imperial" motives of the Sudan Political Service and its purpose in adopting such a nationalist conception of the Sudan in the first place. This interpretation also raises questions about the exact nature of the Political Service's expatriate vision and how that vision may have affected the state structures it put in place in the Sudan—structures on which the Sudanese themselves subsequently built their own independent Sudan.

While the answers to such sweeping questions are beyond the scope of this study, it is at least worth considering the means by which the theory of an "expatriate nationalism" might be proven or disproven, if only to explain the role of the Political Service in Anglo-Egyptian relations after the Second World War. Briefly, it would seem that two propositions must be demonstrated: (1) that the Political Service was not simply an extension of the British national identity and therefore not merely an agent for the exploitation of the Sudan in the interests of Britain; and (2) that the Political Service actually created an alternative self-image that had as its object the creation of a new state in the Sudan, a state that would in turn reflect the Political Service's own "nationalist" vision. It should be clear from the preceding pages that the first proposition has been plausibly demonstrated. Whether the second may also be shown to be true must be the subject of further investigation, but several general observations might profitably be made before leaving the question in abeyance.

In his memoirs, written thirty years later, Robertson recorded his conception of his task in the condominium, as he had learned it in the early days of his career. It is a statement that, for all its retrospective self-service, is consistent with his role in Anglo-Egyptian relations between 1945 and 1953 and may serve as a beginning point for further inquiry:

I had no doubt that the task was an altruistic one. We were to work for the benefit of the people in accordance with the traditions we had inherited and absorbed. . . .

I have often been asked in later years whether in 1922 we were made conscious of an intention to lead the Sudan to self-government in the future . . . I do not remember this goal being put before us. What was . . . made abundantly clear to us was that we were servants of the Sudanese, appointed by the Governor-General and the Sudan Government, to which our loyalty was given; we were not there to forward British aims, except . . . as they accorded with the welfare of the Sudanese. Our duty . . . was to keep the peace, to see that fair dealing was meted out to the people, and that the Sudanese were not sacrificed to foreign enterprise or foreign development.

If this was indeed the duty inculcated in the Political Service from its earliest days, the development of its self-image may well have become rooted in a conviction that its task in the Sudan, its *raison d'être* in fact, was to uplift the Sudanese by forging for them a modern state structure within the boundaries of which an organic sense of Sudanese national identity might develop, particularly as a bulwark against "outside predators" like Egypt.[1]

If the conception of a nationalist phenomenon within the Political Service is accepted, however, it is equally clear that it must be carefully qualified. Clearly the members of the Sudan Political Service did not give up their British citizenship to become Sudanese—though some did make arrangements to retire in their old districts, and many left their bones in the country to which they had become so attached. On the other hand, it might well be argued that the Political Service was able to carry out its task in the Sudan, a task in which no more than 150 men at a time (less than 500 over the entire period of the condominium) ruled some 11 million Sudanese, only by creating an *esprit de corps* founded on a group self-image that would legitimize such an audacious undertaking, if only to themselves. In the process of creating this self-image, they might naturally have created their own "mythology" about the Sudan, its inhabitants, its history, and their own role in that history. Such a mythology, of course, would in turn reflect their own cultural background, which, significantly, was highly paternalistic. Consequently, the Political Service might easily have come to

---

1. Robertson, *Transition*, 8-9.

view the Sudanese as children who had to be carefully parented and taught the skills of citizenship as they slowly grew up.

Such a self-justifying paternalism would require the conception of a unique Sudanese identity that must eventually express itself in the emergence of a modern Sudanese nation. By protecting the fledgling nation until it was strong enough to stand on its own feet within the larger community of nations, and by providing it with a modern state structure in which to pursue its own destiny, the Political Service self-image itself might be fulfilled. In other words, a Political Service "expatriate nationalism" could never be more than a vicarious function of Sudanese nationalism, even a Sudanese "nationalism" projected by the Political Service itself. In the end, of course, if this interpretation of the Political Service is correct, it availed them little. Independence did come, but in a very different form from that which they must have envisioned. However powerful may have been the group identity formed by these expatriate administrators, their self-image and their mythology about the Sudan were but chimeras compared with those of the Sudanese themselves, whether sectarian Muslim or secular nationalist.

Despite the dream that members of the Political Service created in order to justify their alien rule, even the collective consciousness of all five hundred or so British officials over the life of the condominium was no substitute for the reality of eleven million indigenous Sudanese. On the other hand, in adhering faithfully to its own vision and agenda for the Sudan, the Political Service did preserve the Sudanese right to exercize their own sense of national identity and to assert their independence from Egypt. Moreover, although also beyond the scope of this study, the Political Service's view of the Sudan must certainly have influenced the view of the Sudanese themselves, at least initially. Thus, it might well be said that the modern Sudan owes its very existence to the "expatriate nationalist" vision of these British colonial administrators.

As for the original question of Anglo-Egyptian relations, it should be clear from this study that in the Sudan both co-domini were in a sense imperial interlopers. Although the Egyptians may have had a more legitimate claim, the image of a Sudanese identity being created by the Political Service was ultimately effective only to the extent that it approximated reality. However or whenever it may have begun, by the postwar period, a Sudanese national identity, still a bit inchoate perhaps and appealing to a relatively small portion of the population, did indeed exist. Confronted by a recalcitrant Political Service and a truly anti-Egyptian Sudanese nationalist sentiment, for Egypt as for Britain, there proved to be more pressing problems than legitimizing the claim to the Sudan. Rather than Egypt, it was the monarchy, and especially the dynasty established by Muhammad 'Ali, himself an ardent empire-builder, that attached such importance to Egypt's sovereignty over the Sudan. After the fall of the monarchy, there was remarkably little dissent within Egypt when General Neguib and his revolutionary regime decided to repudiate the claim to Sudanese sovereignty, thereby paving the way for an Anglo-Egyptian settlement not only on the Sudan question, but ultimately on the Egyptian question as well.

On the British side too, imperial control of the Sudan without imperial control of Egypt proved an anachronism. Despite suggestions that the Sudan might provide a substitute for the Canal Zone, in the end Anglo-Egyptian agreement was more important. From beginning to end, the interest of the British Government in the Sudan had been tied to its position in Egypt. Once the condominium regime proved too great an embarrassment, indeed a stumbling block rather than a bargaining chip in Anglo-Egyptian relations, London was all too glad to see it go. Despite all the vaunted cries from Whitehall about the rights of the Sudanese, or Gordon's martyrdom and Britain's civilizing mission in the Sudan, the officials of the Foreign Office were pragmatic to the end. Had they been able, they would gladly have compromised the Sudanese position in exchange for an Egyptian treaty.

The Sudan Political Service, on the other hand, not only adhered to the moral rhetoric, but actually believed in it. Their obstinacy, supported by the peculiar status of the condominium, forced the British Government into a position it otherwise would have been happy to avoid. Above all, the Political Service appealed to London's desire not so much to do what was right as to be seen to be doing what was right. In fostering a particular image of Sudanese national identity as part of its strategy, however, the Political Service enabled the Sudanese themselves to play the final cards in the game, and to evict not only the Egyptians once and for all but even the Political Service itself. That the warnings of the Political Service about the probable consequences of such an occurrence were accurate, the subsequent events in the independent Sudan, as well as its present agony, have made all too clear—but such are the ironies of history. What is certain is that the intervention of the Sudan Political Service in Anglo-Egyptian relations between 1945 and 1953 dramatically affected not only the Sudan itself but also the relationship between Britain and Egypt; and without such intervention, the subsequent histories of Africa and the Middle East, indeed of the world, might well have taken a very different course.

Bibliography

ARCHIVAL ABBREVIATIONS

SAD The Sudan Archive, University of Durham
RHL Rhodes House Library, Oxford
PRO The Public Record Office, Kew, England

UNPUBLISHED PRIMARY SOURCES

The Public Record Office, London:

FO 371	General Correspondence
FO 800	Private Papers
FO 78	Turkey (including Egypt)
FO 141	Egypt, Consular Correspondence
FO 633	Papers of Lord Cromer
PREM 11	Prime Minister's Office
CAB 128	Cabinet Meetings
CAB 129	Cabinet Memoranda
CAB 79	Chiefs of Staff, Meetings
CAB 80	Chiefs of Staff, Memoranda

Sudan Archive, Durham University, Durham:
The Baily Papers
The Gillan Papers
The Henderson Papers
The Newbold Papers
The Robertson Papers
The Wingate Papers

Rhodes House Library, Oxford:
  The MacMichael Papers
  The Perham Papers

New College, Oxford:
  The Milner Papers (in the Bodleian Library)

PRIVATE CORRESPONDENCE

Sir Gawain Bell, 1990
K.D.D. Henderson, 1989-90

PUBLISHED PRIMARY SOURCES

Great Britain. *Parliamentary Debates, Lords and Commons*, 1896-1956.
MacMichael, H.A., The Sudan Political Service. Oxford, 1955.
Minutes and Weekly Digests of the. . . Legislative Assembly, 1948-1952. Khartoum.
Parliamentary Papers. Command Series, 1898-1956.
Proceedings of the Advisory Council for the Northern Sudan 1944-1948. Khartoum.
Proceedings of the Senate and House of Representatives, 1954-1956. Khartoum.
Sudan Gazette, 1899-1953. Khartoum.
Sudan Government. *The Sudan: A Record of Achievement*. Khartoum, 1947.
United Nations. *Proceedings of the General Assembly,* 1947-1952.

NEWSPAPERS AND PERIODICALS

The Economist
Journal d'Egypte (al-Misr)
Manchester Guardian
New York Times
Round Table
The Times

PUBLISHED SECONDARY SOURCES: BOOKS

Abbas, Mekki. *The Sudan Question*. London and New York, 1952.
Abdel Rahim, Muddathir. *Imperialism and Nationalism in the Sudan*. Oxford, 1969.
Archer, Sir Geoffrey. *Personal and Historical Memoirs of an East African Administrator*. London, 1963.
Arthur, Sir George. *Life of Lord Kitchener*. 3 vos. London, 1920.
Atiyah, Edward. *An Arab Tells His Story*. London, 1946.
Bakheit, G.M.A. *British Administration and Sudanese Nationalism, 1919-1939*. Cambridge, England, D.Phil., 1965.

Bedri, Babikr. *The Memoirs of Babikr Bedri.* Vol. 1, trans. Y. Bedri and G. Scott. London, 1969. Vol. 2, trans. Y. Bedri and P. Hogg. London, 1980.

Bell, Sir Gawain. *An Imperial Twilight.* London, 1989.

_____. *Shadows on the Sand.* London and New York, 1983.

Bennett, Ernest N. *The Downfall of the Dervishes.* London, 1898.

Beshir, Mohammed Omer. Educational Development in the Sudan. 1898-1956. Oxford, 1969.

_____. *Revolution and Nationalism in the Sudan.* London, 1974.

_____. *The Southern Sudan: Background to Conflict.* New York, 1968.

Boustead, Hugh. *The Wind of Morning.* London, 1971.

Brett, Michael, ed. *Northern Africa: Islam and Modernization.* London, 1973.

Bullock, Lord. *Ernest Bevin.* London, 1983.

Churchill, Winston S. *The River War.* 2d ed., 2 vols. London, 1900.

Collins, Robert O. *King Leopold, England, and the Upper Nile, 1899-1909.* New Haven, 1968.

_____. *Land Beyond the Rivers.* New Haven and London, 1971.

_____. *Shadows in the Grass.* New Haven and London, 1983.

_____. *The Southern Sudan, 1883-1898.* New Haven, 1962.

Croft, Stuart. *The End of Superpower: British Foreign Office Conceptions of a Changing World, 1945-51.* Brookfield, Vermont, 1994.

Cromer, Earl of. *Modern Egypt.* 2 vols. London, 1908.

Daly, Martin W. *British Administration and the Northern Sudan, 1917-1924.* Leiden, 1980.

_____. *Empire on the Nile.* Cambridge, England, 1986.

_____. *Imperial Sudan: The Anglo-Egyptian Condominium, 1934-56.* Cambridge, England, 1991.

_____, ed. *Modernization in the Sudan.* New York, 1985.

Daniel, Norman. *Islam, Europe, and Empire.* Edinburgh, 1966.

Davies, Reginald. *The Camel's Back.* London, 1957.

Deng, Francis. *Africans of Two Worlds: The Dinka in Afro-Arab Sudan.* New Haven and London, 1978.

_____. *The Dinka of the Sudan.* New York, 1972.

Duncan, J.S.R. *The Sudan: A Record of Achievement.* Edinburgh, 1952.

_____. *The Sudan's Path to Independence.* Edinburgh and London, 1957.

Eden, Sir Anthony. *Full Circle.* Boston, 1960.

Evans-Pritchard, E. E. *The Azande.* Oxford, 1971.

_____. *The Nuer.* 2d ed. London, 1974.

_____. *Witchcraft, Oracles, and Magic among the Azande.* Oxford, 1976.

Fabunmi, L. A. *The Sudan in Anglo-Egyptian Relations, 1800-1956.* London, 1960.

Gaitskell, Arthur. *Gezira: A Story of Development in the Sudan.* London, 1959.

Grafftey-Smith, Laurence. *Bright Levant.* London, 1970.

Grandin, Nicole. *Le Soudan Nilotique et l'Administration Britannique, 1898-1956.* Leiden, 1982.

Grenville, J.A.S. *Lord Salisbury.* London, 1964.

Henderson, K.D.D. *The Making of the Modern Sudan: The Life and Letters of Sir Douglas Newbold.* London, 1953.

_____. *Set under Authority.* Somerset, 1987.

_____. *Sudan Republic.* New York, 1965

_____. *A Survey of the Anglo-Egyptian Sudan.* London, 1945.

Henderson, K.D.D., and Owen, T.R.H., eds. *Sudan Verse.* London, 1963.
Hill, Richard. *A Biographical Dictionary of the Sudan.* 2d ed., London, 1967.
________. *Slatin Pasha.* London, 1965.
Holt, P. M. *A Modern History of the Sudan.* London, 1961.
Holt, P. M., and Daly, Martin. *The History of the Sudan.* London, 1980.
Issawi, Charles. *Egypt at Mid-Century: An Economic Survey.* London, New York and Toronto, 1954.
Jackson, H. C. *Behind the Modern Sudan.* London, 1955.
________. *Sudan Days and Ways.* London, 1954.
Jarvis, Major C. S. *The Back Garden of Allah.* London, 1939.
________. *Oriental Spotlight.* London, 1937.
Kent, John. *British Imperial Strategy and the Origins of the Cold War 1944-49.* Leicester, 1993.
Keun, Odette. *A Foreigner Looks at the British Sudan.* London, 1930.
Kirk, George. *Survey of International Affairs, 1939-1946: The Middle East in the War.* London, New York, and Toronto, 1952.
________. *Survey of International Affairs: The Middle East, 1945-1950.* London. New York and Toronto, 1954.
Louis, W. R. *The British Empire in the Middle East, 1945-1951.* Oxford, 1984.
Low, S. *Egypt in Transition.* London, 1913.
MacMichael, Sir Harold. *The Anglo-Egyptian Sudan.* London, 1934.
________. *The Sudan.* London, 1954.
Magnus, Philip. *Kitchener: Portrait of an Imperialist.* London, 1958.
Marlowe, John. *A History of Modern Egypt*, 2d ed. Hamden, 1965.
Milner, Alfred. *England in Egypt.* London, 1892.
Niblock, Tim. *Class and Power in the Sudan.* London, 1987.
Paul, Andrew. *A History of the Beja Tribes of the Sudan.* London, 1971.
Robertson, Sir James. *Transition in Africa.* London, 1974.
Robinson, Ronald; Gallagher, John; and Denny, Alice. *Africa and the Victorians.* London, 1961.
Royal Institute of International Affairs. *Great Britain and Egypt, 1914-1951.* 3d ed. London and New York, 1952.
Sabry, H. Zulfakar. *Sovereignty for the Sudan.* London, 1982.
Sanderson, G.N. *England, Europe, and the Upper Nile, 1882-1899.* Edinburgh, 1965.
Saville, John. *The Politics of Continuity: British Foreign Policy and the Labour Government, 1945-46.* London and New York, 1993.
Schuster, Sir George. *Private Work and Public Causes: A Personal Record.* Cowbridge, 1979.
Shibeika, Mekki. *The Independent Sudan.* New York, 1959.
Slatin, Rudolf C. *Fire and Sword in the Sudan.* London, 1896.
Symes, Sir Stewart. *Tour of Duty.* London, 1946.
Tignor, R. L. *Modernization and British Colonial Rule in Egypt, 1882-1914.* Princeton, 1966.
Trevaskis, Sir Kennedy. *Shades of Amber.* London, 1968.
Trimingham, J. S. *Islam in the Sudan.* London, New York, and Toronto, 1949.
Wai, Dunstan, ed. *The African-Arab Conflict in the Sudan.* New York and London, 1981.
________. *The Southern Sudan: The Problem of National Integration.* London, 1973.
Warburg, Gabriel. *Historical Discord in the Nile Valley.* London, 1992.

_____. *Islam, Nationalism, and Communism in a Transitional Society.* London, 1978.

_____. *The Sudan under Wingate.* London, 1971.

Weiler, Peter. *Ernest Bevin.* Manchester, 1993.

Wingate, Colonel Sir Francis. *Mahdiism and the Egyptian Sudan.* London, 1891.

_____. *Ten Years Captivity in the Mahdi's Camp, 1882-1892.*

Wingate, Ronald. *Wingate of the Sudan.* London, 1955.

Woodward, Peter. *Condominium and Sudanese Nationalism.* New York. 1979.

_____. *Sudan, 1898-1989: The Unstable State.* Boulder and London, 1990.

Wylde, A. B. *'83 to '87 in the Sudan.* London, 1888.

Yusuf Fadl Hasan. *Sudan in Africa.* Khartoum, 1985.

Zulfo, I. H. *Karari: The Sudanese Account of the Battle of Omdurman.* London, 1980.

PUBLISHED SECONDARY SOURCES: ARTICLES

Collins, Robert O. "The Sudan Political Service: A Portrait of the Imperialists." *African Affairs* 71 (1972).

Daly, M. W. "The Egyptian Army Mutiny at Omdurman, January-February 1900." *Bulletin of the British Society for Middle Eastern Studies* 8, no. 1 (1981).

Hill, R. L. "The Gordon Literature." *Durham University Journal* 47, no. 3 (1955).

Ibrahim, H. A. "Imperialism and Neo-Mahdism in the Sudan: A Study of British Policy towards Neo-Mahdism, 1924-1927." *African Affairs*, January 1985.

_____. "The Mahdist Risings against the Condominium Government, 1900-1927." *International Journal of African Historical Studies* 12, no. 3 (1979).

_____. "The Sudan in the 1936 Anglo-Egyptian Treaty." *Sudan Notes and Records* 54 (1973).

Kirk-Greene, A.H.M. "The Sudan Political Service: A Profile in the Sociology of Imperialism." *International Journal of African Historical Studies* 15, no. 1 (1982).

Mangan, J.A. "The Education of an Elite Imperial Administration: The Sudan Political Service and the British Public School System." *International Journal of African Historical Studies* 15, no. 4 (1982).

Robinson, Ronald. "Non-European Foundations of European Imperialism: Sketch for a Theory of Collaboration." In *Studies in the Theory of Imperialism*, ed. Roger Owen and Bob Sutcliffe. London, 1972.

Robinson, Ronald, and Gallagher, John. "The Imperialism of Free Trade." *Economic History Review*, 2d ser. 6, no. 1 (1953).

_____. "The Partition of Africa." In *New Cambridge Modern History*, vol. 11, *Material Progress and World-Wide Problems, 1870-1898*, ed. F. H. Hinsley. Cambridge, 1962.

Sanderson, G. N. "Sudanese Nationalism and the Independence of the Sudan." In *Northern Africa: Islam and Modernization*, ed. Michael Brett. London, 1973.

Woodward, Peter. "In the Footsteps of Gordon: The Sudan Government and the Rise of Sayyid Abd al-Rahman al-Mahdi, 1915-1935." *African Affairs* (January 1985).

Index

About the Author

W. TRAVIS HANES III is Visiting Assistant Professor of History, Southwestern University, Georgetown, Texas. Dr. Hanes's articles have appeared in *Journal of Imperial and Commonwealth History* and *Journal of World History*.

ISBN 0-313-29341-4

90000>

EAN

9 780313 293412

HARDCOVER BAR CODE